IMAGES
of America

AROUND SAN ANTONIO

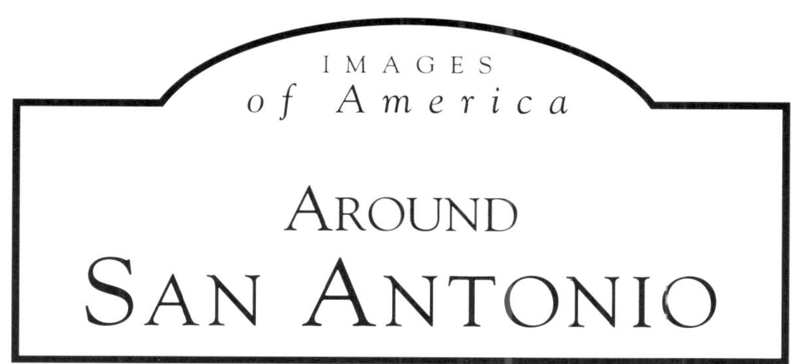

Around San Antonio

Pauline T. Newton

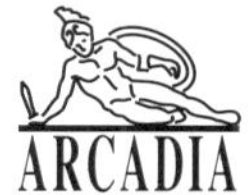

ISBN 0-7385-0311-8

Published by Arcadia Publishing,
an imprint of Tempus Publishing, Inc.
2 Cumberland Street
Charleston, SC 29401

Printed in Great Britain.

Library of Congress Catalog Card Number: 99-066662.

For all general information contact Arcadia Publishing at:
Telephone 843-853-2070
Fax 843-853-0044
E-Mail arcadia@charleston.net

For customer service and orders:
Toll-Free 1-888-313-BOOK

Visit us on the internet at http://www.arcadiaimages.com

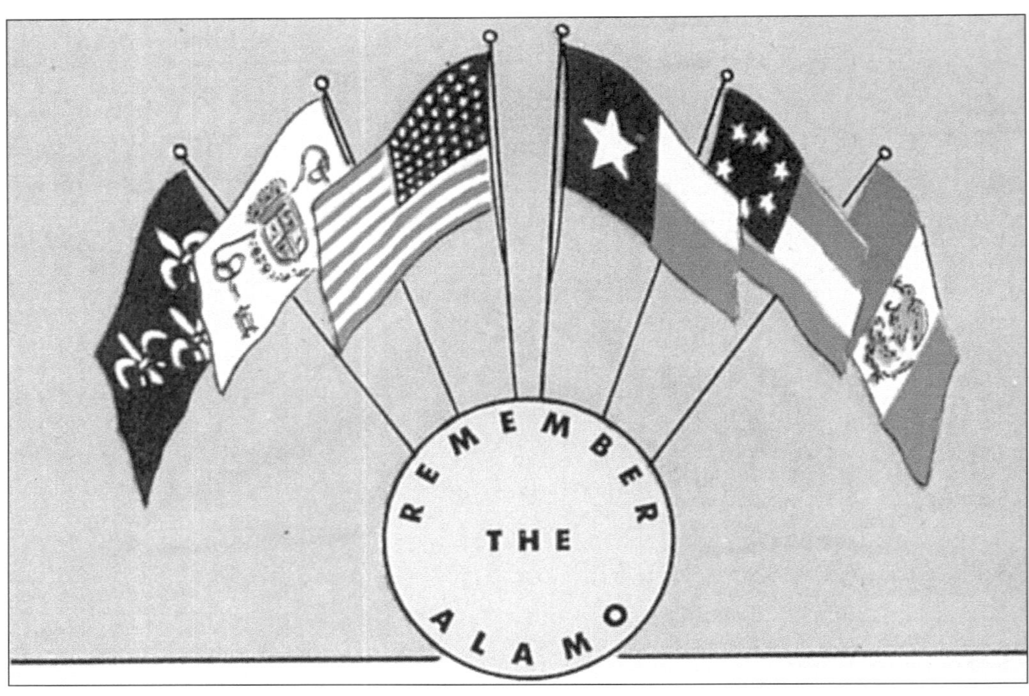

Cover: Courtesy Texas Department of Transportation.

CONTENTS

ACKNOWLEDGMENTS

Dedicated historians, librarians, and volunteers enabled me to make *Around San Antonio* a reality, and my appreciation goes to Mark Barnes, Archivist, St. Philip's College; Anne Cook, Photo Librarian at Texas Department of Transportation Library; and Sister Francisca Eiken, Archivist at Sisters of the Charity of the Incarnate Word. I also would like to thank Dora Guerra, Interim Head of Special Collections and Archives at Our Lady of the Lake University; Louis M. "Rocky" LaRocco, owner of Broadway 50-50; Marjorie George, Communications Officer at the Episcopal Diocese of West Texas; Brenda Johnson, Registrar at Camp Capers; John M. Manguso, Director, Fort Sam Houston Military Museum; Harry Orem, former superintendent of the Alamo Heights Independent School District; Stanley Schmidt, former president of Alamo Cement Company; Martha Utterback, Assistant Director at the Daughters of the Republic of Texas Library at the Alamo; and Nelle Lee Weincek, Photo Archivist at the San Antonio Conservation Society Foundation. All of them tirelessly offered wonderful pictures and suggestions, as did Brother Robert Wood, Archivist at St. Mary's University; Pamela Wadsworth, Director of Development and Alumni Relations at Texas Military Institute; Ann Marie Thornton, Public Information Officer at San Antonio College; and Janice Sabec, Senior Archives Assistant at Elizabeth Huth Coates Library, Trinity University. Historians Ssgt. Jason W. Axberg, 12th Flying Training Wing at Randolph Air Force Base, and Ssgt. Patrick D. Longe, Brooks Air Force Base, also deserve recognition for their assistance.

Brice Woods, one of my oldest friends, and her family submitted some great images of real Texans. Walter Tallafuss, my cousin, sent some good advice, and Eunice Lewis, Carlita Hughes Kosty, and Cynthia Davenport Woodland, family friends, loaned wonderful pictures. Richard Weaver, a long-time friend, encouraged me to submit my work to Arcadia. I am grateful to him and to Jack Karp for their suggestions. And Neale Lunderville showed constant support and faith in me. Allison Carpenter, my editor, also deserves recognition for her assistance.

Thanks to my aunt, Nancy Lambert Davenport; my uncle, Joseph B. Lambert; and especially my parents, Thille Lambert Newton and Geoffrey Paul Newton, for their wonderful family photos and patient replies to my endless questions.

This book is dedicated to the memory of my maternal grandparents, Joseph Idus Lambert and Elizabeth Kirwan Lambert.

INTRODUCTION

One hundred years ago, in 1900, my grandfather, Joseph Idus Lambert, and his family shook the dust from their feet and surveyed their new home: Center Point, Texas. Texas, he said in his memoirs, "was a beautiful world . . . with the cotton fields in the summer, the . . . spring garden of vegetables, and the berries in the wood nearby." Under the ruthless sun, he shelled pecans, picked unyielding cotton buds, and kept a lookout for savage Mexican bandits as he rode in the United States Cavalry. In later years, he and his wife, Elizabeth Kirwan Lambert, settled in San Antonio and nourished a thriving community of descendants that still ramble through the plains of Texas, tracing their heritage back to that day in 1900.

Determined to gain a solid education, endure two world wars, adapt to a rapidly growing social scene, and stay out of debt, my grandparents cultivated a deep respect for their land and its history. With their children and, later, grandchildren, they explored San Antonio's five missions, paid frequent visits to the graves of their loved ones, and volunteered in fund-raising events, including Fiesta, a ten-day celebration. In their letters and memoirs, they wrote of nights in covered wagons, the troubles and debts of their families due to the early deaths of their fathers, and the beauty of the landscape and its historical monuments. These reminiscences also revealed their persistence and pride. I did not realize how important the heritage and traditions of my family were until I began to read my grandparents' memoirs and look at their pictures.

Yet, I grumbled each year when my parents announced the annual trip to the missions or the cemetery. This past June, my parents, my five-year old niece, and I picked our way through burrs and worn-down stones in search of our relatives' graves. Unlike me, my niece did not grimace when my parents told her how my grandfather, her great-grandfather, picked cotton balls until the hot soil burned the soles of his feet. When we finally found the graves, an image of my niece, a grown woman with children, flashed through my mind. Someday, she, like her ancestors, will lead her children though burrs and graves, telling them the story of how their great-great-grandfather cultivated the unruly Texas soil and taught his descendants the importance of its history.

The pictures and postcards in *Around San Antonio* retrace my family's footsteps from the 1900s until the early 1960s and reveal places my family members have traveled and lived, such as Center Point, Fort Clark, Dripping Springs, Leakey, Waring, and the Hill Country, in addition to San Antonio, home to various festivities, schools, historical sites, and military bases. Although my family's history is unique, other families may recall similar experiences as they read this book. With this purpose in mind, I hope that local ranchers, military citizens, old-timers, and newcomers will enjoy my sketch of the history of the families, lands, and origins around San Antonio. And the book will continue to keep alive my grandfather's wish to cultivate a never-failing pride in Texas.

—Pauline T. Newton

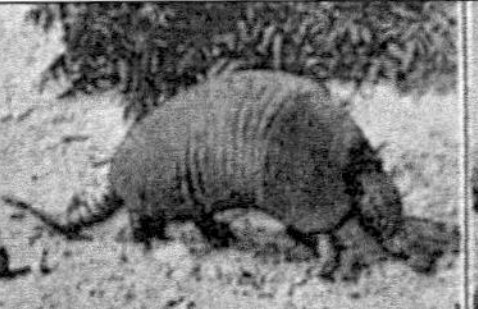
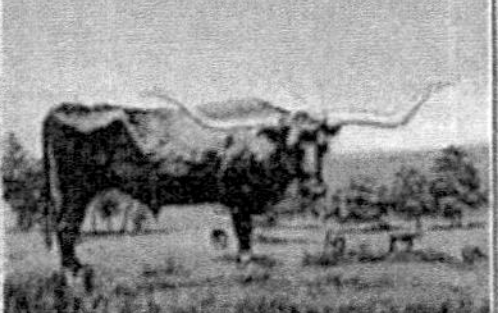
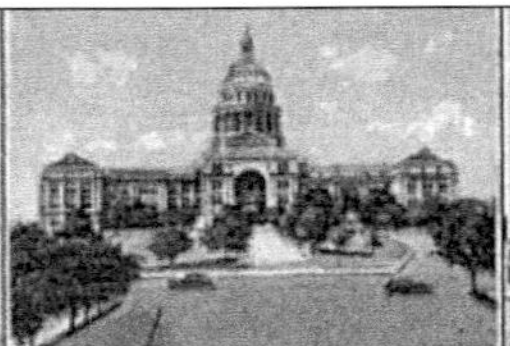
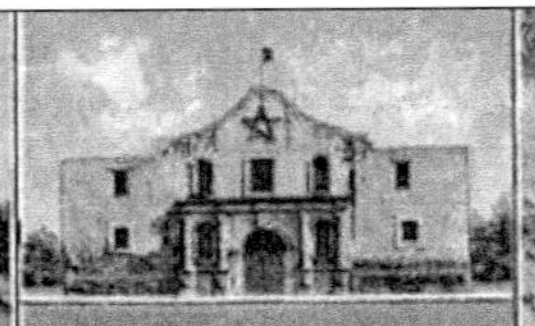
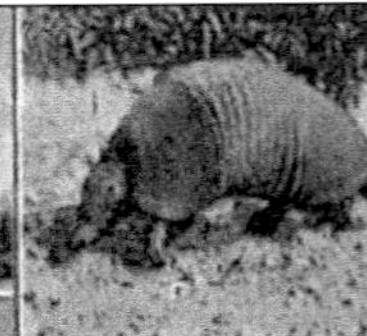
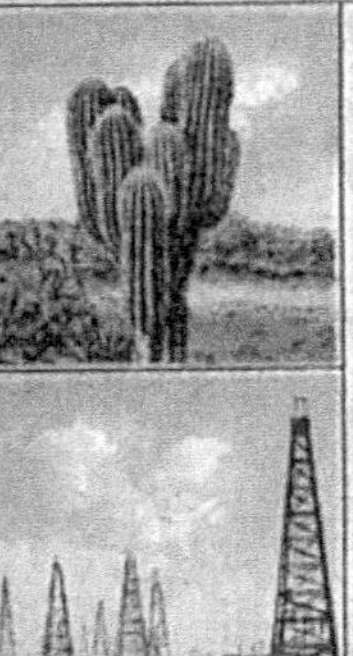

"DOWN IN TEXAS"

We're down here in old Texas,
Where you never have the blues
Where the bandits steal the jitneys
And the Marshals steal the booze
Where buildings horn the skyline,
Where the populace is boost
Where they shoot men just for pastime
Where the chickens never roost,
Where the stickup men are wary
And the bullets fall like hail;
Where each pocket has a pistol
And each pistol's good for jail;
Where they always hang the jury,
Where they never hang a man
If you call a man a liar you
Get home the best you can;
Where you get up in the morning
In a world of snow and sleet
And you come home in the evening
Suffocating in the heat;
Where the jitneys whiz about you
And the street cars barely creep;
Where the burglars pick your pockets
While you "lay me down to sleep"
Where the bulldogs all have rabies,
And the rabbits they have fleas
Where the big girls like the wee ones
Wear their dresses to their knees,
Where you whist out in the morning
Just to give your health a chance,
Say "Howdy" to some fellow who
Shoots big holes in your pants;
Where wise owls are afraid to hoot
And birds don t dare to sing
For it's hell down here in Texas,
Where they all shoot on the wing.

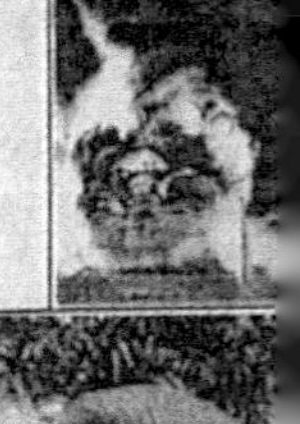
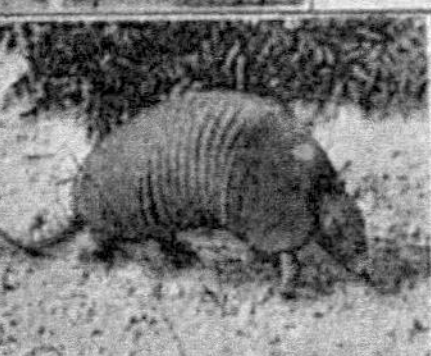
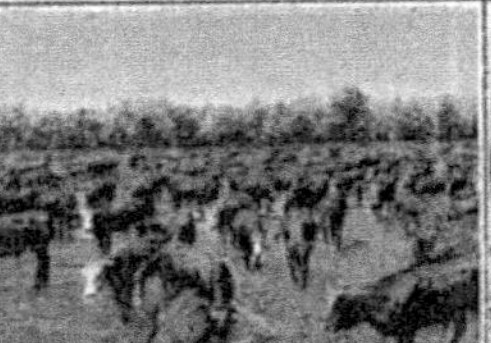
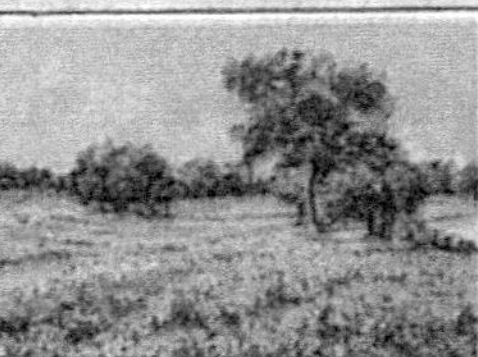
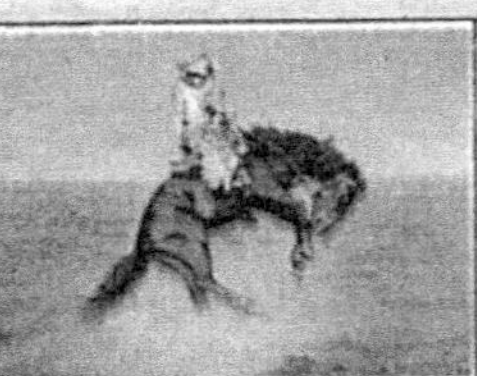
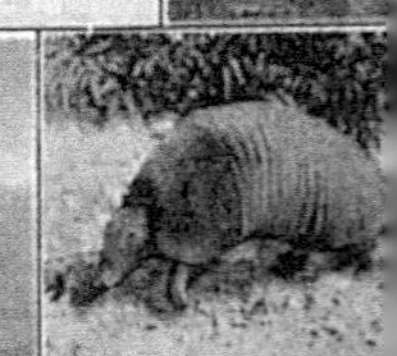

One

DEEP ROOTS:

CENTER POINT

Whenever looking at pictures of Center Point, home of 32 Texas Rangers and of my grandfather, Joseph Idus Lambert, I hear the voice of my grandmother, Elizabeth Kirwan Lambert: "We have to adjust our points of views to an era before airplanes, before automobiles, and-this far west-almost before trains." Joseph Idus recounts his memories of living in Center Point in his memoirs: "we rented small farms near the village. My brothers did not make much money renting land . . . they drudged away at some other person's fields year after year. . . My mother worked about the house toiling day in and day out." Yet he shares his joy in studying diligently at the local school and roaming the nearly-untouched countryside to his heart's content.

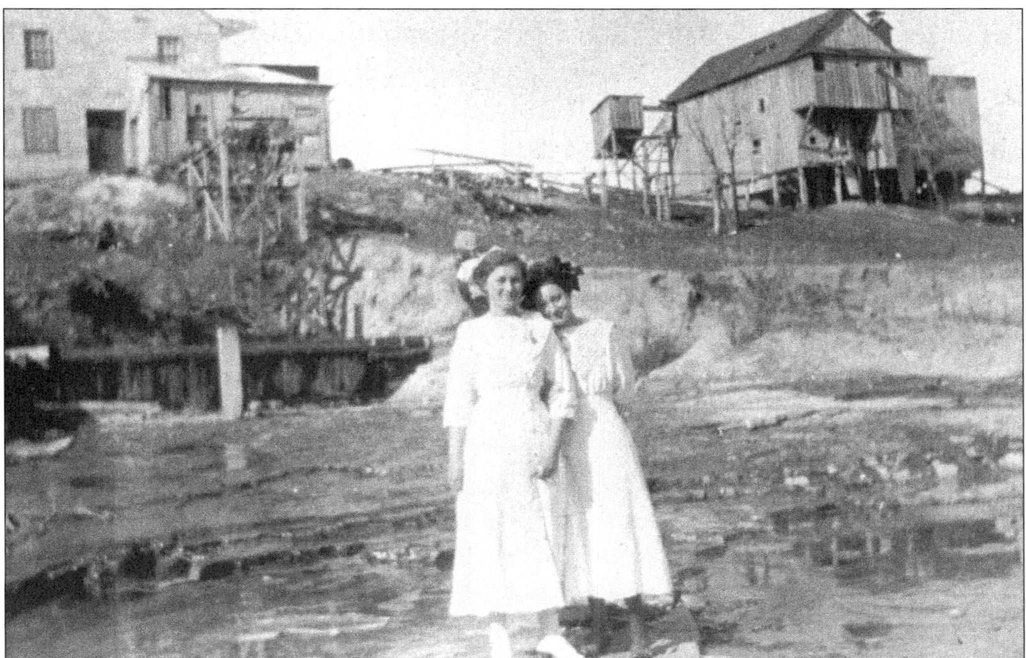

Rowena (left) and Margherita stand by the Mill Stream in Center Point. The Mill Stream, like all other sights in the town, charmed Joseph Idus and his family when they arrived in 1900. In his journals, Joseph Idus recalls, "I moved at the age of five to the little village of Center Point, Texas, Kerr County, which sits majestically on the banks of the Guadalupe River, about 60 miles northwest of San Antonio." (Courtesy Joseph B. Lambert.)

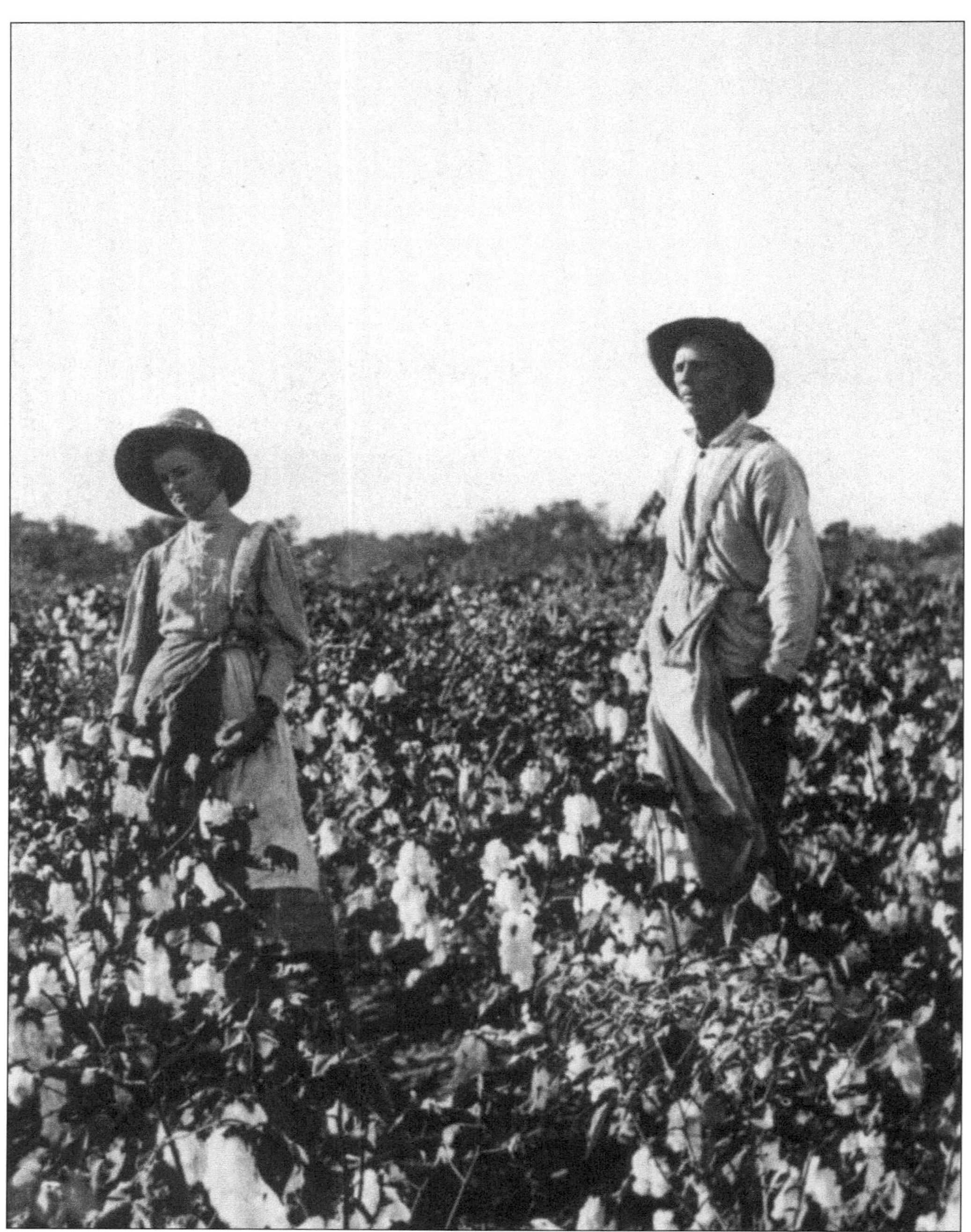

Joseph Idus optimistically remembers the hard labor that he and his family performed in order to make ends meet: "The first thing I remember in this world . . . was the picking of 36 pounds of cotton in one day. I considered it a stupendous amount of cotton for one boy to pick in a day at so early an age . . . . it gave me so much pleasure to pull the cotton out of the burr, and to watch my sack fill as I dragged it along the cotton row." Like Joseph Idus and his family, these unidentified workers also plucked cotton for hours on end. (Courtesy Daughters of the Republic of Texas Library, CN96.262.)

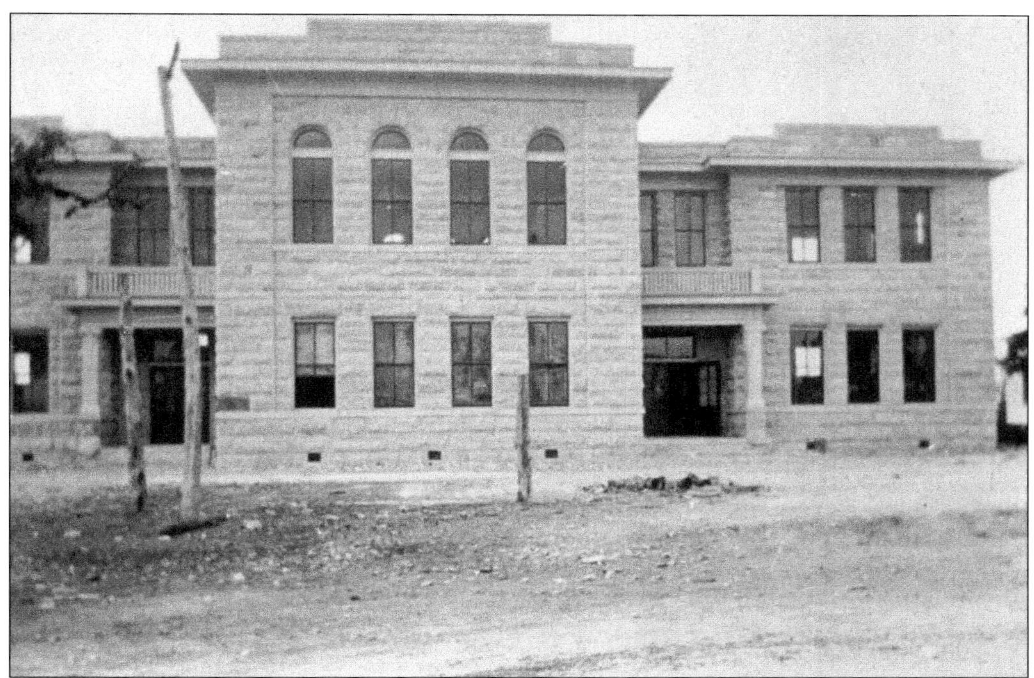

Joseph Idus graduated from Center Point High School in 1912. Here, he recognized the value of a solid education. In his journals, he wrote, "I won first honors in the graduating class by making the highest average. I was valedictorian of my class of ten students and made a speech." (Courtesy Joseph B. Lambert.)

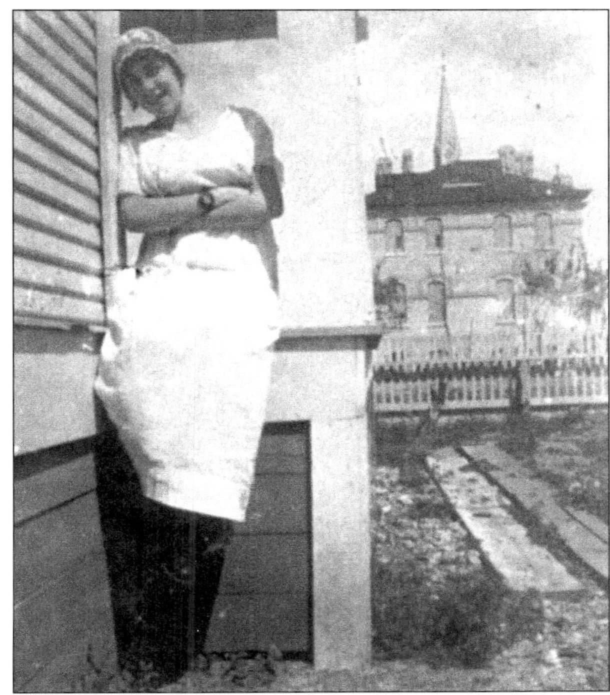

This unidentified woman, perhaps taking a break from her household duties, demonstrates the garb that many women wore during the 1910s. Pioneer women in Center Point and other small towns in Texas constantly worried about attacks from Indians, Mexicans, and rattlesnakes as they cared for their families. (Courtesy Joseph B. Lambert.)

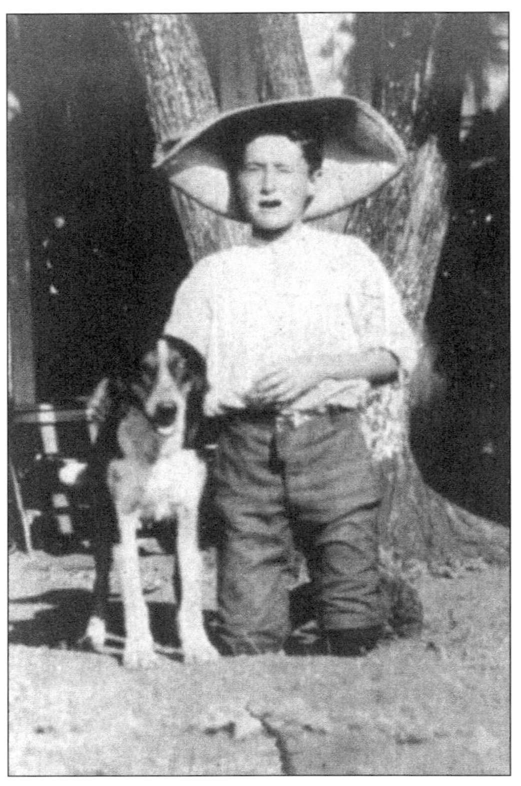

As a youth, Joseph Idus spent his days "eating pecans and sleeping, or spending many hours . . . in the woods or about the village." He also passed many afternoons playing and resting with his dog under the shade of this tree next to his house in Center Point. (Courtesy Joseph B. Lambert.)

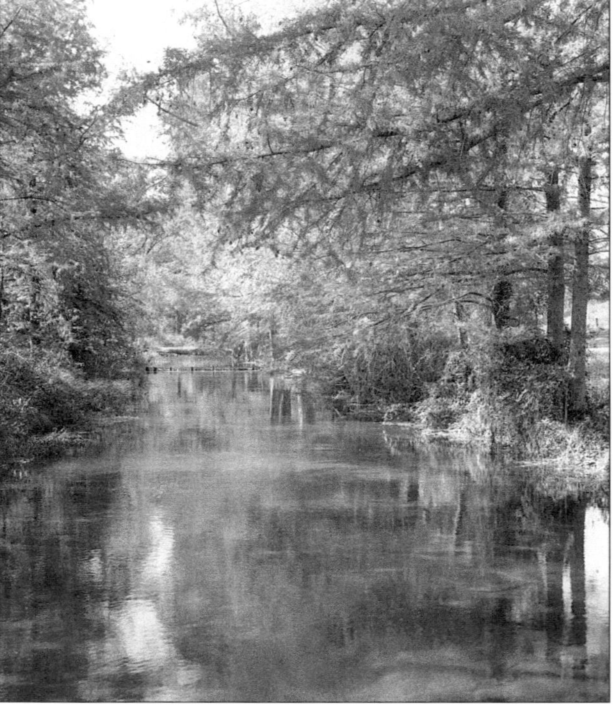

Joseph Idus often swam and fished in the Guadalupe River with his friends. Not only have I, too, swam in the Guadalupe River, but I have hiked through part of the river when it has dried up. After wandering through the hill country along the river, a friend and I dared one another to jump over several freshly-dug animal holes in the banks. (Courtesy Texas Department of Transportation.)

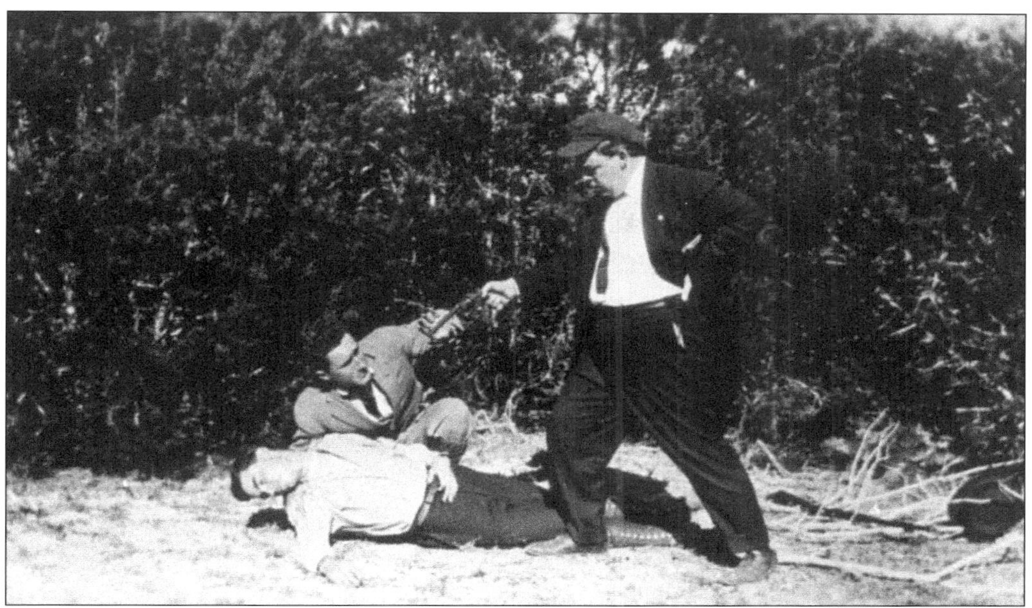

These potential Texas Rangers, who Joseph Idus and his friends identified as Hurley, Reynolds, and Tucker, strut and play with their rifles and pistols along the banks of Barton Creek near Austin in these 1915 shots. My grandfather was in college during this time; after he joined the Texas National Guard and the United States Cavalry less than a year later, few could catch him in a relaxed pose. He was a dignified, dedicated soldier. In the above shot, Joseph Idus is the one who leans over the "dead" man, Hurley, and holds up a hand to Reynolds's gun. Below, Joseph Idus holds a pipe in his mouth as his gun hangs from his belt; Reynolds and Tucker stand to his right respectively. (Both courtesy Joseph B. Lambert.)

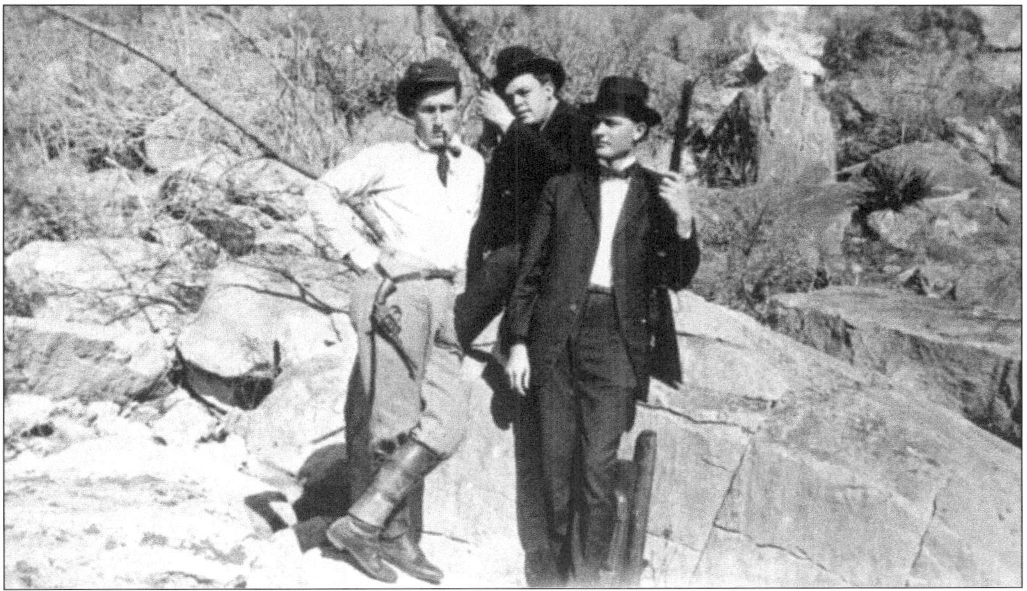

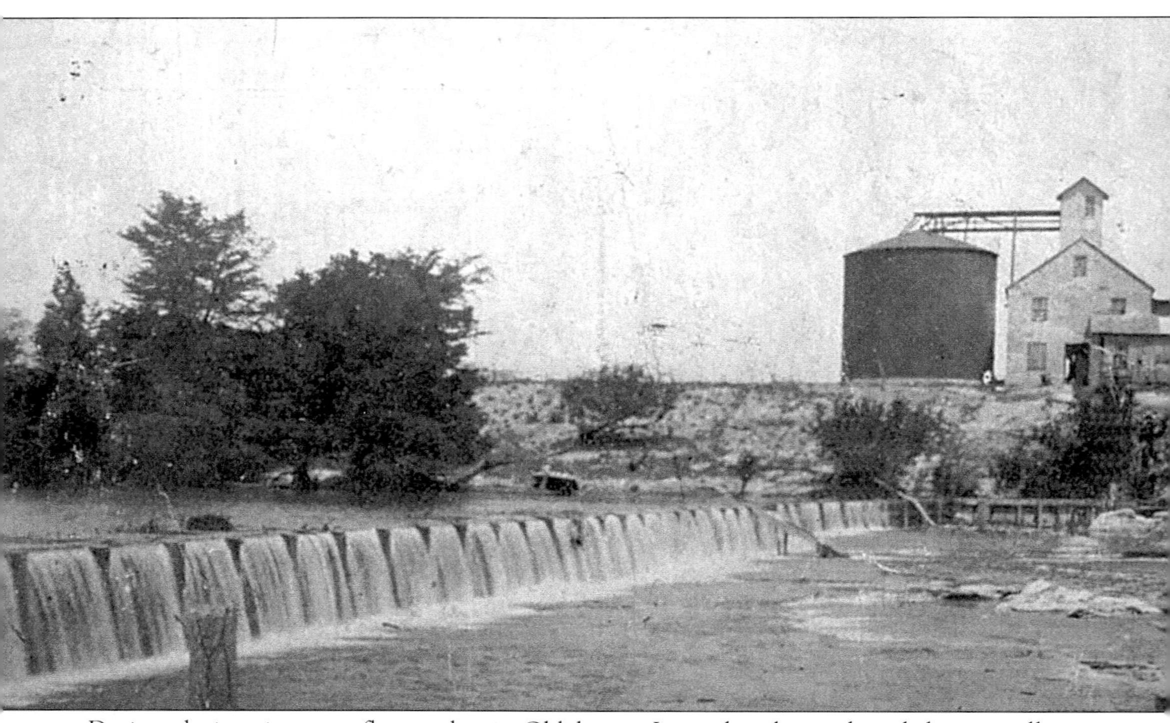

During closing time at a flea market in Oklahoma, I impulsively purchased this partially-torn card, thinking "I'll never find another image of Center Point" and handed it to the seller. Later, when I turned the card over, these words caught my eye: J.M. Lambert. I scanned for a signature: Lottie. This postcard was written by my grandfather's sister, Charlotte Lambert, to my grandfather's oldest brother, John Morgan Lambert. Although both moved to El Paso in the early 1900s, they still frequently returned to Center Point to visit my grandfather and his mother. The card was probably sent before World War I.

Two

DEEP IN THE HEART OF TEXAS:

SAN ANTONIO

After my grandfather left Center Point, he moved with the army to numerous places until he, his wife, and their three children finally settled in San Antonio. Like my grandfather, I spent many afternoons visiting historical monuments and sites in San Antonio. Since I grew up digging holes in search of 18th-century remnants of Mexican and Texan artifacts behind my 20th-century house, San Antonio's potpourri of old and new buildings never surprised me until I returned to the city after college. When I looked past the people and cars scurrying past me on Commerce, St. Mary's, and Houston Streets in the heart of the downtown business district, the contrast of steel rods and ancient stones startled me. I examined these structures, wondering how each has changed the façade of the city in its own time. New buildings may rise and fall, but the spirit of those who first came to San Antonio and fought for Texas's independence still remains.

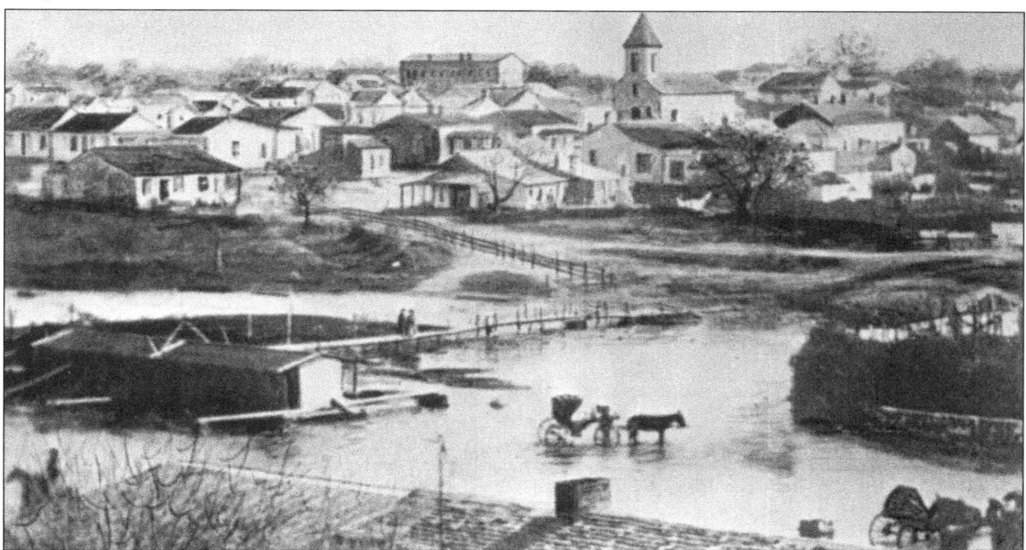

Today, few could recognize this early view of San Antonio from Market Street, near Navarro Street, looking southeast. The steeple belongs to St. John's Church. Although this 1880s image is a photograph, someone touched up the image with a pencil or pen. (Courtesy Daughters of the Republic of Texas Library, Grandjean Collection, 60.)

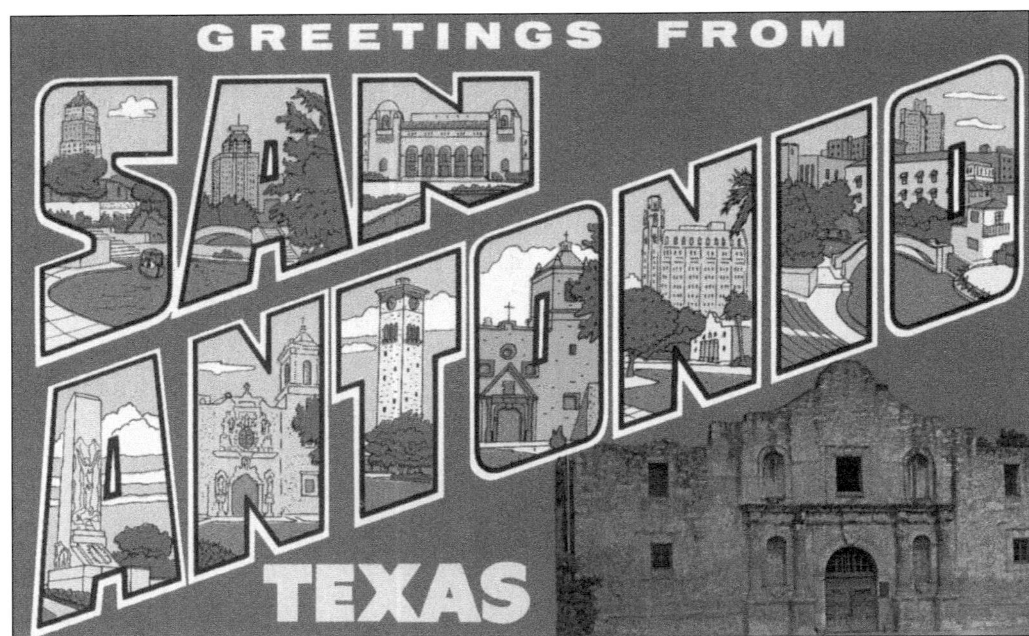

After the 1960s, many new buildings such as the Rivercenter Mall and hotels, the Alamodome, the Institute of Texan Cultures, and the Tower of the Americas sprang up in downtown San Antonio, and in this card, these now-familiar landmarks are absent, although each one of the featured structures remain in good condition despite years of floods, droughts, and depressions.

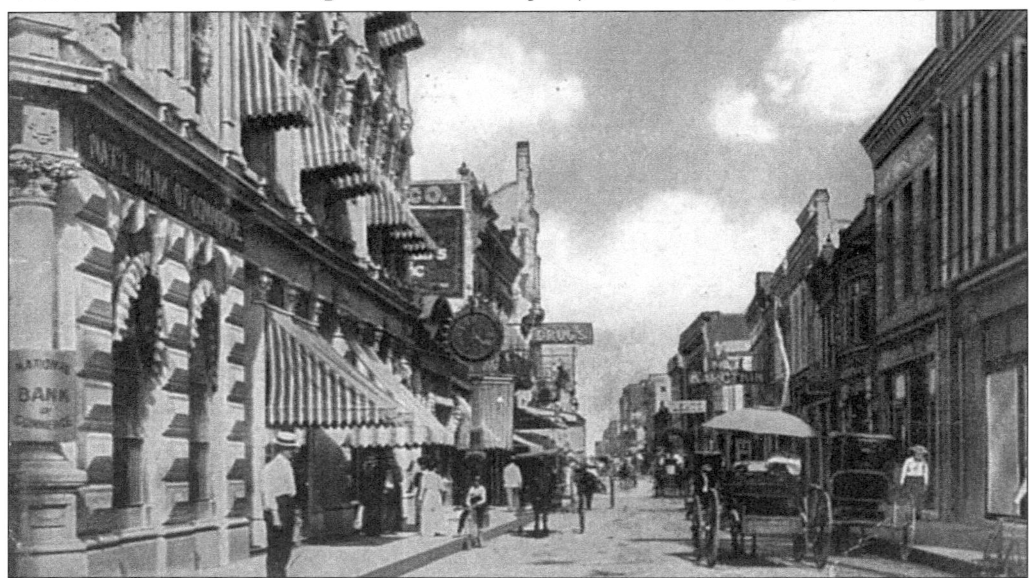

The National Bank of Commerce, pictured on the left front side of this postcard, is only one of many banks on this avenue that San Antonians have frequented since 1917, the postmarked date of this card. The entire structure was called the Kampmann Building. The clock on the sidewalk near to the bank, known as the Hertzberg Clock, now stands on the northwest corner of St. Mary's and Houston Streets. Although recently-installed electric lights make this 1878 timepiece readable at night, it still must be wound by hand.

The Hertzberg Clock is now located on this part of Houston Street, which intersects St. Mary's Street. The "Majestic" sign marks the site of the Majestic Theatre Building, constructed in 1929, and in the far distance stands a white structure with a turret. Known as the Medical Arts Building until 1985, the Emily Morgan Hotel has an interesting V-shape.

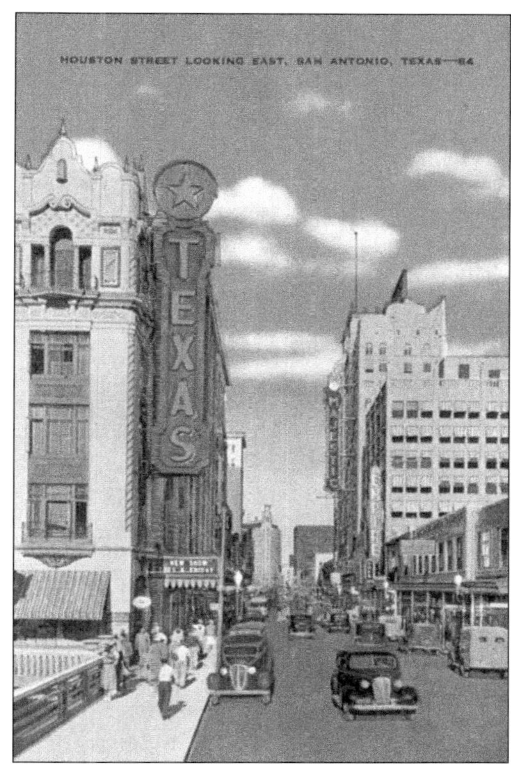

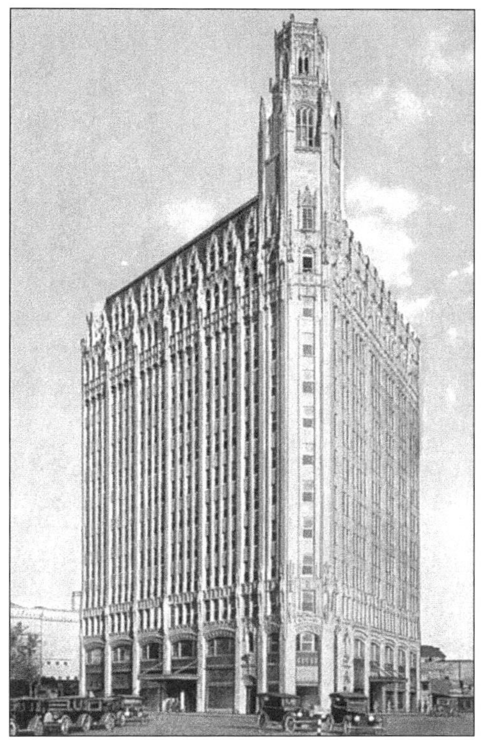

This close-up shot of the Emily Morgan Hotel shows the hotel's Gothic details. According to a tall tale, Emily Morgan helped the Texans to secure their independence by attracting and holding the attention of Santa Anna, the Mexican army's leader who had made her his personal servant. When Santa Anna fell asleep, she took with her the Mexican army's battle plans and carried them to General Sam Houston, who then defeated the Mexican Army in the Battle of San Jacinto, April 21, 1836, and secured Texas's freedom. She was the inspiration for "The Yellow Rose of Texas" song.

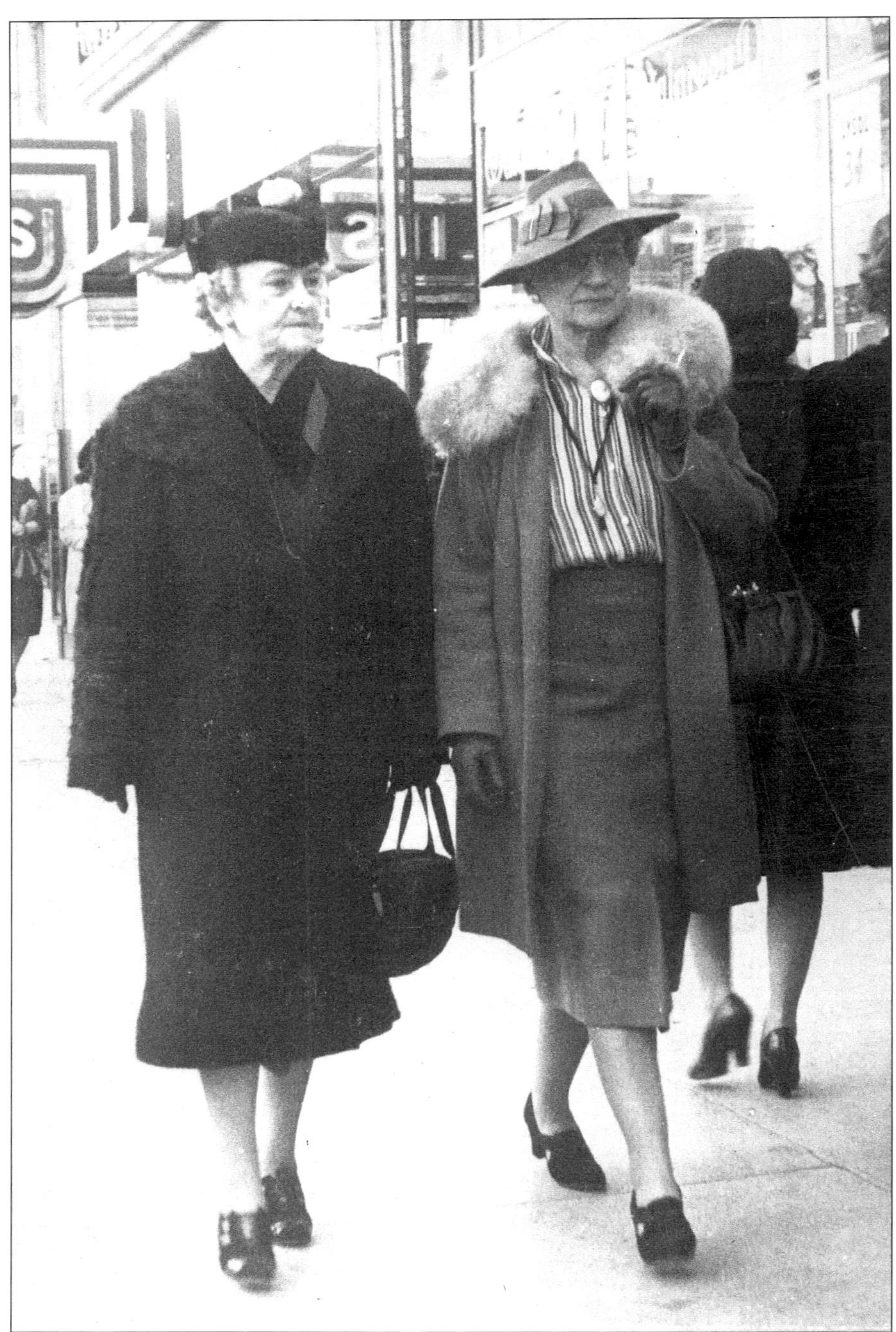

In stylish hats and coats representative of the late 1940s, Mrs. Winston (left) and Corrie Stallings walk down Houston Street. Corrie and her husband, Dr. Samuel Luther Stallings, a well-respected San Antonio dentist, and their children moved to San Antonio in the 1910s. The descendants of the Stallings and my grandparents still attend the same schools and gatherings and often have coordinated fund-raising events such as candle-making for San Antonio and its inhabitants. (Courtesy Carlita Hughes Kosty.)

Located on the corner of Houston, Travis, and St. Mary's Streets, the Camberley Gunter Hotel was completed in 1909, although the last three stories were added in 1927. This central location has been the site of a hotel since the 1830s and still attracts visitors as well as San Antonians who rent rooms solely to watch Fiesta parades or events.

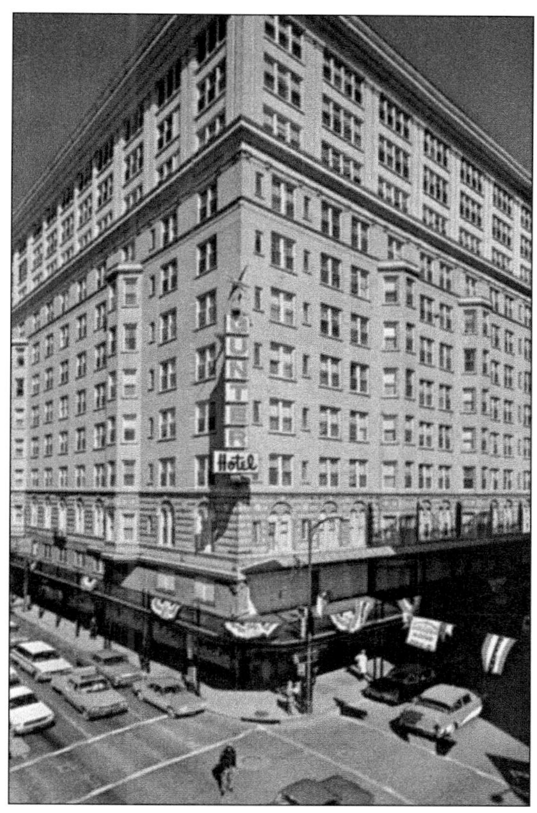

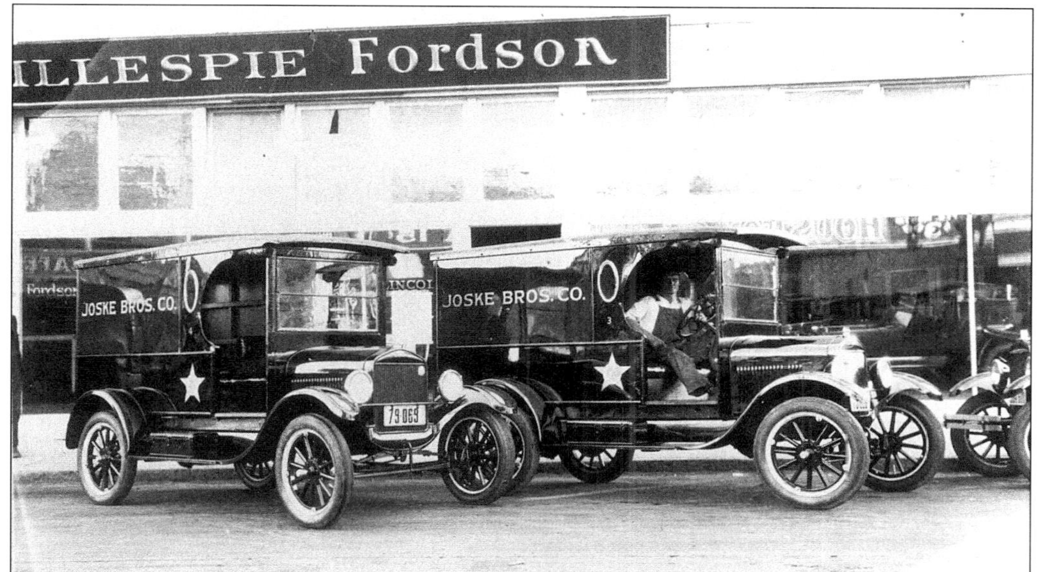

Judging by the make of the Joske Brothers Ford wagons, the picture was taken prior to World War II. Joske's department store, located on Alamo Plaza, was known as "The Largest Store in the Largest State" until Alaska joined the United States. (Courtesy Broadway 50-50 and Louis M. LaRocco and Frank R. Little.)

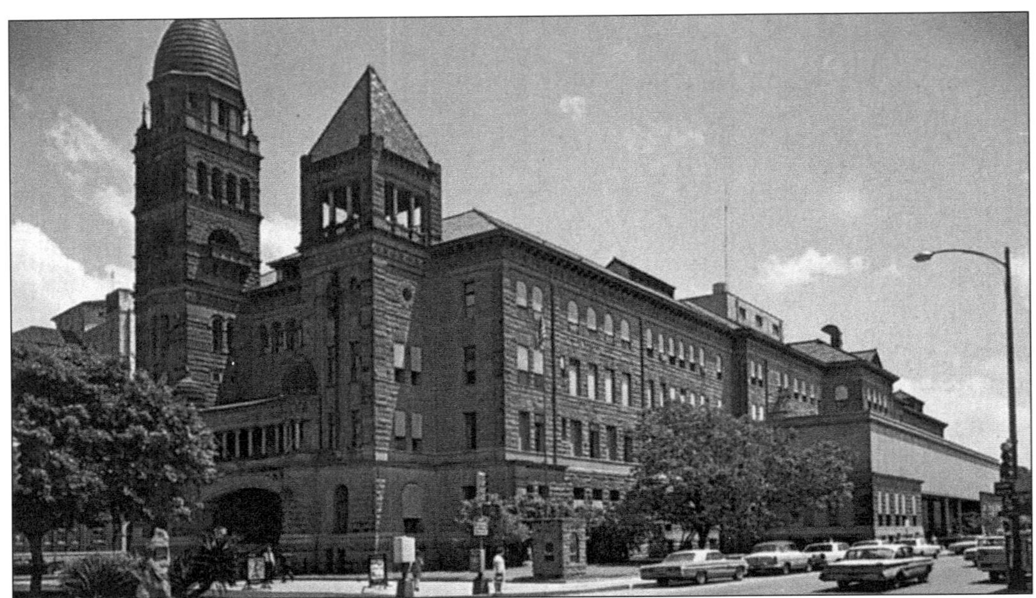

By combining granite, Pecos red sandstone, and Romanesque architecture, James Riely Gordon created one of the most beautiful buildings in San Antonio. The Bexar County Courthouse, along with its seven-story beehive tower, was completed in 1896.

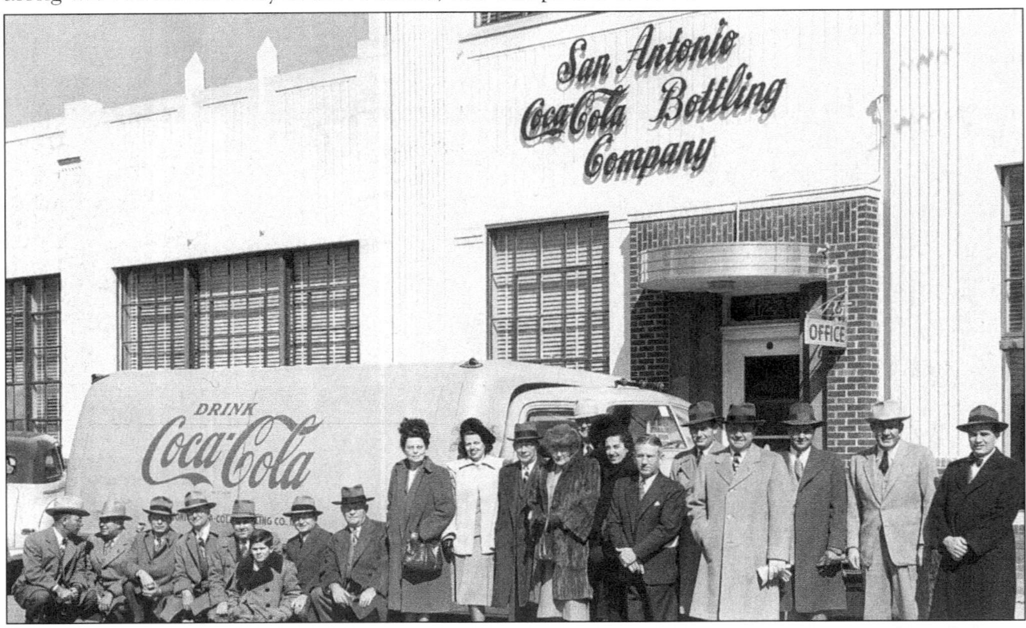

The Biedenharn family was the first to bottle Coca-Cola in a bottle at its original Vicksburg, Mississippi plant. They purchased the first San Antonio Coca-Cola Bottling Company plant in 1931. Here, several executives of Hobbs stand with Coca-Cola's representatives during the 1947 introduction of "Protecto Body" GMC truck by Hobbs Company. Addie and Albert Biedenharn are pictured 12th and 13th from the left, and 15th from left is Sam Johnson, president of Laredo Coca-Cola Bottling Company. Albert Biedenharn Jr. is pictured 19th from the left. (Courtesy P. Randolph Mayo Jr.)

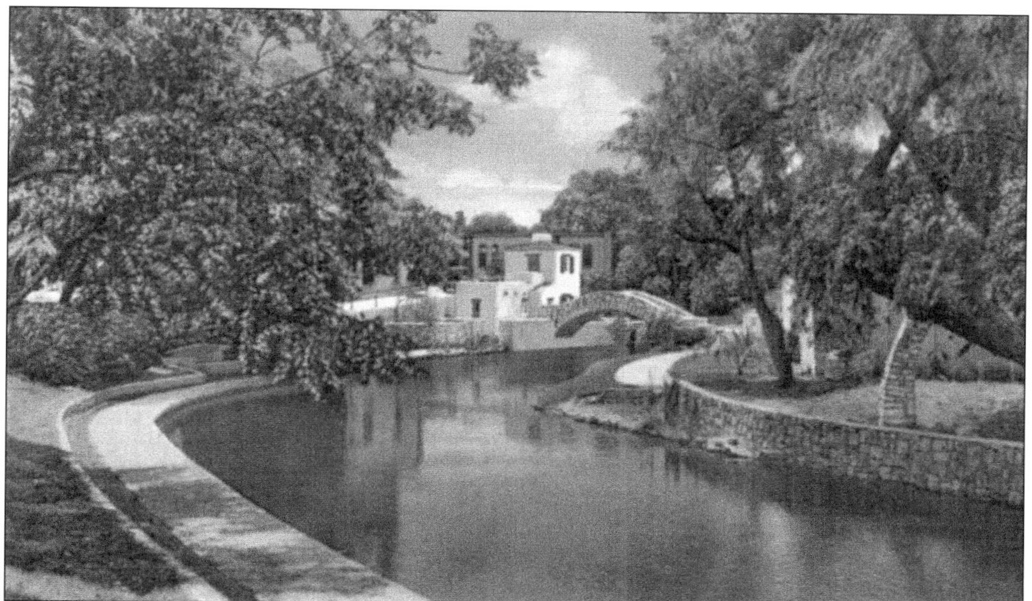

Paseo del Río, or the Riverwalk, almost became a paved street, but thanks to the San Antonio Conservation Society's determined efforts to preserve the area, the horseshoe-shaped walk is lined with cypress trees, colorful lights, and restaurant tables. During the holiday season, my favorite time to walk alongside the river, one can listen to carols and have a drink at a local cafe.

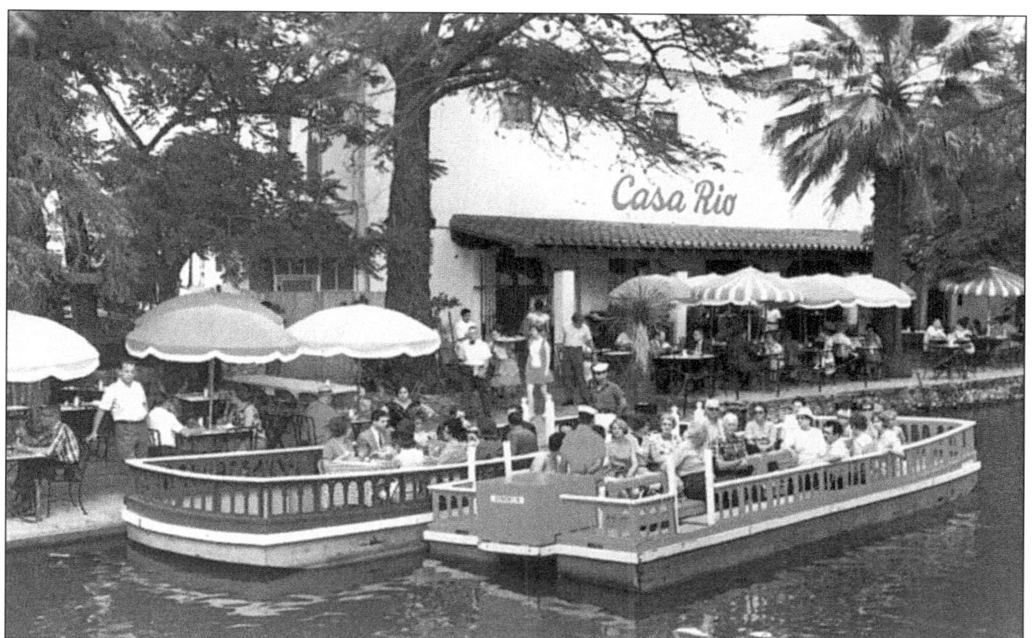

After walking along the river, my friends and I sometimes stop at Casa Río for drinks, chips, and salsa. I always request a seat by the river. One Fourth of July morning, a friend and I sat here and drank beers in honor of our nation's birthday as we watched tour boats float down the river.

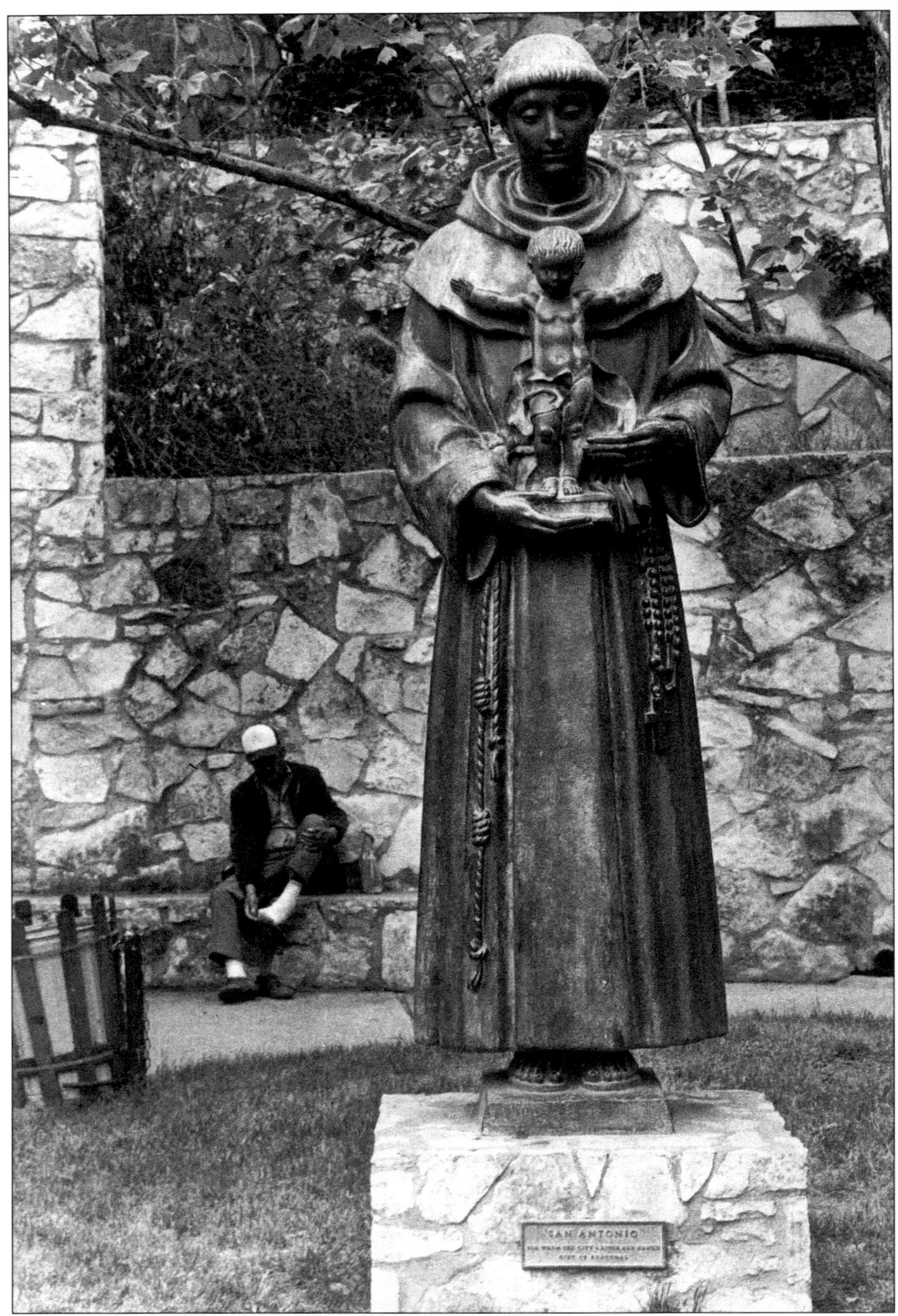

This statue of St. Anthony of Padua, which graces a niche along the north bank of the San Antonio River extension, was given to the city by the people of Portugal. San Antonio was named after the day of St. Anthony of Padua, June 13, in 1691. Numerous benches and shady areas give people like this unidentified man a place to rest or to enjoy an ice cream cone. (Courtesy San Antonio Conservation Society Foundation.)

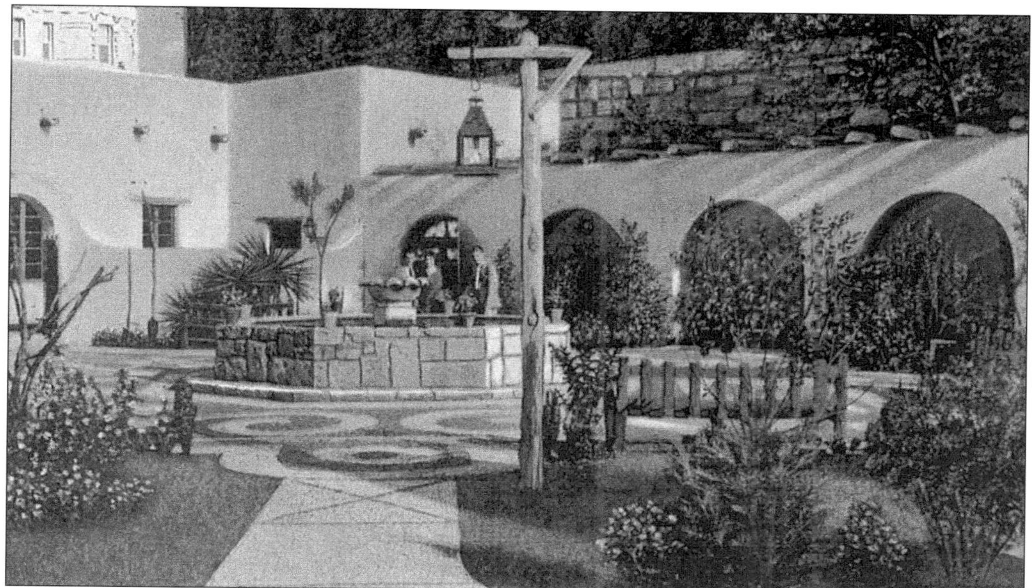

When the Spaniards built the Spanish Governor's Palace in the 1700s, they intended to use the palace as a residence for the city's presidio, or fort commander. Even though the palace has changed hands numerous times, the San Antonio Parks and Recreation Department, which gained responsibility for this building and its grounds in the early 1930s, has preserved the fountain and mosaic tiles, as shown in the above image. Several rooms in the governor's mansion retain the colonial style of the mid-18th century; this reception room, seen below with its adobe walls and intricately designed furniture, is no exception.

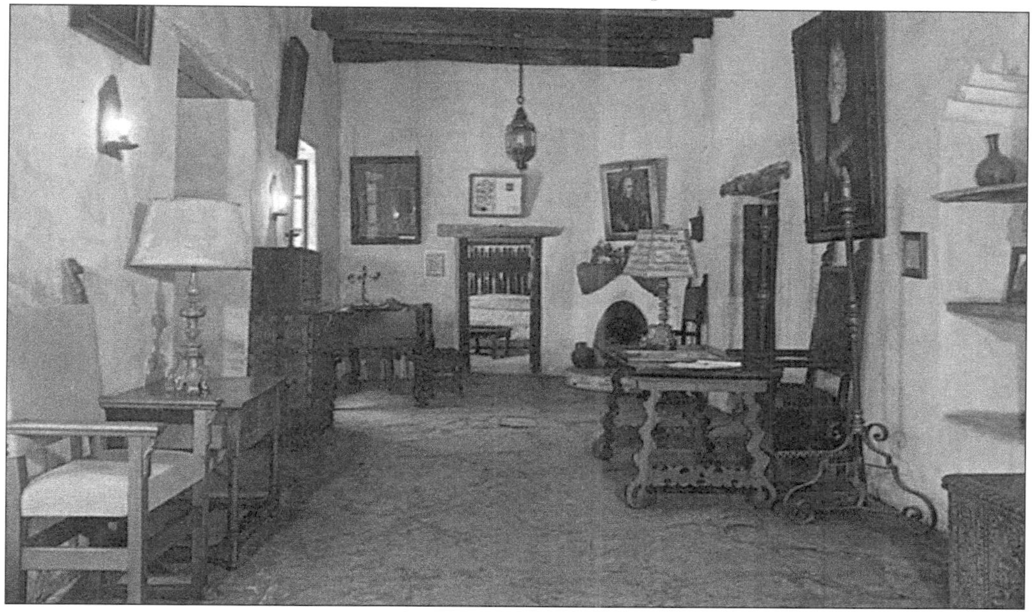

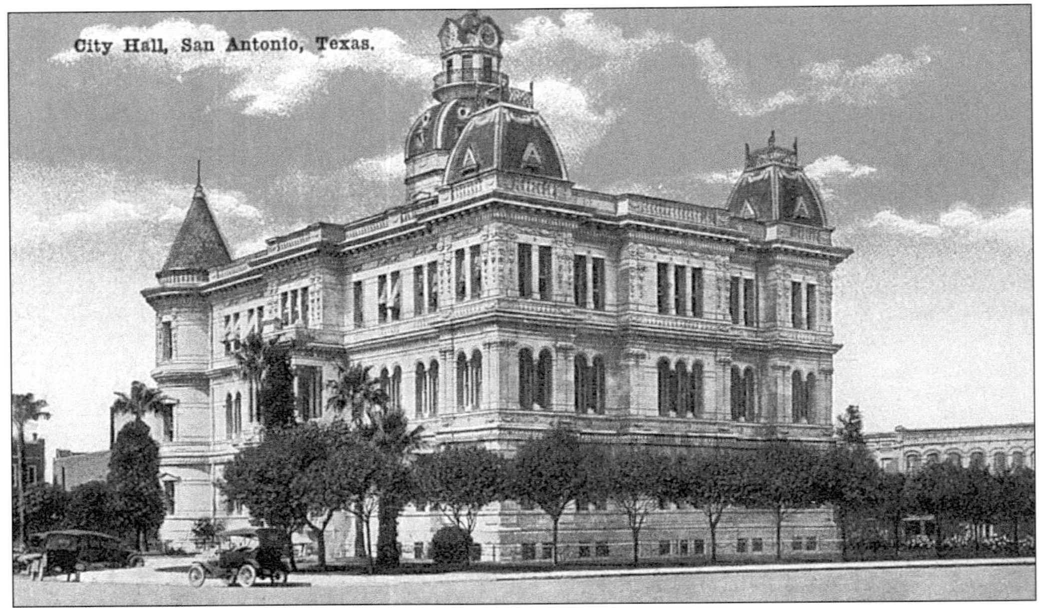

Now turret-less and tower-less and shrouded by trees, San Antonio City Hall does not boast the fine architectural features that it once did. In a 1927 effort to preserve the building from ruin, architects added a fourth floor to this edifice when they removed the135-foot octagonal tower and its cupola.

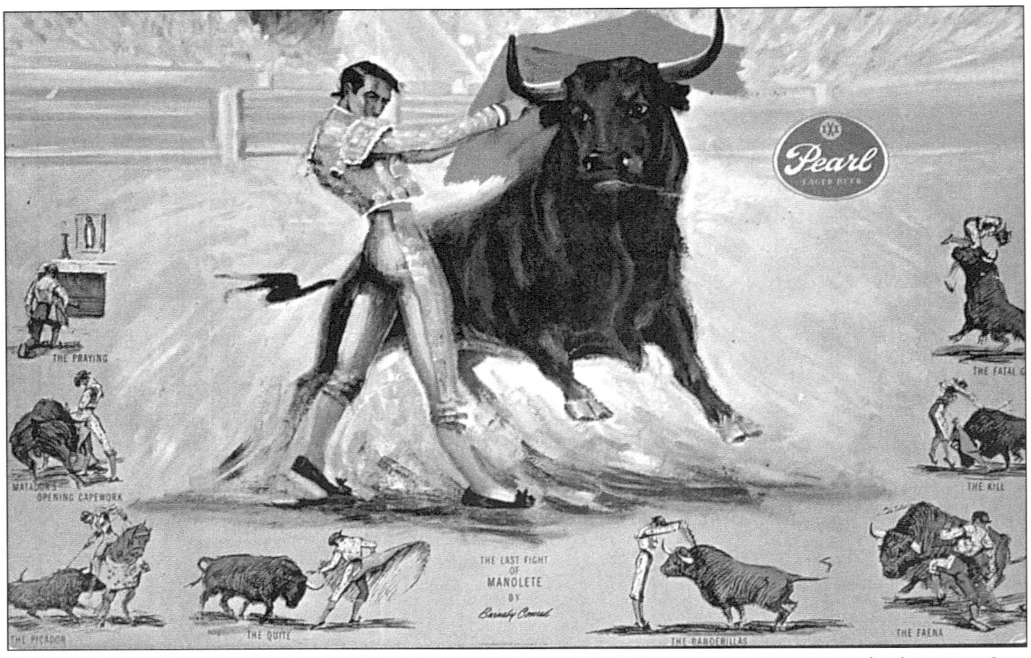

The seal on this postcard of a bullfighter is from Pearl Brewery, a renowned plant in San Antonio. The three "X"s on the seal indicate that the beer is of a high quality. Although San Antonians drank Pearl during various events, the owners struggled to stay in business during Prohibition and the Great Depression by bottling soft drinks or making advertising signs.

The limestone and classical features of the United States Post Office and Courthouse exemplify one of the many different types of architectural styles, including Gothic, classical, and Spanish colonial, that decorate the heart of San Antonio. This view of the post office is from Alamo Plaza, part of which can be seen in the foreground.

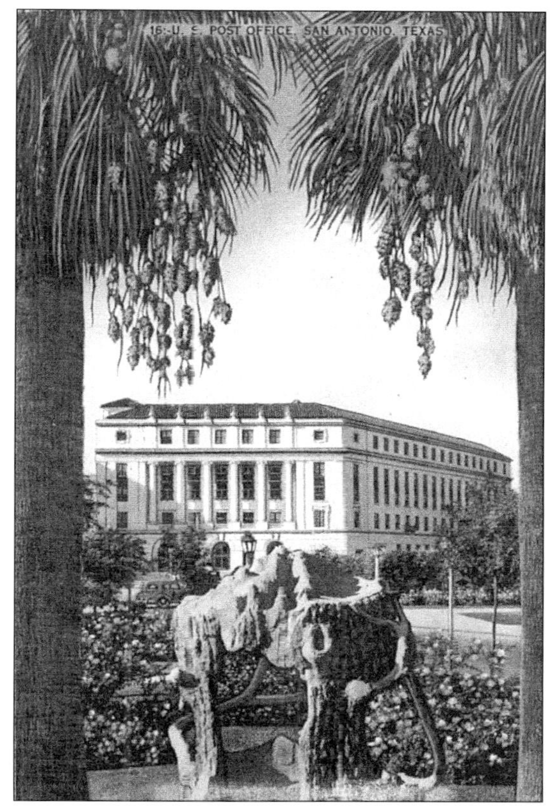

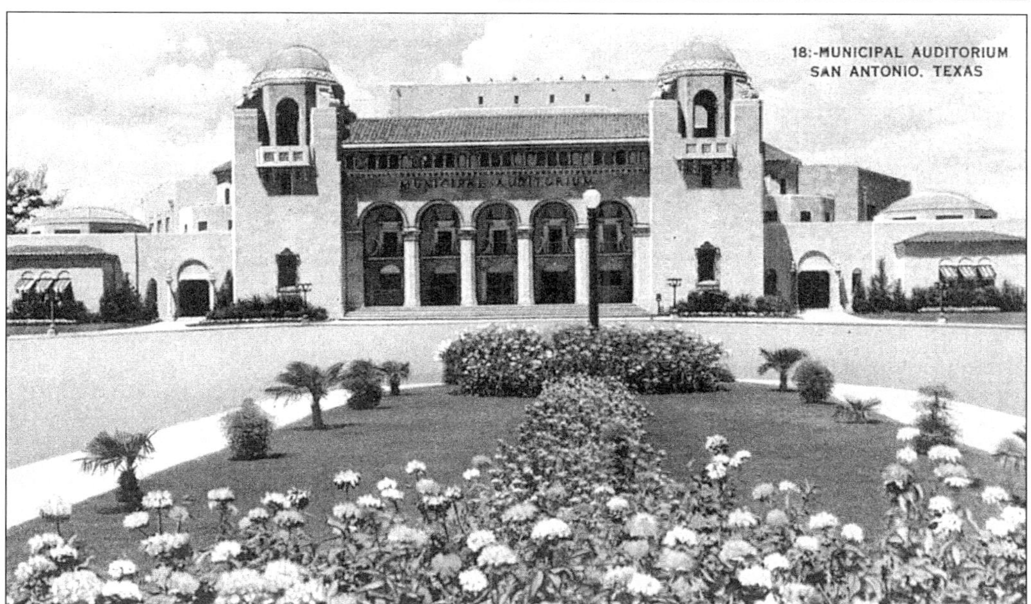

"Dedicated to World War Heroes" and built between Alamo and St. Mary's Streets, the colonial-style Municipal Auditorium initially cost $1.2 million. The auditorium caught on fire in 1979. Today, the newly renovated auditorium still hosts theater shows and concerts.

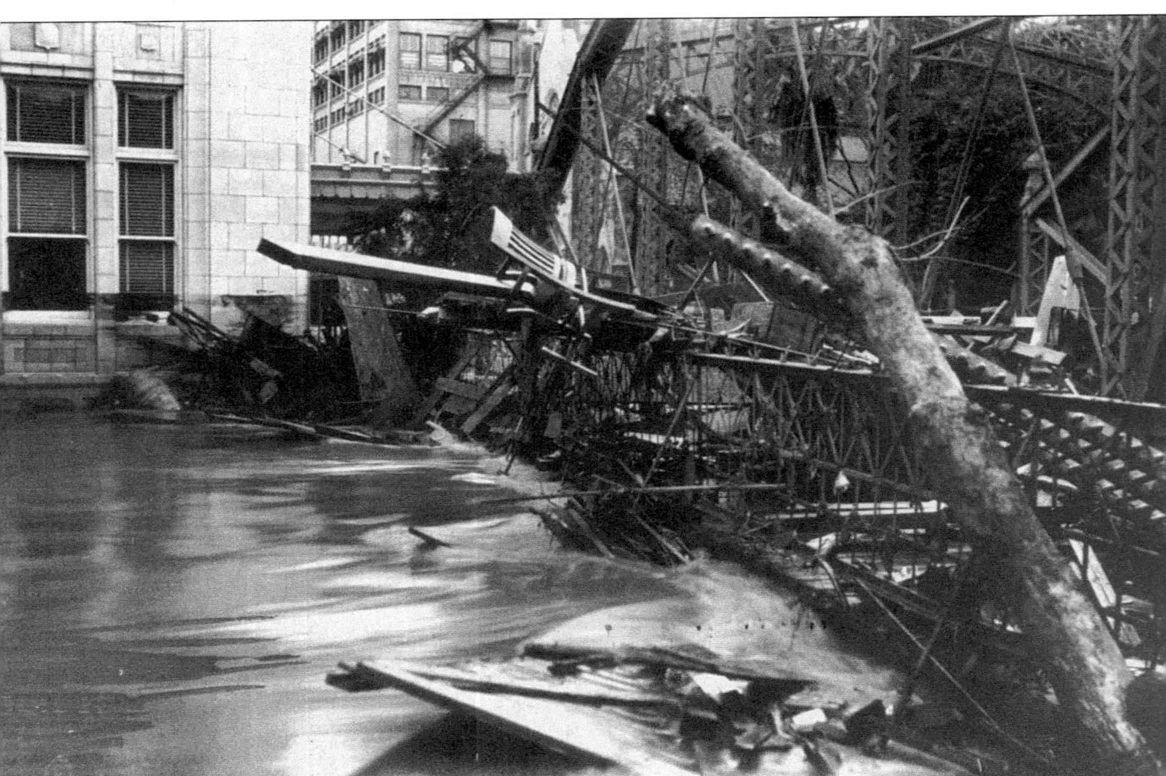

Floods rampage down the streets of San Antonio nearly every ten years, and in this 1921 photo, the waters reached St. Mary's Street Bridge. The September 9th flood stormed in after nearly seven inches of rain and left more than 50 people dead. Seventy-seven years later, long after the city built a dam and higher bridges, another flood destroyed 600 homes and left many destitute. (Courtesy Daughters of the Republic of Texas Library, Aniol Collection, 19–21.)

The flagpole and smokestack at the top of the Smith-Young Tower (also called the Transit Tower or the Tower Life Building) were removed in the 1960s and replaced with an antenna. Since several creeks from the San Antonio River, which is pictured in the foreground, once surrounded the tower, the area was nicknamed Bowen's Island until the creeks were paved.

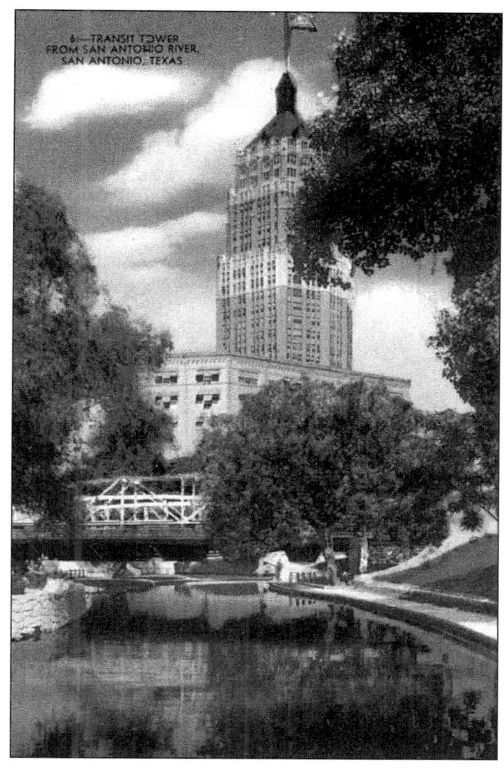

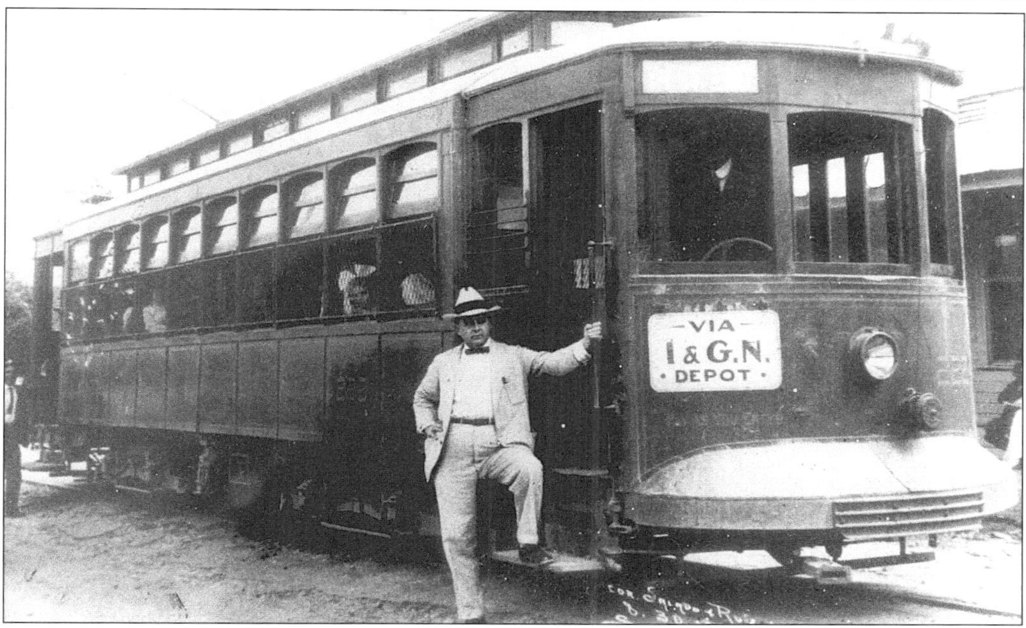

The destination of this 1910s trolley is the West End. Until the Great Depression, San Antonians relied on trolley cars as their main form of public transportation. Today, the city's transit system is called VIA. (Courtesy Broadway 50-50 and Louis M. LaRocco and Frank R. Little.)

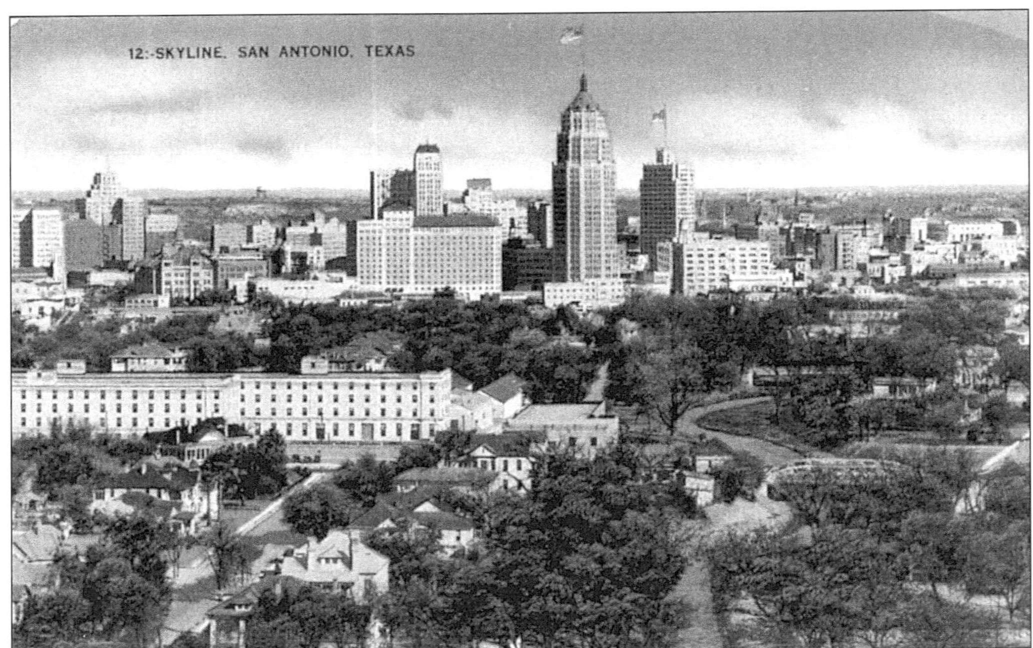

The skyline on this card lacks numerous now-familiar sites, many of which were built in the late 1960s. The tallest structure here is the Tower Life Building. To the left of it stands the former Plaza Hotel. Today, one can view the skyline not only from the 750-foot Tower of the Americas, which is now the tallest building, but from a spectacular lift in a garden on the north side of the city.

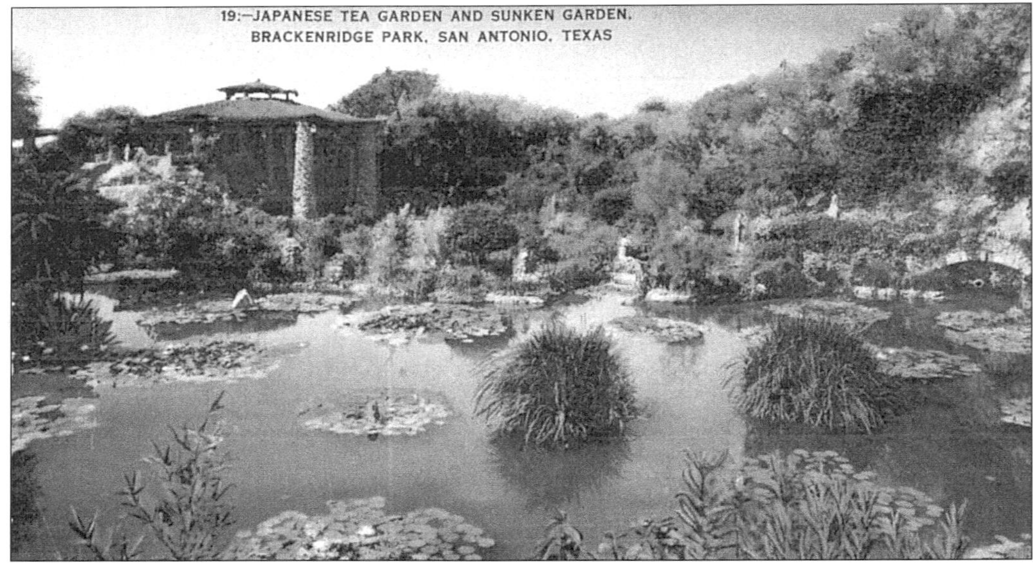

The best way to view Brackenridge Park's Japanese Sunken Gardens, completed in the 1910s by prison labor, is from a skyride, which carries one from the San Antonio Zoo over the gardens. The ride was built after this postcard was designed, but the gardens are still breathtaking, even though I always fear that I will fall into the water lily pond, which was once the pit of a quarry in the late 1800s.

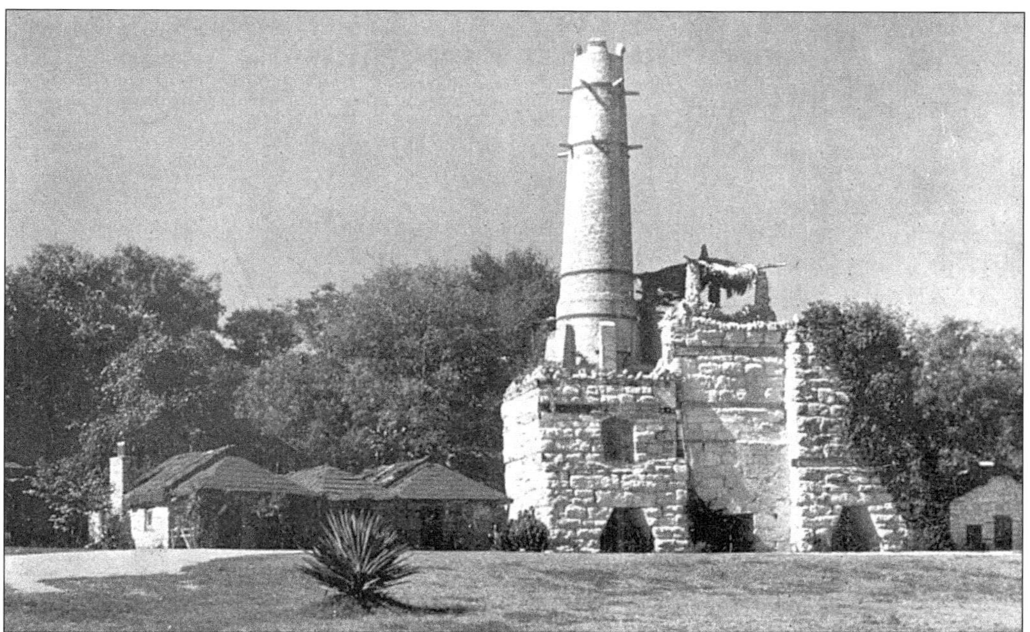

The original lime kilns and one of the smokestacks still remain from the first San Antonio Portland Cement Company, the first plant of its kind built on the west side of the Mississippi. Around 1907, the plant, which was founded by a French chemist, George Kalteyer, moved to what became known as Cementville, and this area became part of Brackenridge Park.

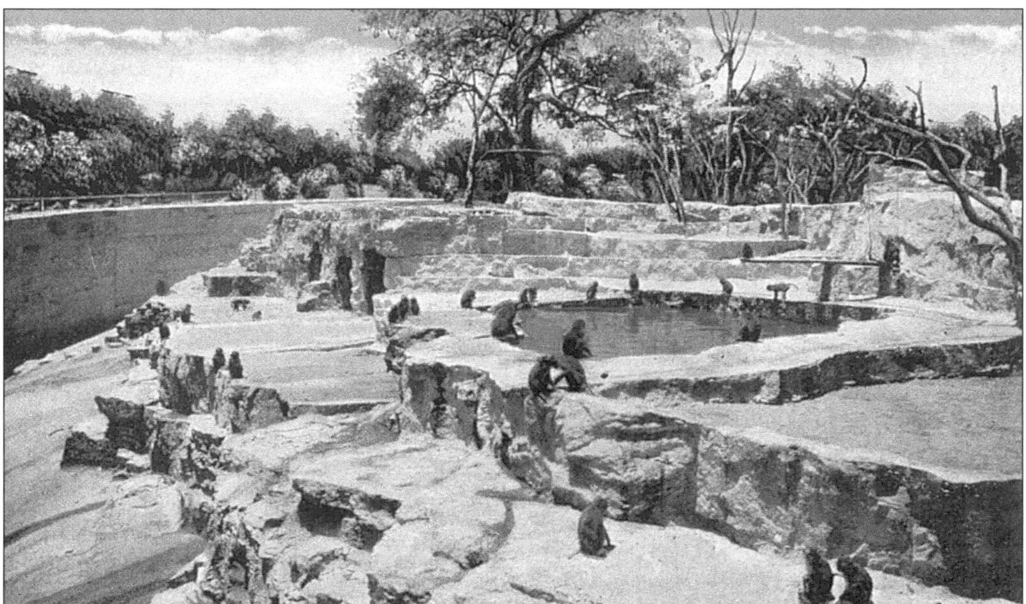

As children, my cousins and I always anticipated visiting Monkey Island in Brackenridge Park, even in 100-degree weather. We drank our cokes quickly, then refilled the cups with water that we splashed onto one another as we chased each other through the 70-acre zoological gardens that also featured enormous elephants, Komodo dragons, and whooping cranes.

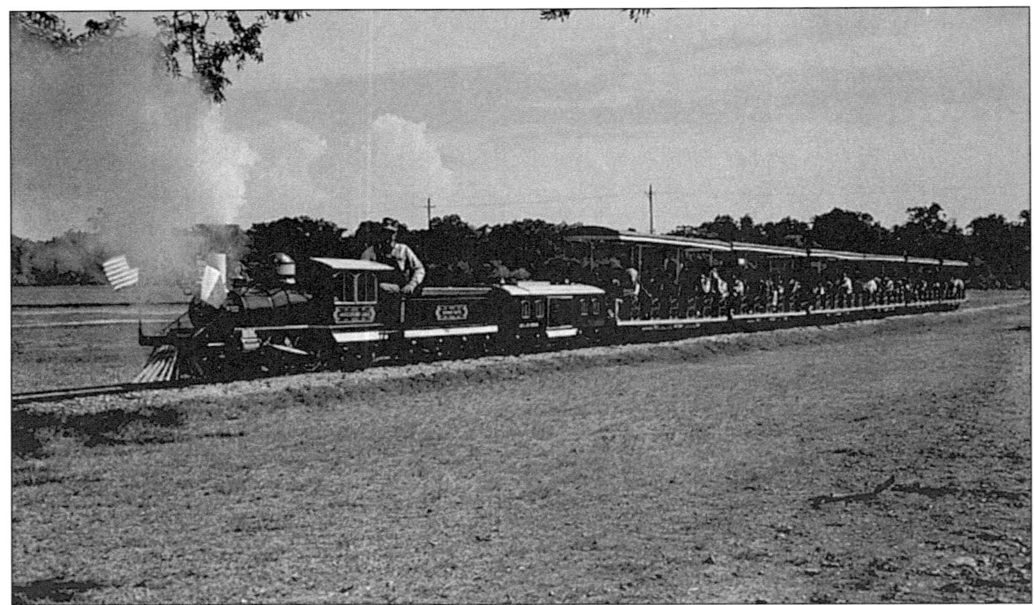

If we were not careful, this train would roar by my cousins and me before we could hop on it. If we did not jump on this miniature train modeled after the 1865 steamer, *Ole Smokey*, we took turns on the carousel in Kiddie Park or rode horses on the trails.

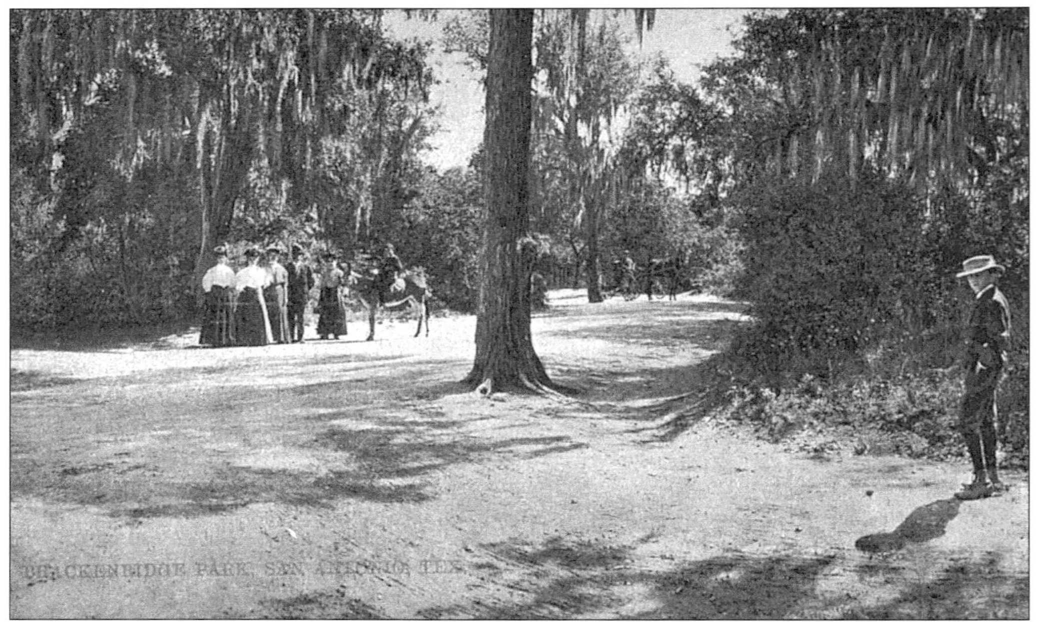

Shady trees and trails still allow horseback riders, bikers, and picnickers to enjoy the 343-acre land donated by George W. Brackenridge in 1899. Observant walkers may notice swimming holes and springs that once comprised the headwaters of the San Antonio River. Part of the park is used as a golf course, which hosted the first Texas Open in 1922.

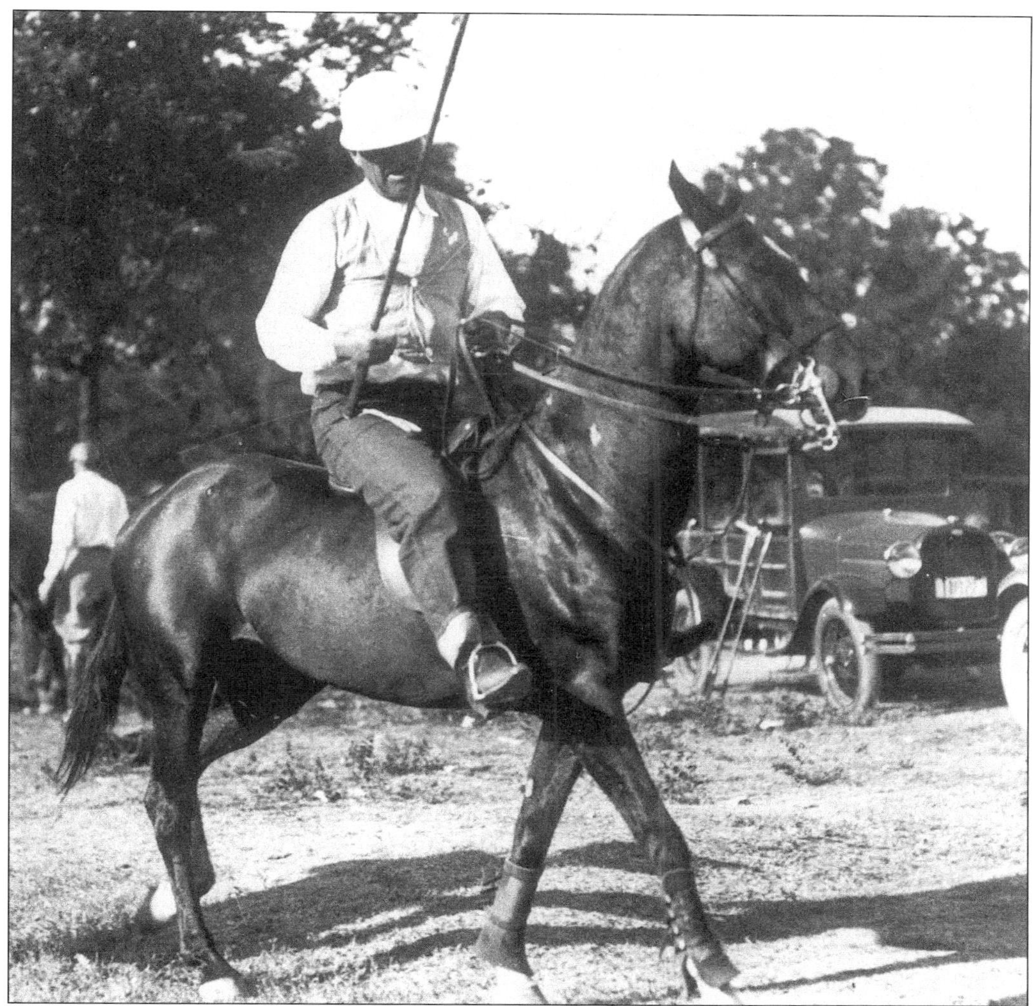

Will Rogers, perhaps the greatest cowboy of all time, played polo at Brackenridge Park in the 1910s when this picture was taken. Although Rogers was not a Texan, his roping and riding skills awed most Texans; he could throw three lassos and rope a horse's legs and head as well as the rider—simultaneously. (Courtesy Broadway 50-50 and Louis M. LaRocco and Frank R. Little.)

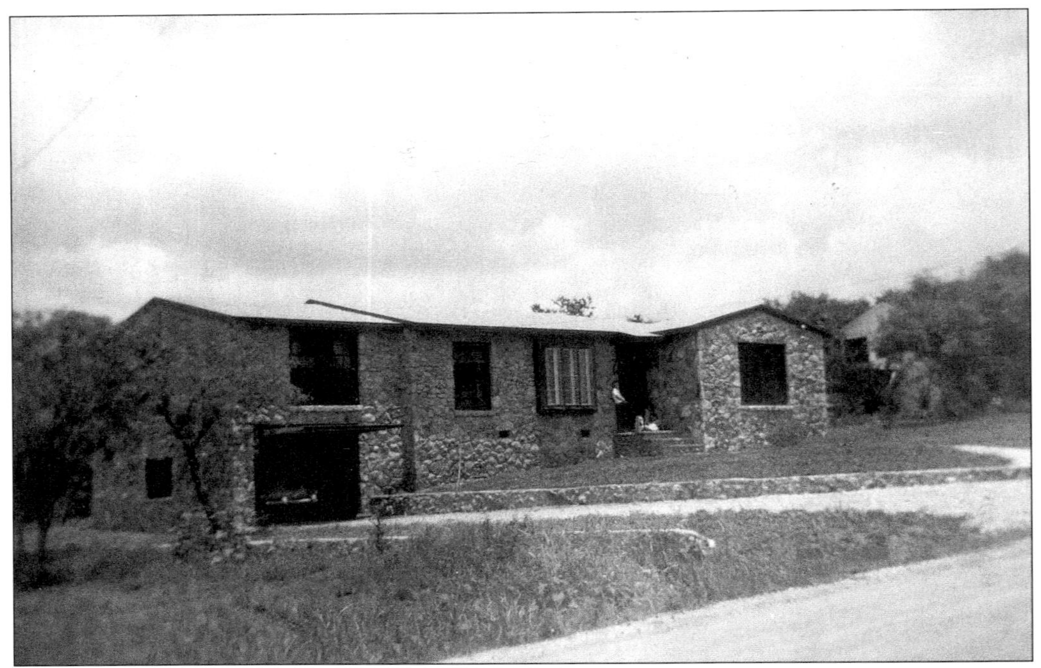

As downtown continued to expand after World War II, people like my grandparents migrated further away from the center of the city. They moved from their temporary post-war Erie Street home and settled into 126 Sunset Road, the house in which they lived after the war. This rock house still stands only one block from my parents' current house on Lawndale. (Courtesy Thille Lambert Newton.)

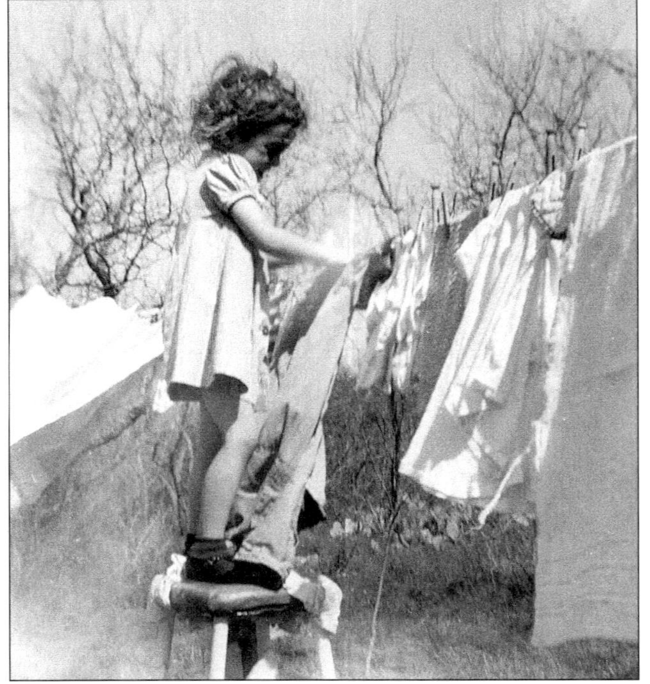

In the backyard of the Sunset Road house, my aunt Nancy hangs the laundry on the line. Even though the Second World War had ended, she still was expected to do her share of the household chores, just as her older siblings were too. (Courtesy Nancy Lambert Davenport.)

Three

DEEP IN THE HALLS OF ACADEMIA:

MUSEUMS AND SCHOOLS

By no means do I remember the stifling atmosphere of classrooms. I sketched lily pads in the gardens at the McNay Art Institute, perused Trinity University's history books in its vast library, attended the Nutcracker at the University of Incarnate Word, and studied Impressionist paintings in the Witte Museum. My grandparents, who escorted me on many of these expeditions, taught me that San Antonio's post-secondary schools and museums offer a range of hands-on tasks and subjects. Although a handful of educational institutions, including Palo Alto College, The University of Texas at San Antonio, and The Institute of Texan Cultures, sprang to life after the 1950s, some institutions' roots trace as far back as the 18th century. This chapter will focus on these older schools and museums, including St. Mary's University, where my grandfather earned his masters in history in 1948. By example of their respect for education, literature, and art, my grandfather and grandmother, Elizabeth Kirwan Lambert, a professional librarian, instilled in their descendants a love for learning.

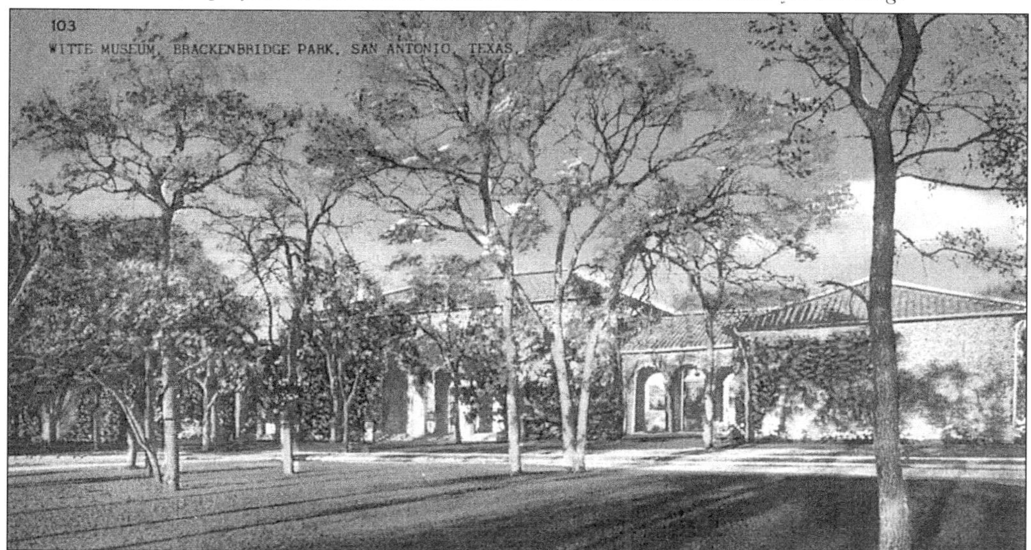

A haven for natural scientists of Texas, the Witte Museum features a diverse array of paintings and interactive exhibits. After an afternoon of studying Texas's landscape and wildlife at this museum, I like to walk in Brackenridge Park, looking for native shrubs or animals.

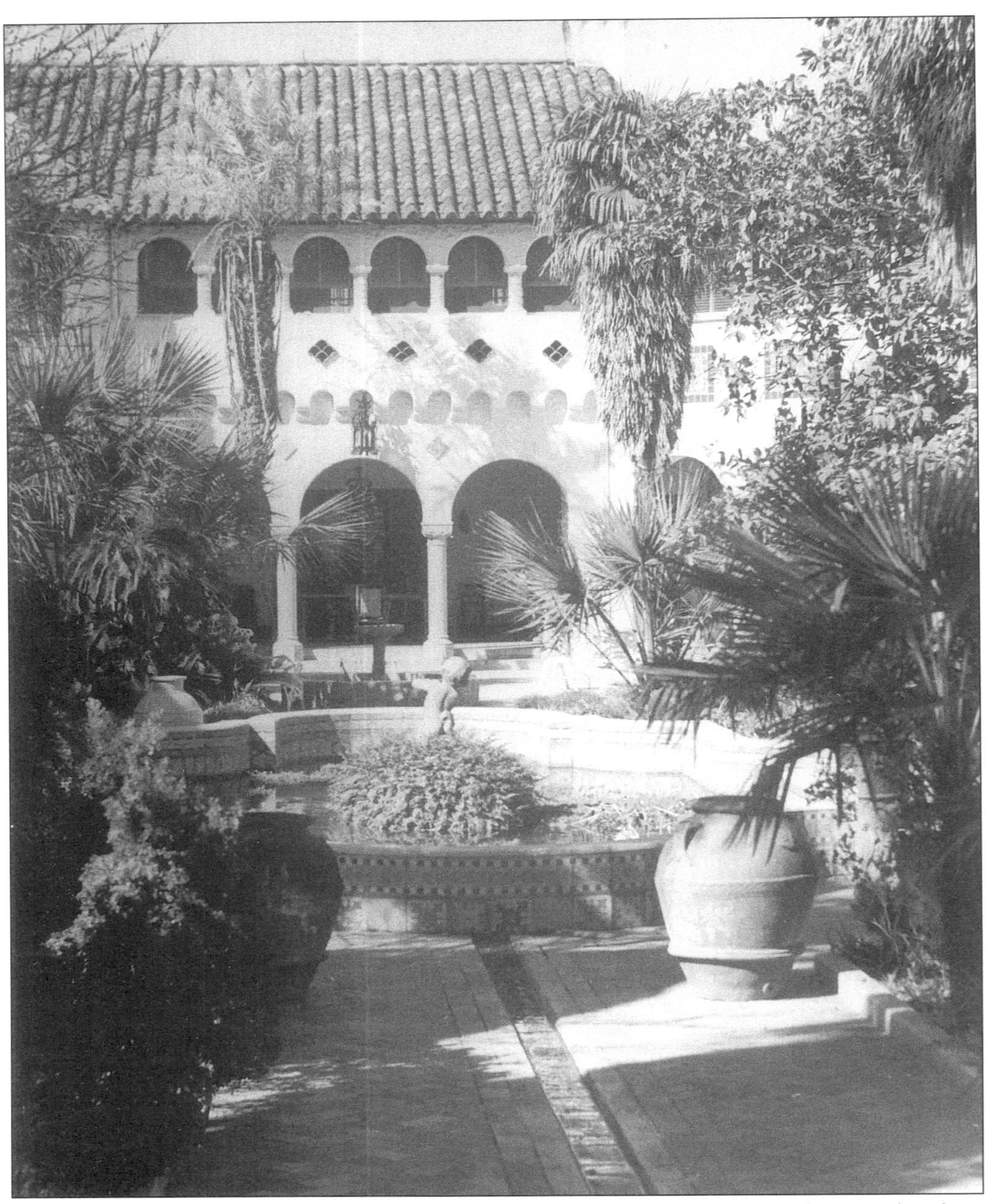

The Spanish-style house, patio, and grounds are as spectacular as the exhibits inside of my favorite museum, the Marion Koogler McNay Museum. This picture of the enclosed patio does not do justice to the complex Spanish tiles and spacious balconies. I took drawing and sculpture classes in the institute beside the original house and walked in the gardens with friends. (Courtesy Daughters of the Republic of Texas Library, Ramsdell Collection, Fred Schmidt photograph, CN99.175.)

If a cowboy brought in a free rack of horns or some snakes' rattles, he could count on a few beers way back in the 1880s when Albert Friedrich opened the Buckhorn Saloon. Visitors could see the antlers on the walls or venture into the curio store, which housed an odd assortment of items. Although the saloon was purchased by Lone Star Brewery after it closed, visitors still can view the collection at a new location on Houston Street. The postcard at right shows various rooms, including the bar and, below, the curio store.

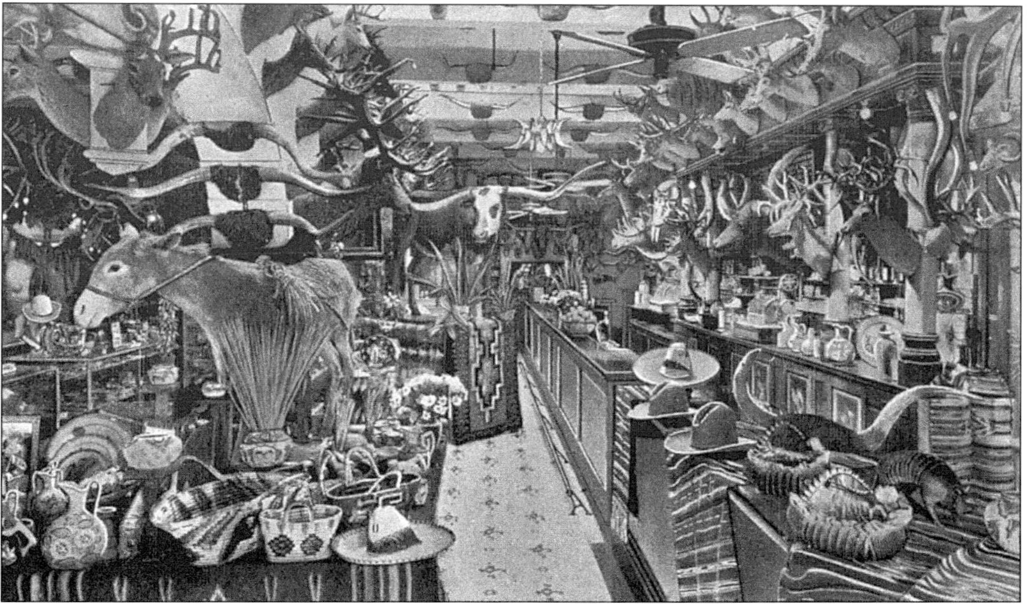

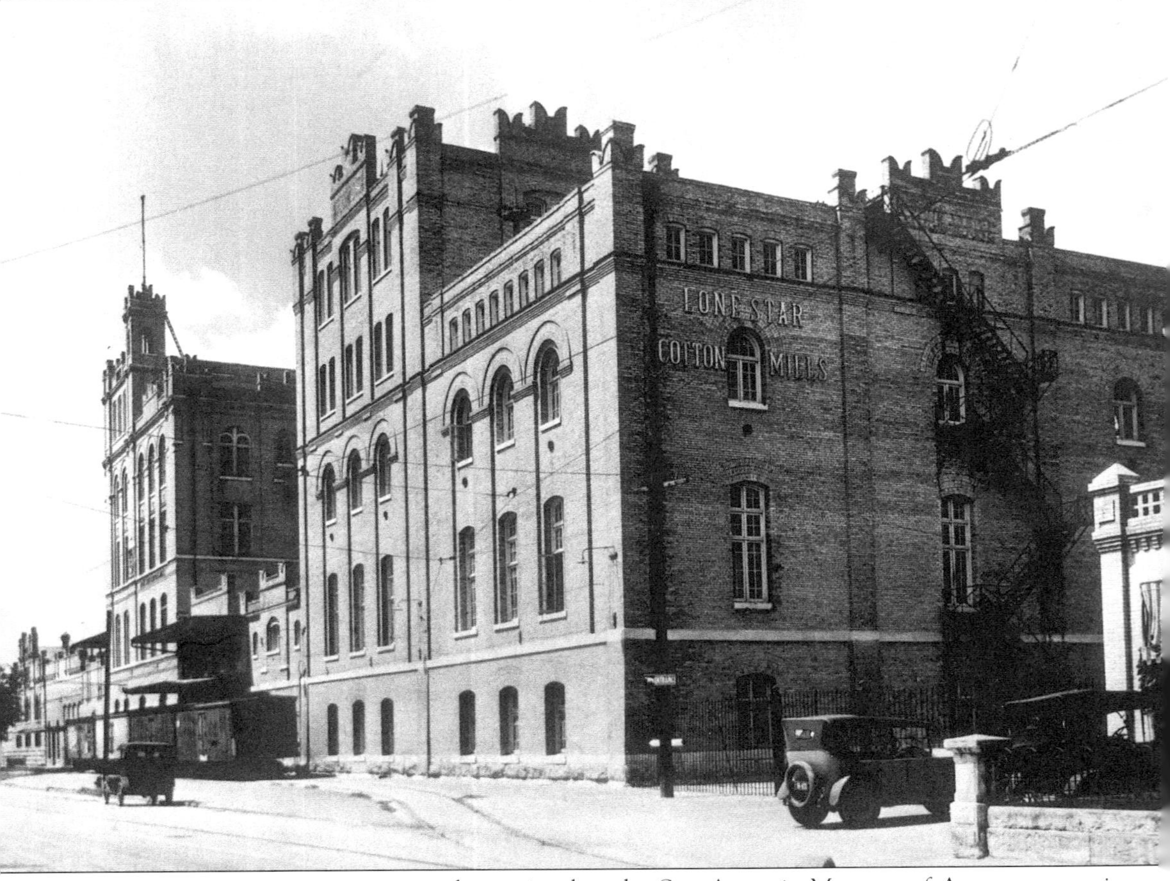

Not many museums once were breweries, but the San Antonio Museum of Art now occupies this building, which once was the Lone Star Brewery. The brewery company abandoned this site during the 1940s. The entire structure was preserved, even though the restoration of the museum required some internal changes. During Prohibition, when this picture was taken, the brewery complex temporarily became the Lone Star Cotton Mills. (Courtesy San Antonio Conservation Society Foundation.)

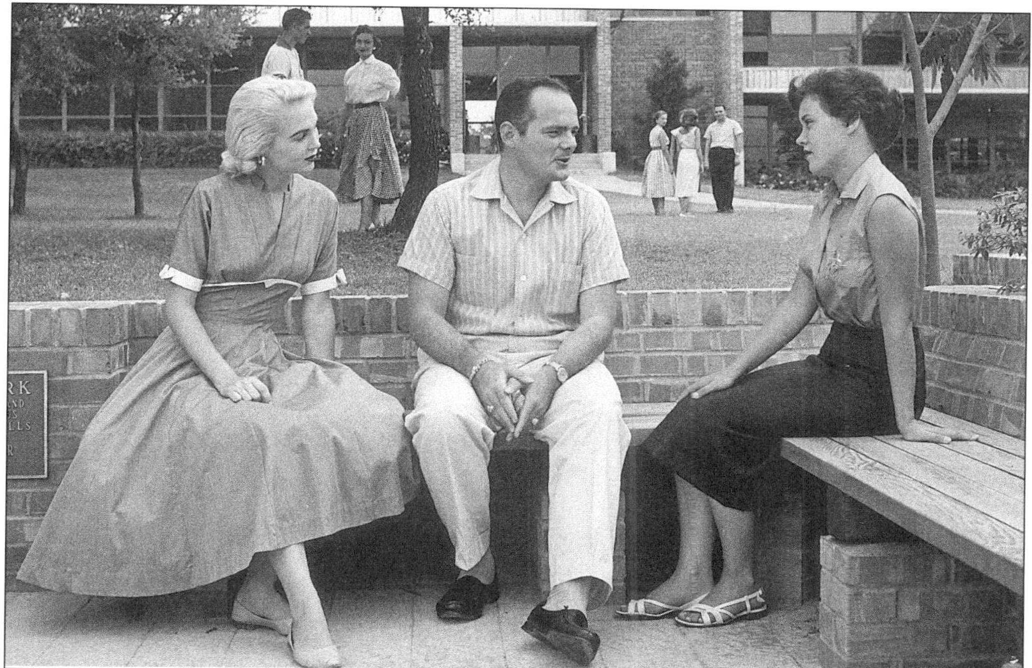

Seated in front of today's Preston Gaines Northrup Hall, the first completed building at Trinity University, three students talk with one another. In this 1950s shot, students may appear older, since some had fought in World War II or in the Korean War prior to attending college. (Courtesy Elizabeth Huth Coates Library, Trinity University.)

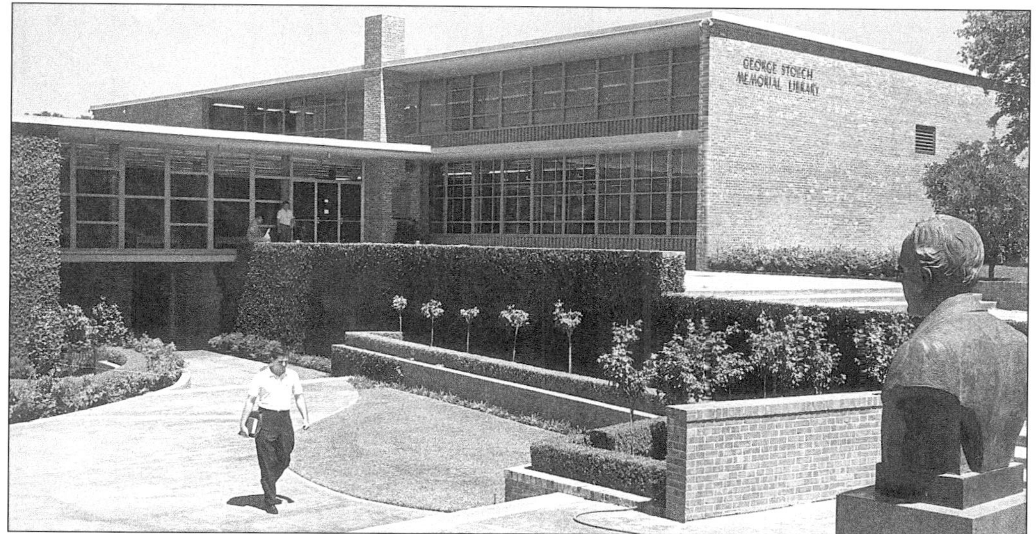

The George Storch Memorial Library, one of the first buildings built at Trinity University, was completed in 1952. Since the current library is the Elizabeth Huth Coates Library, this building (the old library) is now called the Storch Memorial Building and is used for classes and offices for the Education Department. Originally founded by Presbyterians in 1869, Trinity relocated several times in the northeast region of Texas until it settled in its present location in San Antonio in the early 1950s. (Courtesy Elizabeth Huth Coates Library, Trinity University.)

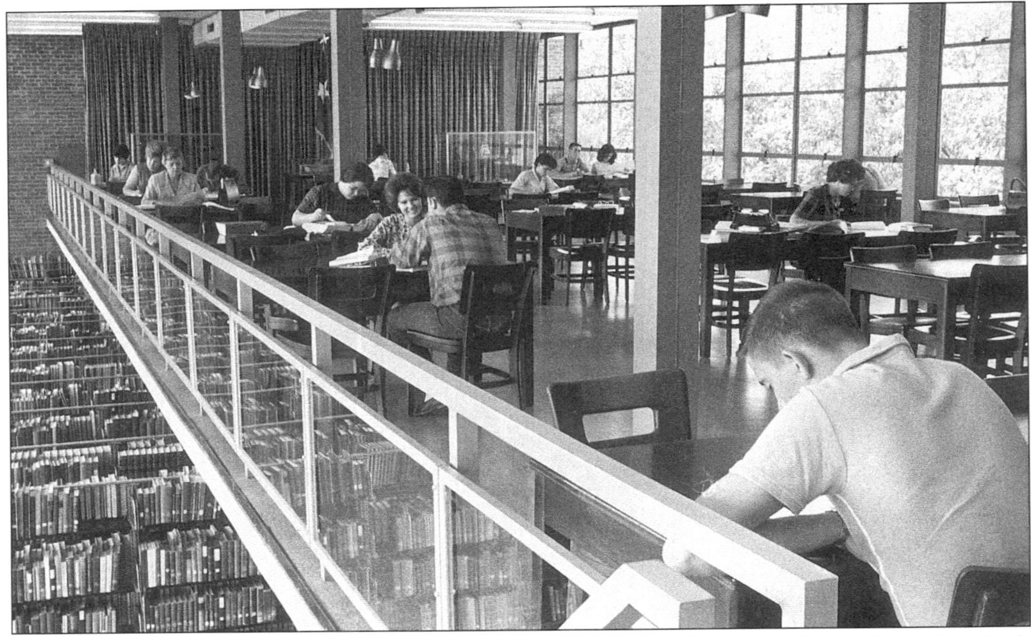

Like the current library, Storch Library provided students with niches for studying. My high school friends and I spent many Saturday afternoons wandering through book stacks at Trinity University when we needed research for papers. When we grew weary, we ran outside to a nearby fountain or slope and spied on the college students walking around campus. (Courtesy Elizabeth Huth Coates Library, Trinity University.)

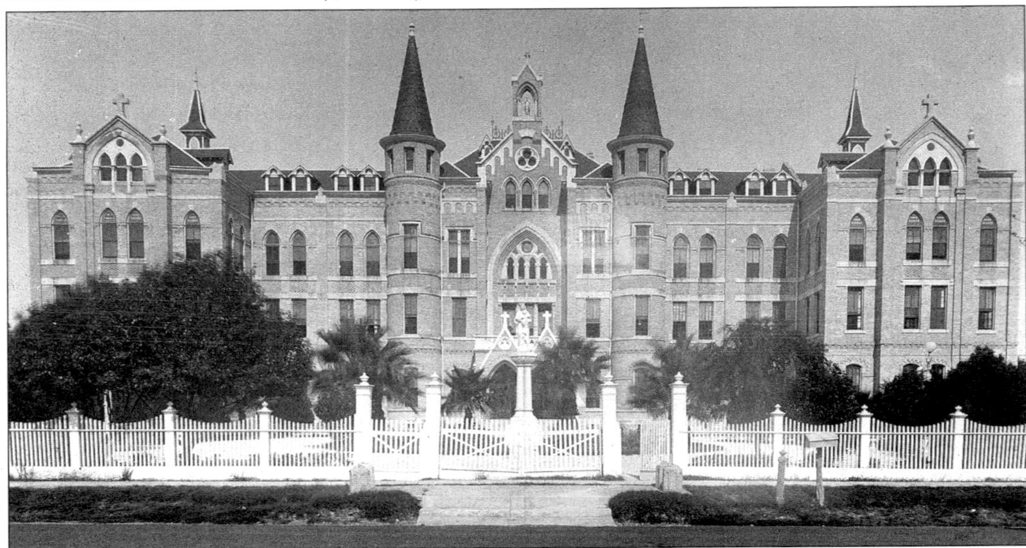

Our Lady of the Lake's Main Building, built by James Wahrenberger in the early 1900s, is a spectacular sight to behold. The Gallic structure was originally constructed for the Society of the Sisters of Divine Providence. This Catholic order of women founded Our Lady in the mid-1890s, and in 1918, the school was listed as an approved junior college; however, by the mid-1920s, it had become a four-year liberal arts institution. (Courtesy University Archives, Our Lady of the Lake University Library.)

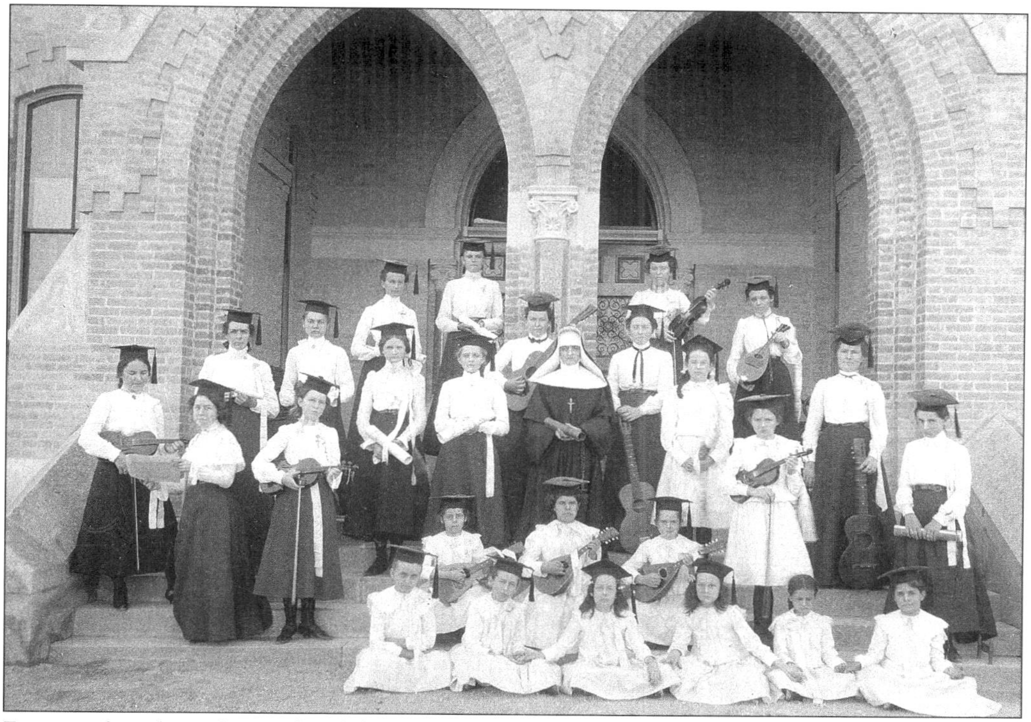

From its first days, Our Lady of the Lake University offered students the opportunity to study the fine arts, including music and art. Above, this 1901 music class gathers for a group picture, and below, students in this 1940s art class work diligently. (Both courtesy University Archives, Our Lady of the Lake University Library.)

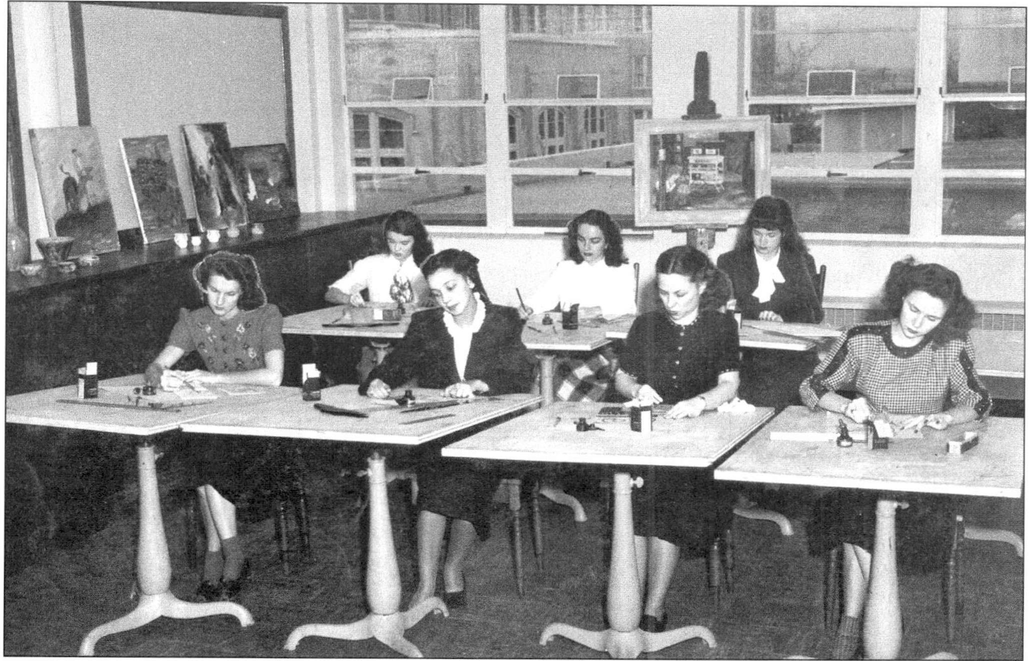

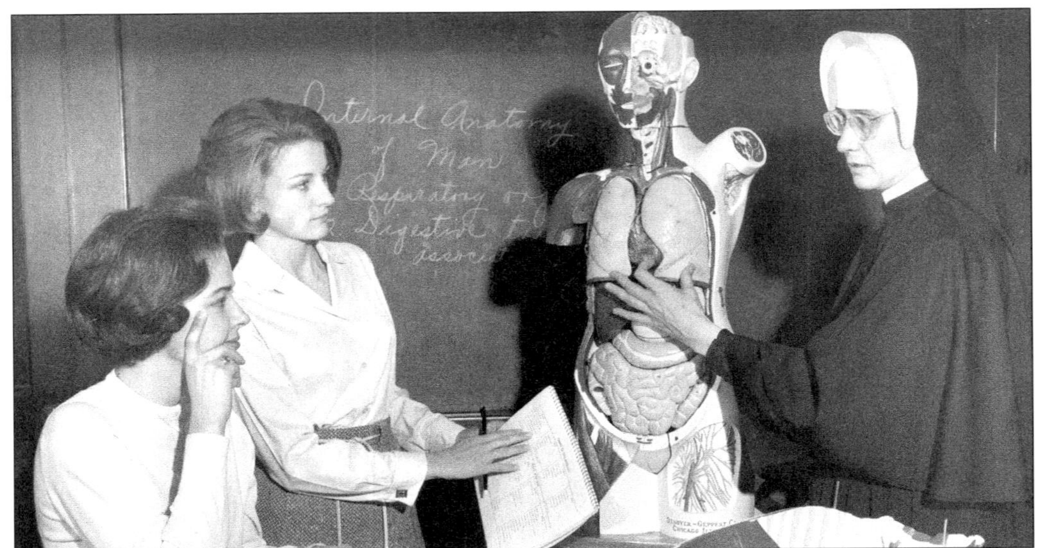

With Sister Elizabeth Anne, these two students at Our Lady of the Lake University study internal anatomy. Even in the early 1900s, the university offered students several courses in the natural sciences, including chemistry and physics. (Courtesy University Archives, Our Lady of the Lake University Library.)

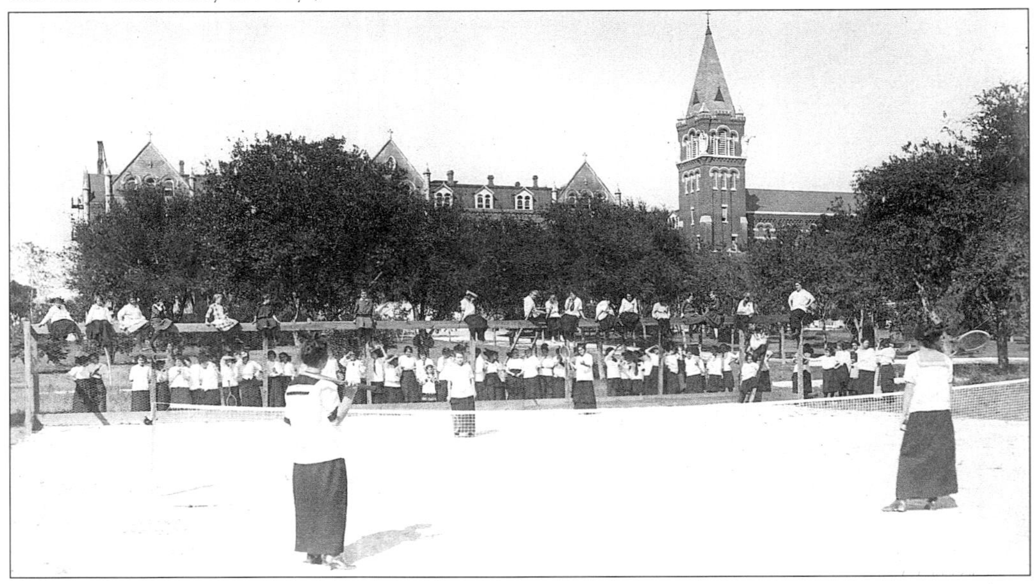

The first Sisters of Charity of the Incarnate Word came to San Antonio in 1869, and as their vision to minister to the sick and the poor grew, so did plans to establish a school. By borrowing money and squirreling funds, the sisters purchased Brackenridge Villa and the surrounding estate, which consisted of approximately 280 acres. A few years later, in 1900, they completed the Incarnate Word Convent, pictured behind the students playing tennis, on the left. The chapel on the right was constructed in 1906. The sisters reserved part of the convent for dormitories and classrooms, but in the early 1900s, they decided to call Incarnate Word School, which served the elementary and high school levels, the College and Academy of the Incarnate Word and eventually established a college. (Courtesy Incarnate Word Archives.)

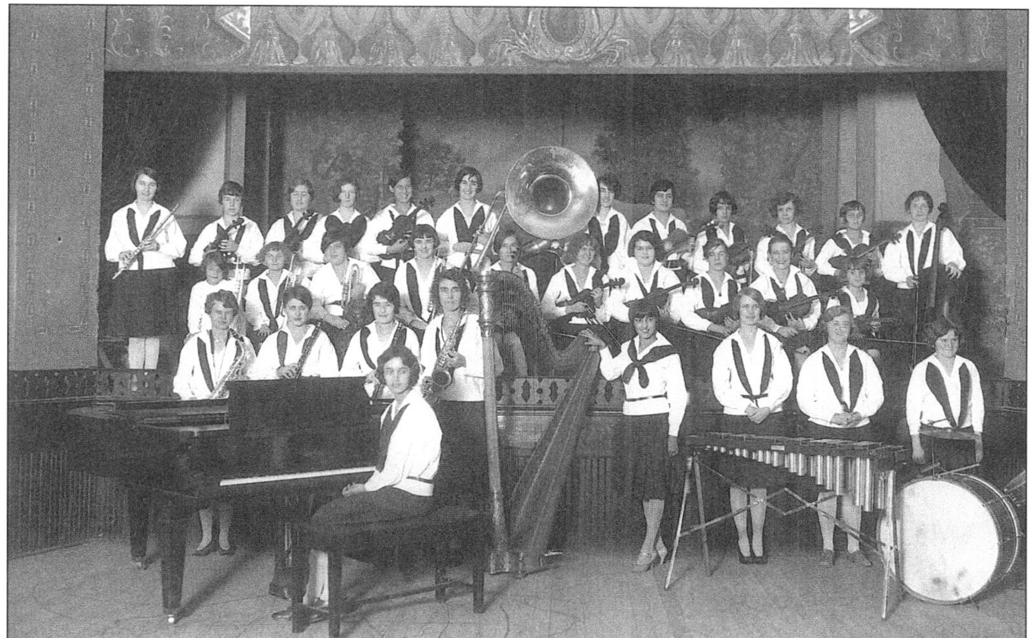

This early-1900s picture of Incarnate Word's college students was taken in St. Cecilia's Hall, which once stood behind the convent and chapel. Today, Incarnate Word's fine arts division, including music, still demonstrates talent; my family and I have attended various recitals at the school. (Courtesy Incarnate Word Archives.)

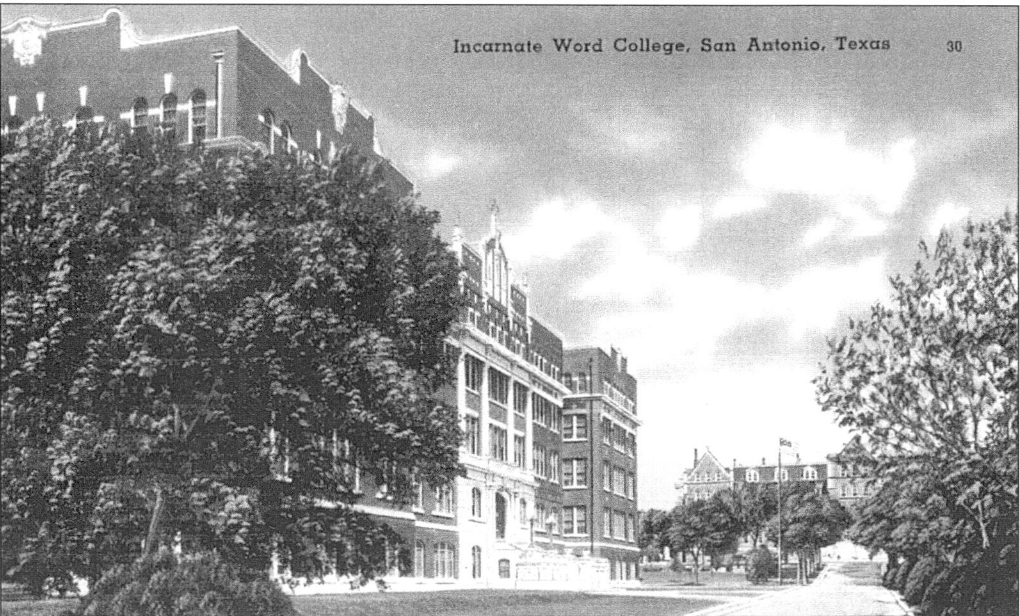

Colbert Hall, the administration building at the University of Incarnate Word, stands on the left in this photograph, facing the street of Broadway. In the distance, on the right, stands the convent, which no longer exists today. During the holiday season, Colbert Hall and the grounds in front of it are a spectacular sight to behold; the trees are decorated with festive lights.

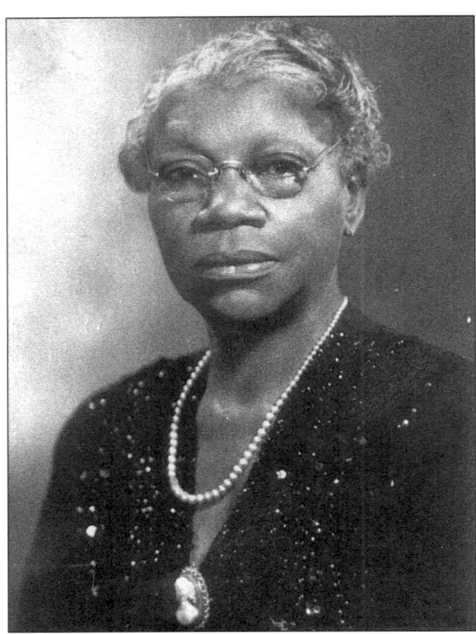

Miss Artemisia Bowden assumed leadership of St. Philip's College for over 50 years (1902–1954), and under her guidance, the college developed into a prominent educational institution. St. Philip's celebrated its centennial anniversary in 1998. (Courtesy St. Philip's College Archives.)

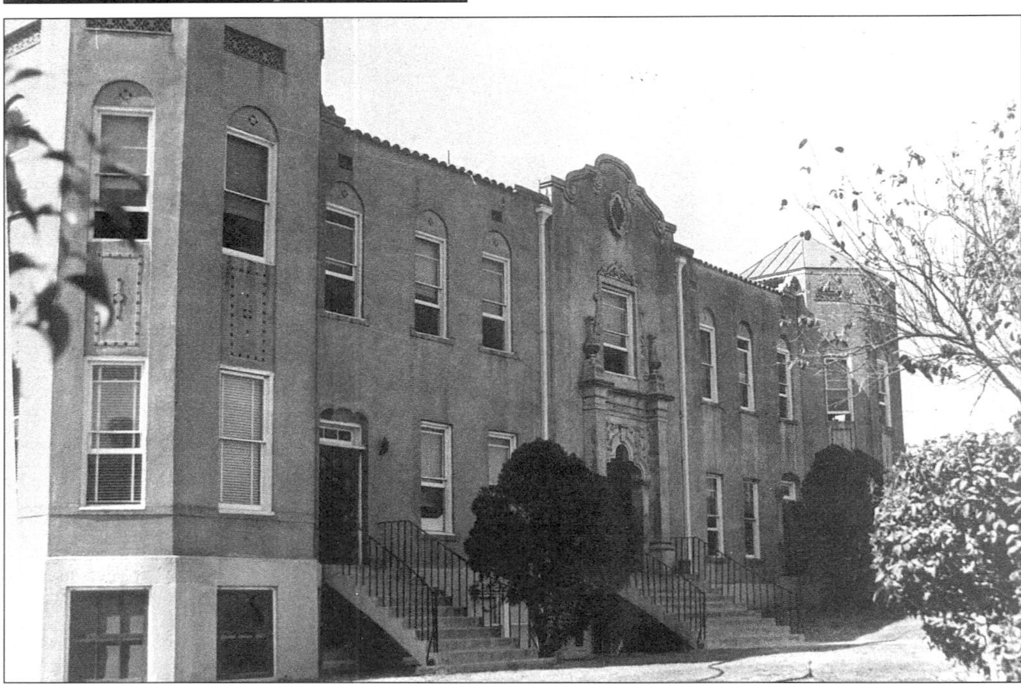

Named after the Right Reverend James Steptoe Johnston, the Bishop of the Diocese of West Texas and the founder of St. Philip's College, the Johnston Memorial Building, built in 1927, was demolished in 1949 to make way for what is now the physical education building. Once a women's college in the late 19th century, the school evolved into a private junior college serving the needs of the black community of San Antonio. In the early 1940s, the college became affiliated with San Antonio College, and today, nearly 9,000 students attend the college. (Courtesy St. Philip's College Archives.)

Established in 1858 as a German-English school, this structure was home to San Antonio College beginning in 1926. After the Great Depression and World War II, the college moved to a larger location on San Pedro Avenue where it stands today. (Courtesy San Antonio College Library.)

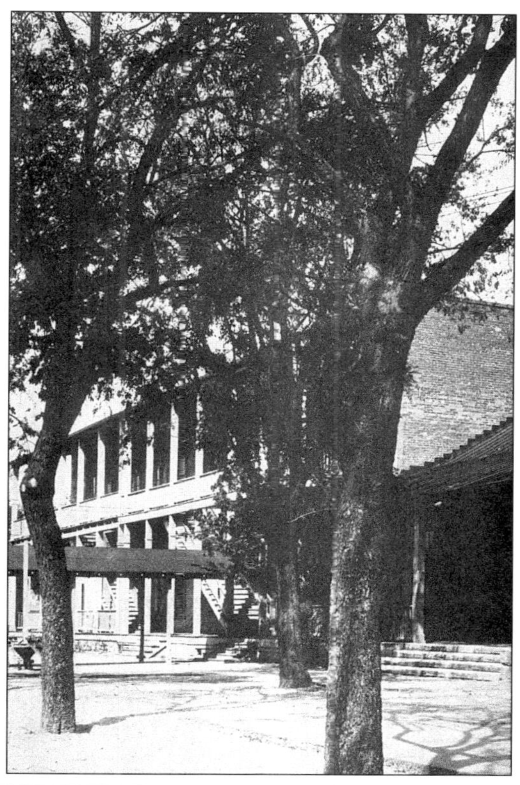

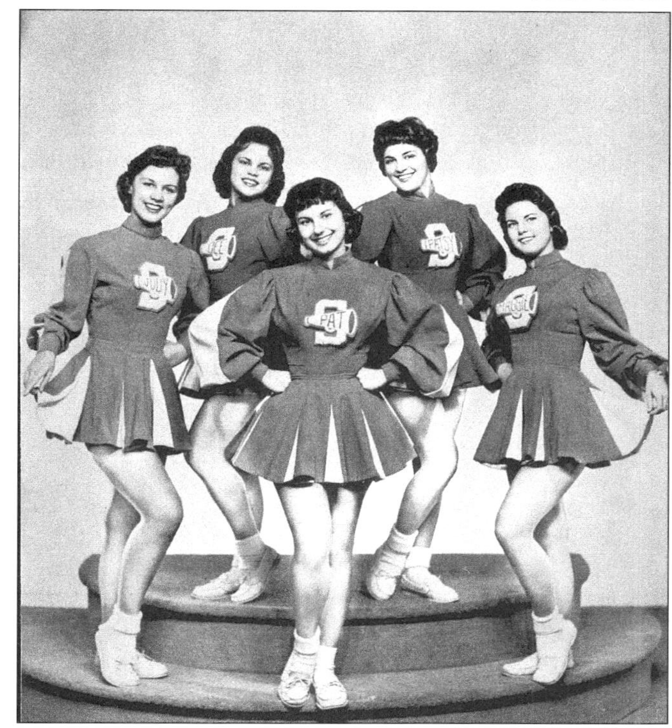

From left to right Judy, Pat, and Maggie (front row) and Gee and Patsy (back row) led the yells at games in 1960. The cheerleaders were chosen by the student body at an assembly. (Courtesy San Antonio College Library.)

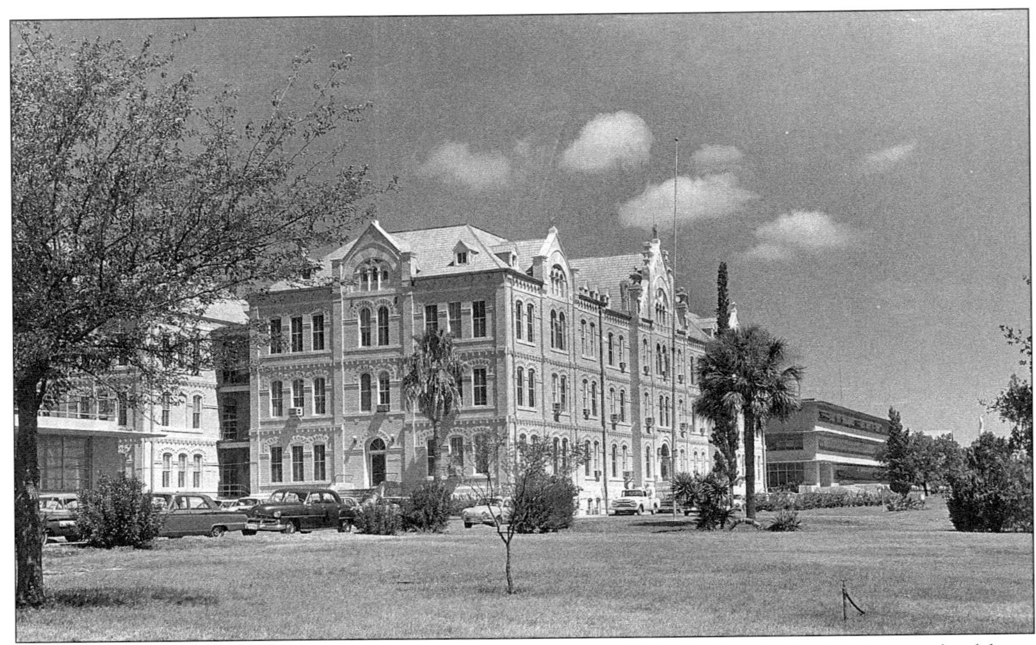

This shot of St. Louis Hall, the administration building, and Garni Hall, the science building, at St. Mary's University was taken in the 1950s. Although the university dedicated Garni Hall in 1952, the administration building was constructed in the 1890s, when the college expanded and moved part of its school from its central location in San Antonio to a larger, more rural area. The rural school, situated in Woodlawn Hills, was named St. Louis College until the rest of the school moved to the same location. (Courtesy St. Mary's University Archives.)

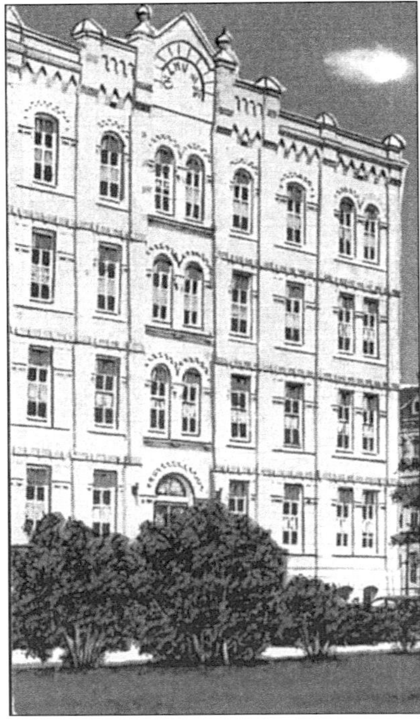

Located on the campus of St. Mary's University, Chaminade Hall was named after the founder of the Society of Mary, Reverend William Joseph Chaminade. Once a dormitory, this 1921 structure now houses offices.

Four

DEEP-SET STONES:

THE MISSIONS

The five Spanish-style missions of San Antonio were constructed in the early 1700s by Spaniards who desired to Christianize the American Indians and stake new land. The Spaniards, however, were the first of many colonists who attempted to seize property and control in Texas. Five other groups have staked their flags into Texas ground—France, Mexico, the Confederacy, the Republic of Texas, and the United States—and Texans battled every one of them until they joined the United States. Texans' determination to preserve their land and heritage did not fully materialize until Colonel James Bowie chose to disobey the orders of General Sam Houston to destroy the Mission San Antonio de Valero, or the Alamo, as the Mexican general, Santa Anna, stormed toward San Antonio. With this decision, Bowie set an example for generations of Texans to follow: never give up. Every time I visit the still-standing façade of the Alamo today, I imagine Colonel William Travis, along with Bowie, Davy Crockett, and other heroes, daring each man, woman, and child literally to cross a dirt line to demonstrate their decision and determination to protect the Alamo. Since nearly every defender sacrificed his or her life to save this fort in 1836, future Texans, including my grandfather, still keep alive the spirit and gusto of these brave men.

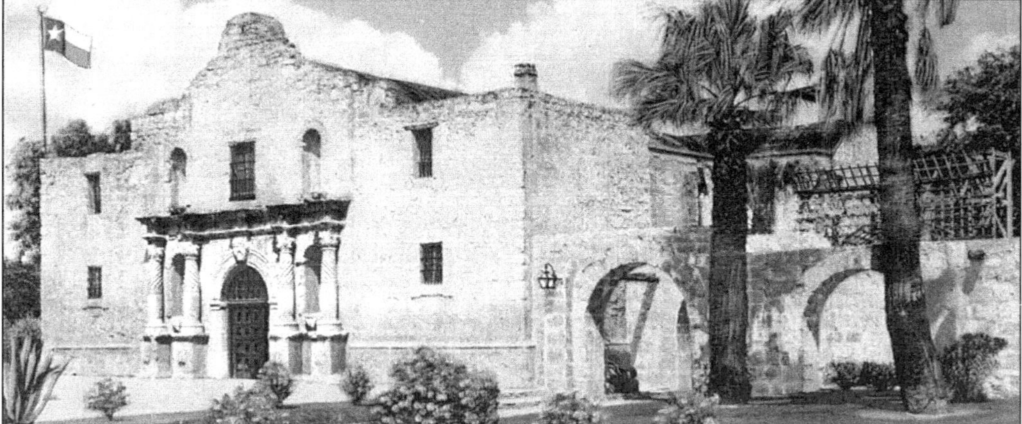

The moment out-of-state visitors and natives step onto the grounds of the Alamo, they sense the deep-rooted patriotism of those who died in defense of San Antonio and Texas's land and heritage. These 200 defenders held nearly 2,000 Mexican troops at bay for 13 days. Even during the world wars, members of the Texas National Guard, including my grandfather, Joseph Idus Lambert, under the guidance of General John J. Pershing, still protected their land from the Mexicans and other imposters. In a July 3, 1916 entry in his diary, he sadly remarked, "So many Americans both in the United States and in Mexico have been killed [by Pancho Villa and his bandits] that it seems a disgrace to the nation to speak of peace."

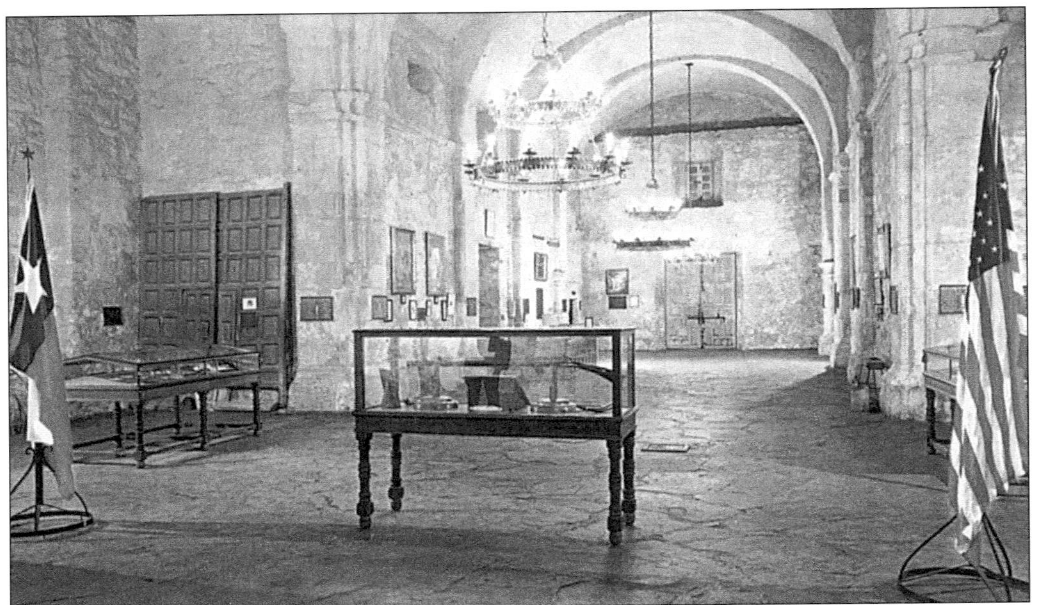

On the left side of the Alamo's interior, a modern-day Lone Star flag stands as a reminder of the gusto of those who died for Texas's freedom. Other artifacts in the Alamo include gunpowder horns, knives, and letters written by brave men in their last hours.

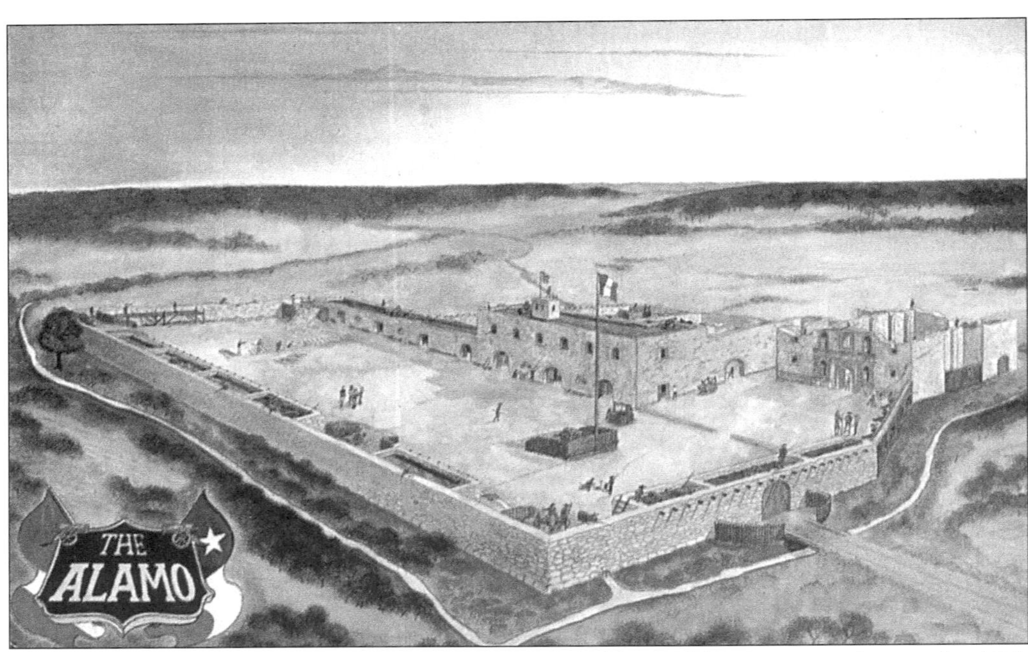

Today, most of the land around the fort is surrounded by buildings or trees, but in the 18th century, the first Alamo mission was located near a stream of the San Antonio River. It was moved to its present location in hopes of protecting it from flooding. The other missions, all along the river, were built within 9 miles of each other and, like the Alamo, had protective walls, churches, and living areas designed for the American Indians and the missionaries.

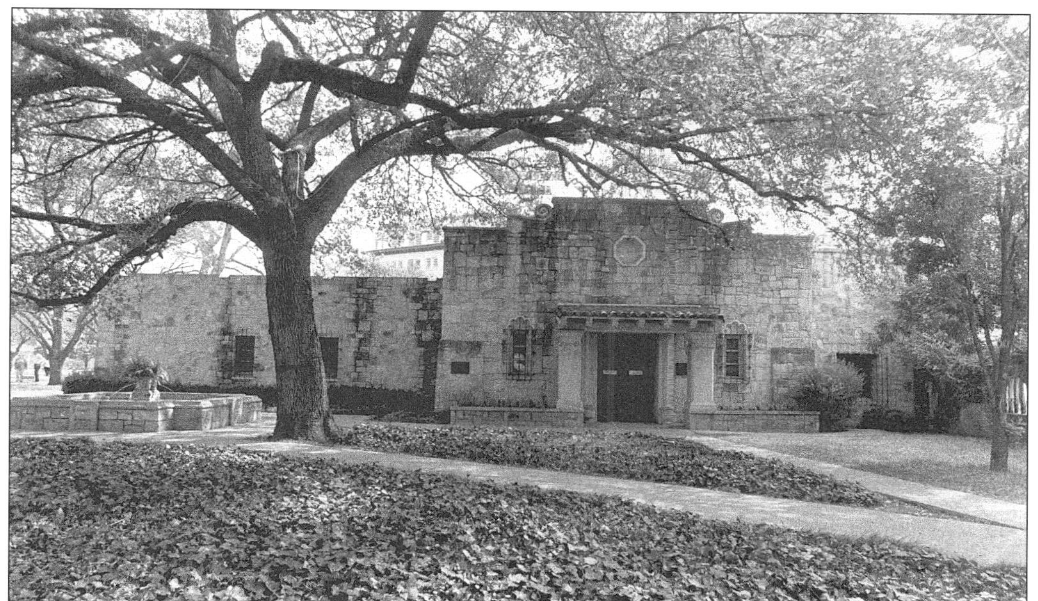

The Daughters of the Republic of Texas Library at the Alamo houses a wonderful collection of archival materials for curious researchers of Texas and its history. The library is part of the Alamo complex and is located to the right of the Alamo church, behind the arcade. Part of the mission of the Daughters of the Republic of Texas is to "perpetuate the memory and spirit of the men and women who achieved and maintained the independence of Texas," and to "encourage historical research into the earliest records of Texas . . ." (Courtesy Daughters of the Republic of Texas Library, Joe Elicson photograph, 1982.)

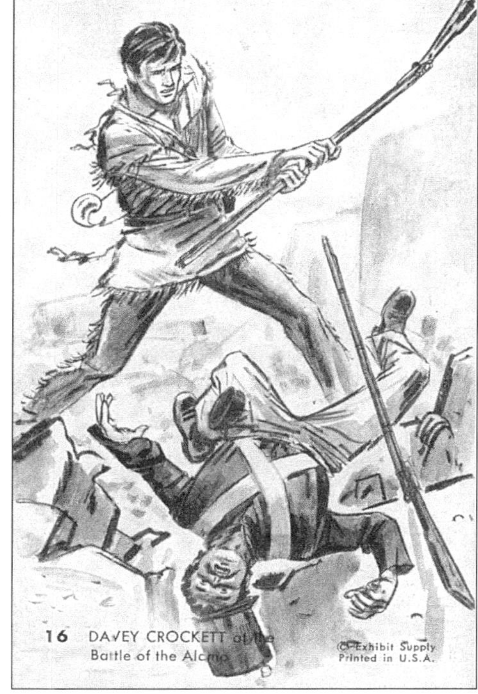

Always dressed in deerskin and armed with his rifle, "Old Betsy," Davy Crockett is remembered by modern Texans as one of the Alamo's greatest heroes. Whenever I think of Davy Crockett, I imagine the brave deeds and sacrifices of the Alamo's men and women and am inspired.

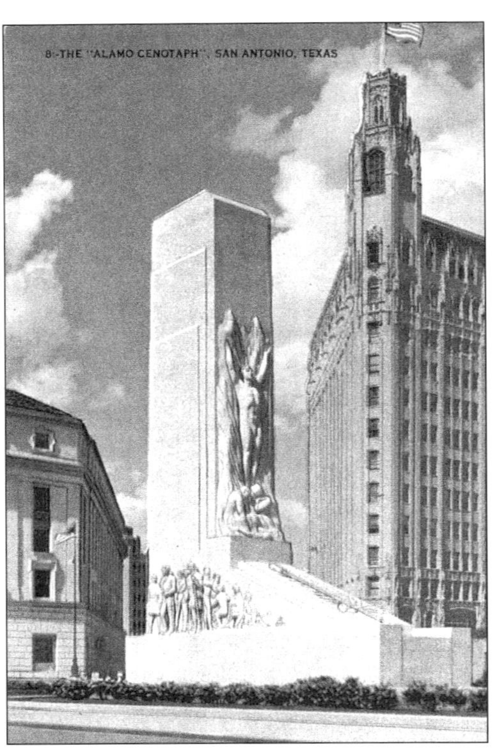

Inscribed on this 60-foot marble structure, the Alamo Cenotaph, are the names of the heroes of the Alamo. According to a tall tale, the bodies of the Texas heroes were burned by General Santa Anna at this site.

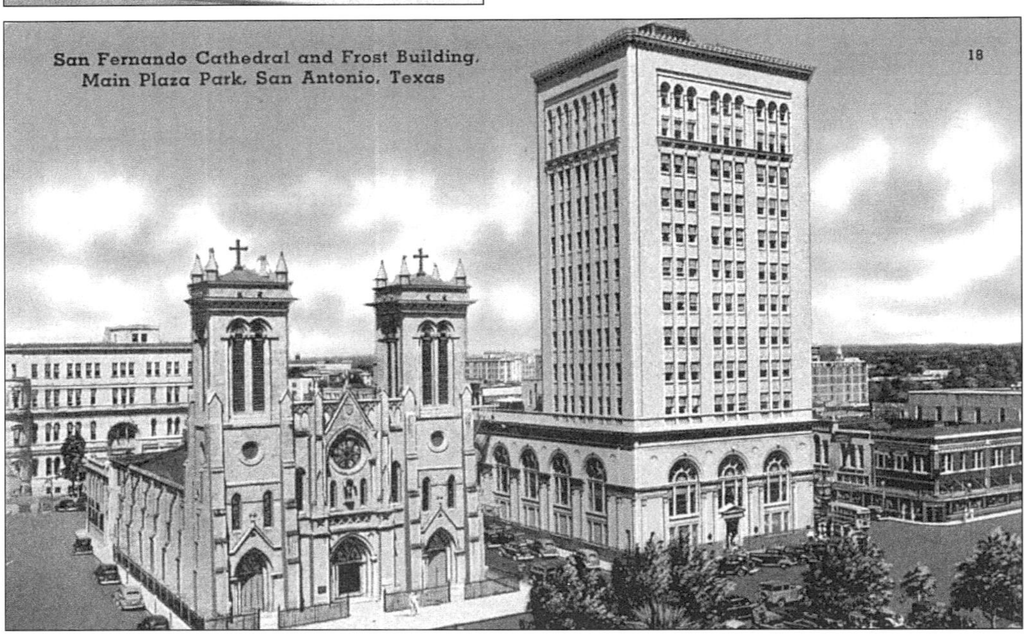

According to another legend, "the bones of the Martyrs of the Alamo are buried under the high altar" of San Fernando Cathedral. Like the five missions, this cathedral was built by the Spaniards in the 18th century; San Fernando became the parish church for the Spaniards and the American Indians. The Old Frost National Bank Building, completed in 1922, stands to the right of the cathedral.

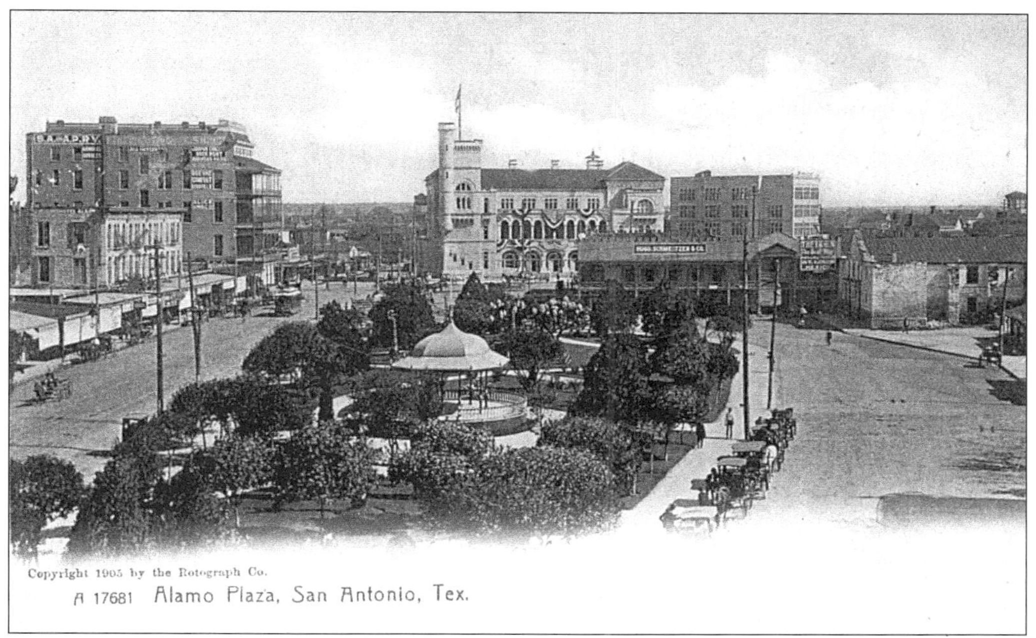

This 1905 scene of Alamo Plaza, formerly the enclosed courtyard of the Alamo, was taken the year that the state of Texas appointed the Daughters of the Republic of Texas to preserve the Alamo and its history. Today, reconstructed fortress walls surround part of the Alamo, and the area directly in front of the Alamo is no longer used as a street. The Hugo, Schmeltzer & Co. building on the right front flank of the Alamo has been demolished, as has the Romanesque post office behind it. A modern post office that houses federal offices now stands in this location.

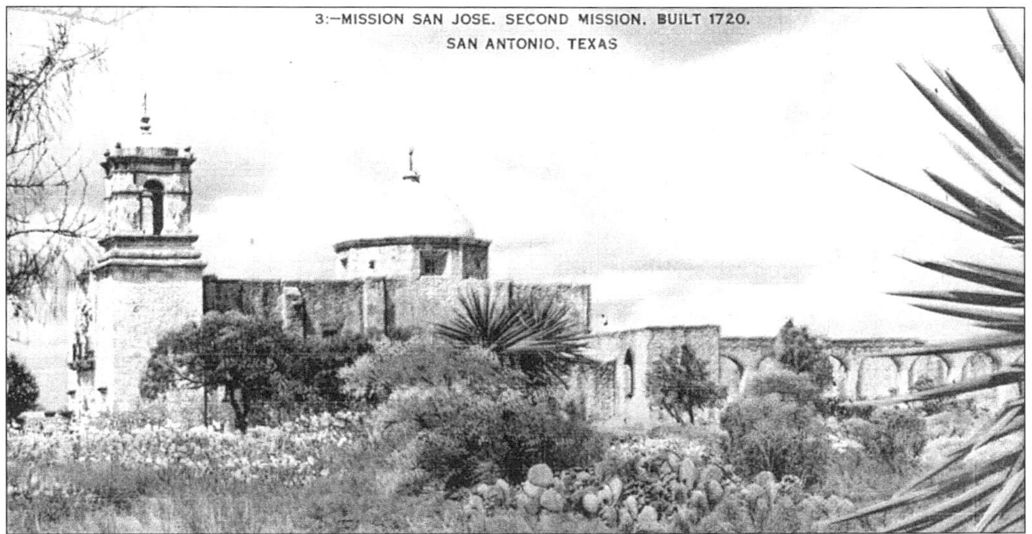

Mission San José y San Miguel de Aguayo, my favorite mission, is situated on the rim of San Antonio, and its dusty paths, old wells, and American Indian artifacts offer cryptic corners that I love to explore. Although the mission was founded in 1720 and reconstructed in the 1920s, one can still trace the pattern of painted Spanish tiles and sit atop a 1790s flour mill.

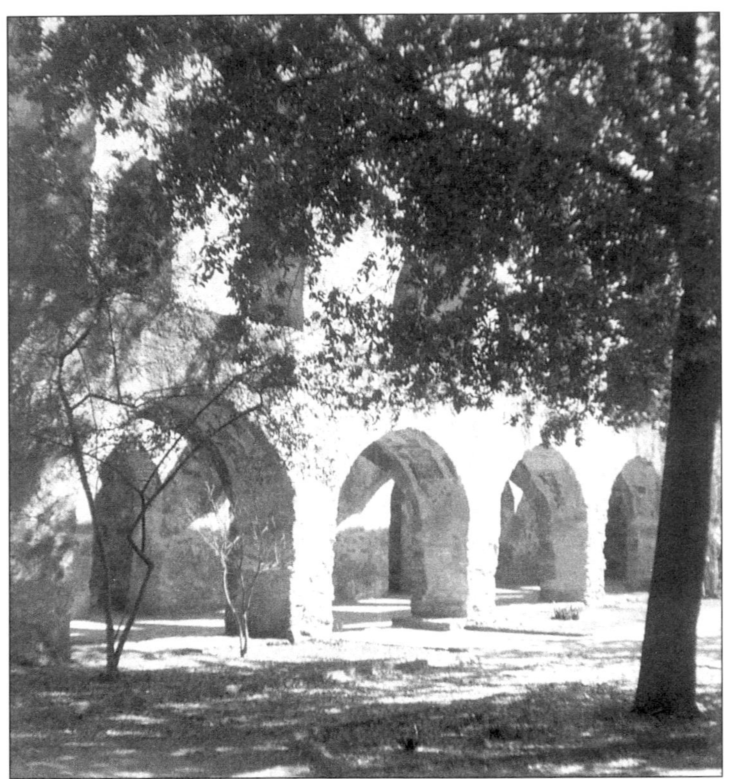

As a child, after skipping through San José's Church and peering into the tiny American Indian dwelling rooms, I would run behind the mission to watch the light and shadows change on the walls of the cloisters. (Courtesy Thille Lambert Newton.)

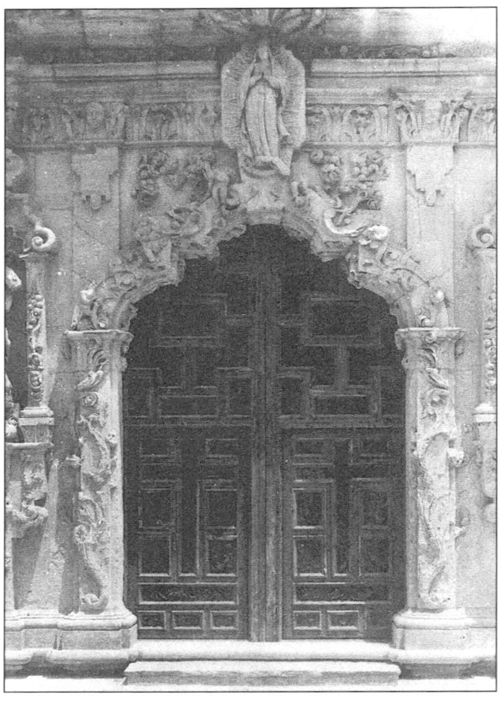

Supposedly carved by Pedro Huizar, the portal at San José, which leads into the domed church, is perhaps one of the most interesting carved images in the state. The figure on the keystone is the Virgin of Guadalupe.

I always imagined that a lovelorn conquistador created Rosa's Window, often called the Rose Window, as he thought of his lover who remained on the other side of the Atlantic. Although a plaque credits Pedro Huizar for sculpting the window, research suggests that he did not arrive at San José until 20 years after the window's completion. This mysteriously beautiful window, with its unusual leaf patterns, draws me back to San José again and again.

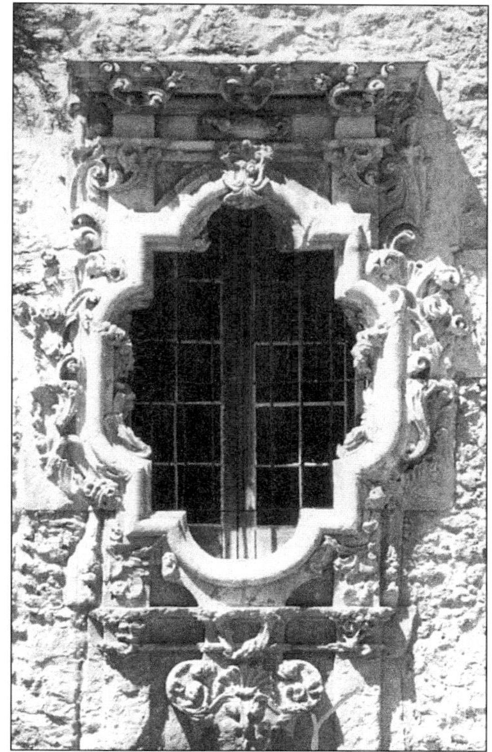

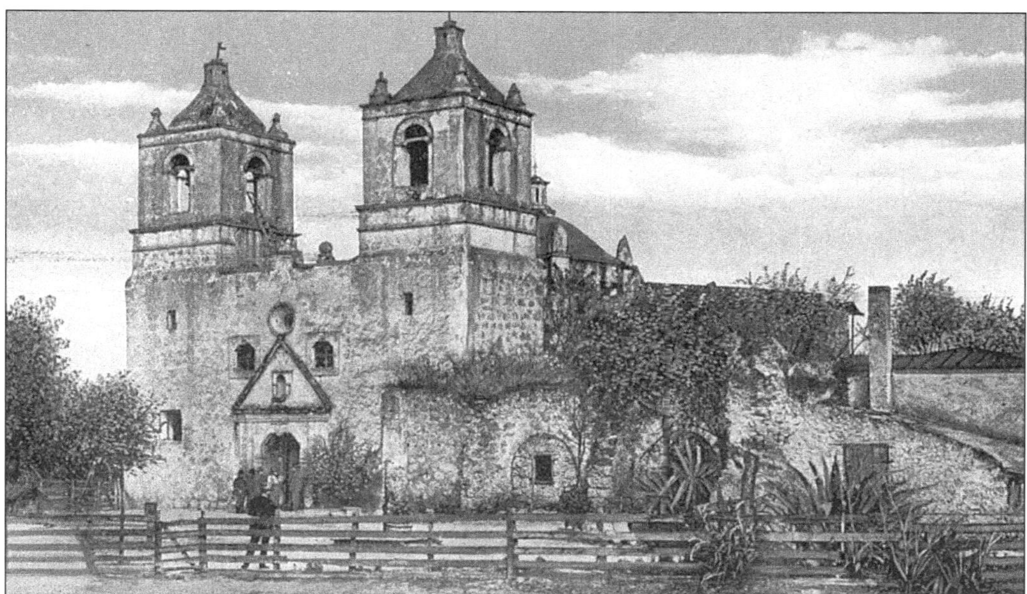

Named after "the Virgin Mary and the Spanish Viceroy Don Juan de Acuna," Mission de la Nuestra Señora de la Purísima Concepción de Acuña has required the least amount of reconstruction of all the missions. Prior to the Battle of the Alamo, the Texans and Mexicans fought the Battle of Concepción on the grounds; under the guidance of Colonel James Bowie, the Texans forced the Mexicans to make a hasty retreat.

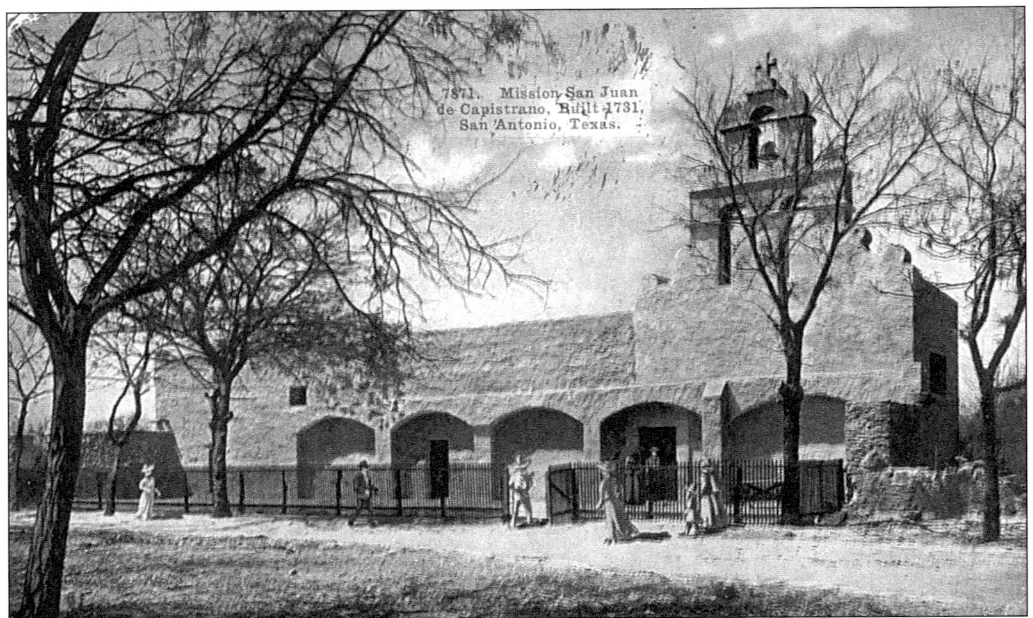

Above, Mission San Juan Capistrano, founded in 1731, "was named after Santa Giovanni de Capistrano, a friar of the Franciscan Order." The ruins of foundations for an incomplete larger church lie on the east side of the mission. Originally founded in east Texas, the mission moved closer to San Antonio and currently is located within a mile of Mission Espada. Below, the postcard of the same mission shows parts of the structure that remained before its restoration in the latter half of the 20th century.

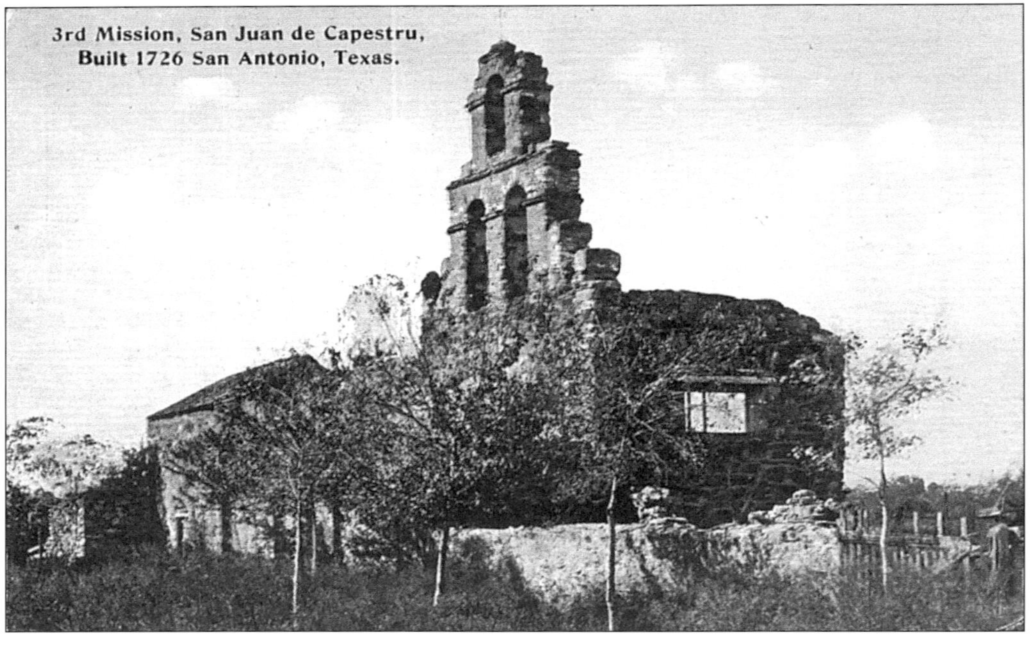

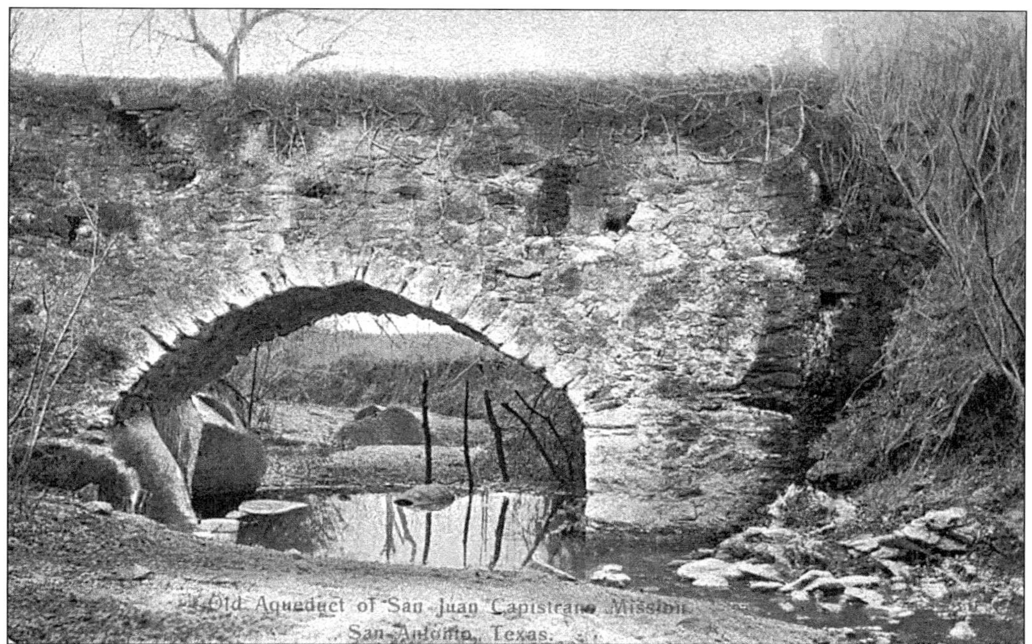

Although the postcard labels this aqueduct as the "Old Aqueduct of San Juan Capistrano," it appears to be the Espada Aqueduct, which is actually located closer to Mission San Juan than to Mission Espada. In San Antonio's heat, water resources can dry up quickly, and aqueducts near these missions, as well as at northern locations including Brackenridge Park, often provided residents with their main sources of water. Although the Edwards Aquifer is the city's primary reservoir today, those who live near the Espada Mission still rely on the aqueduct for some of their water needs.

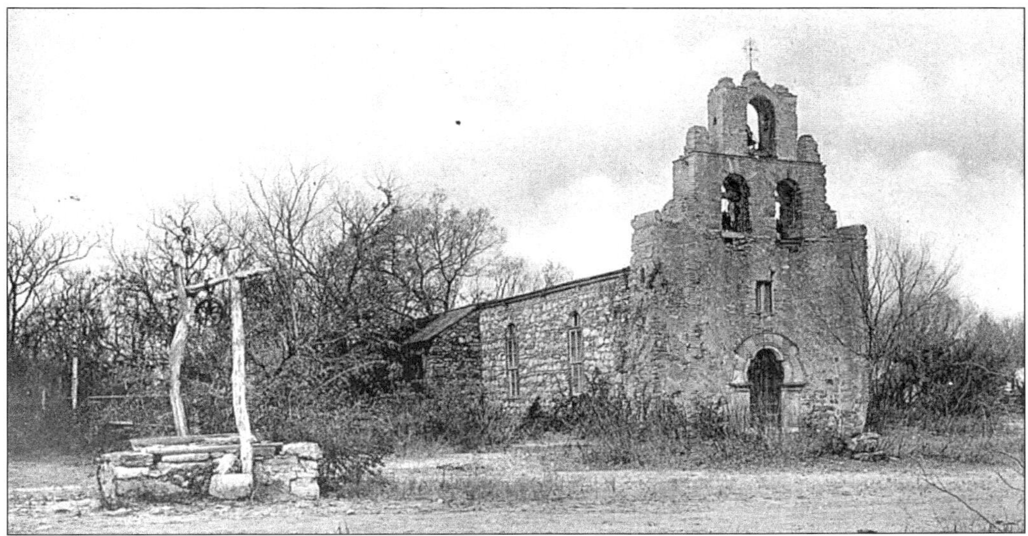

Mission San Francisco de la Espada, the southernmost mission, is still relatively isolated from the heart of the city. On a five-mission tour, I visited this mission last. Tired and thirsty, I peered into the old well situated on the left side, wondering how the American Indians and Spaniards endured the dusty climate.

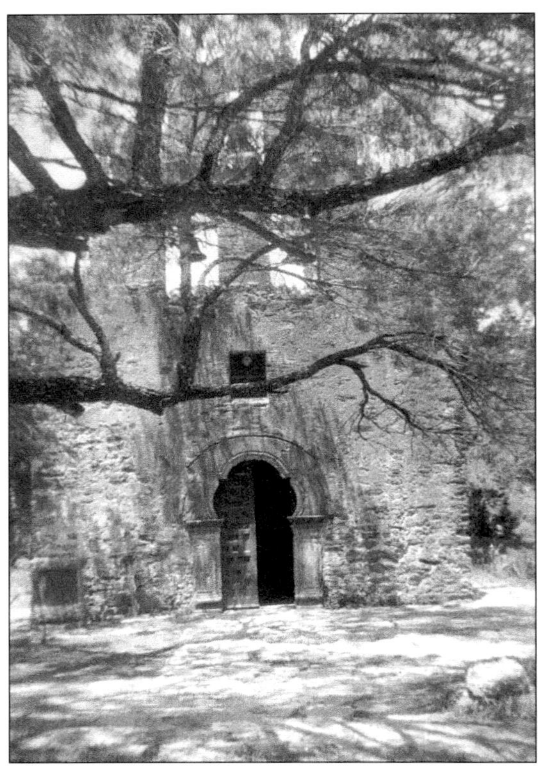

Does the doorway of Mission Espada look too top-heavy or disproportionate? Architects have long debated about the erroneous structure of this entrance. If one switches the two lower stones of the arch, they fit with the other stones but do not rest properly on the pilasters below them. An architect may have damaged or mislaid the stones or decided to construct a smaller entrance at the last minute. (Courtesy Thille Lambert Newton.)

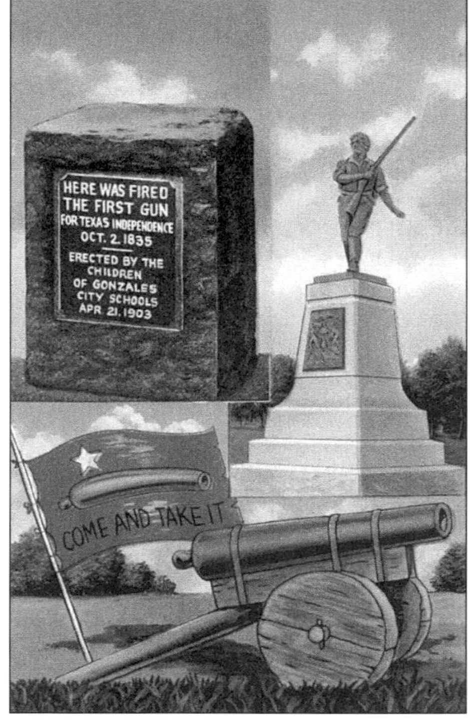

The fight for Texas's independence began in the town of Gonzalez, situated approximately 70 miles northeast of San Antonio. "Mexican authorities at San Antonio gave colonists at Gonzales . . . a cannon for protection of the settlement against the Indians . . . when relations between Mexico and Texas were strained, authorities demanded that the 'loaned' cannon be returned. . . 150 Mexican dragoons came to take it by force. The first battle of the Texas revolution resulted." Ironically, no one seems to know where the cannon, sketched in the lower part of the postcard, is located today. The monument on the right was dedicated in 1910 to Texas's heroes.

Five

Deep in Old San Antone:

La Villita

For such a tiny, busy spot—one square block—La Villita certainly seems larger. Home of the famous "Night in Old San Antonio®" (NIOSA®) event during Fiesta week and haven for local artists, La Villita's history traces back to the early 18th century, when Spanish colonialists lived in houses here. Contested by floods and age, the little village nearly dissipated, but little old ladies in sneakers, formally known as the members of the San Antonio Conservation Society, have restored and preserved several areas in the little village. During most days in the year, I like to visit the Little Church and to look at works on display by various artists, but during Fiesta week, I drink margaritas and eat tacos and sopapillas as I listen to mariachis and watch dancers. Fiesta, held during the week of the 21st of April, the anniversary of the Battle of San Jacinto in which Texas won independence from Mexico in 1836, is a smashing, whirlwind ten-day event during which Texans celebrate their freedom with flowers, parades, band parties, and much more. The spirit and enthusiasm of participants, attendees, and sponsors has not changed since the first celebration in 1891. ¡Viva Fiesta!

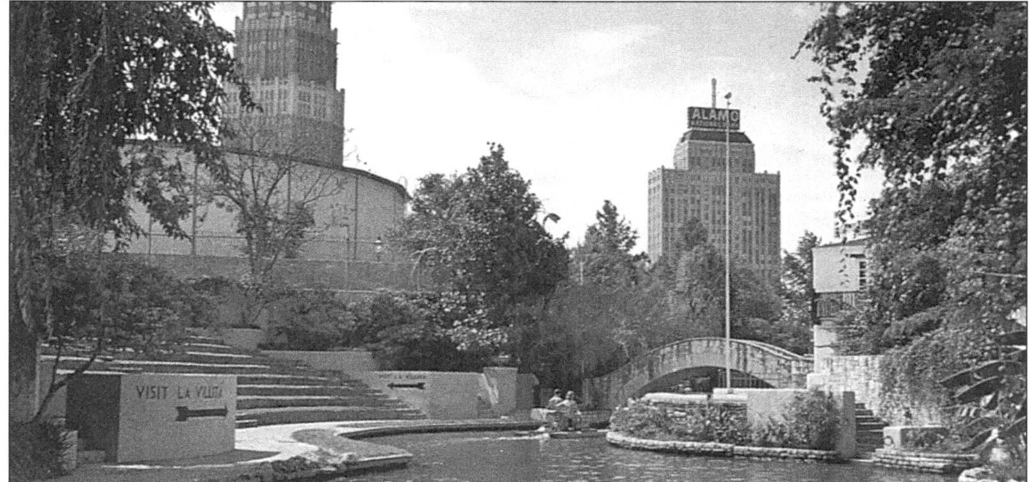

Like Alice in Wonderland, whenever I step off the Riverwalk and climb the steps of the Arneson River Theatre, I find myself in a different world—La Villita. The round structure on the right, the La Villita Assembly Hall, was built in 1959, but most of the other buildings are small Spanish colonial-style houses, shops, and churches.

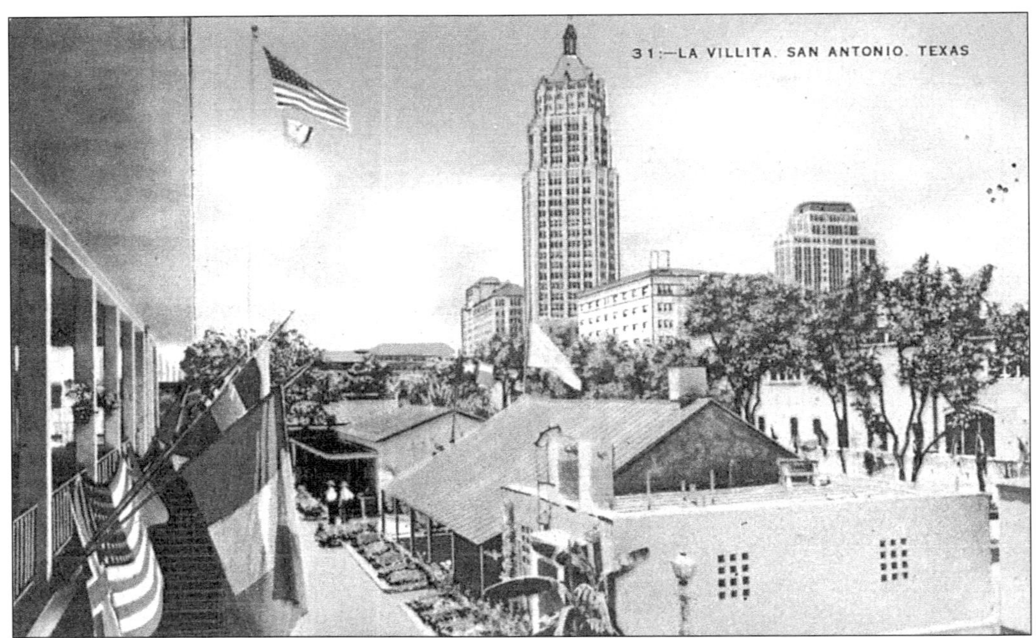

Although La Villita is surrounded by high buildings, no one should miss a trip to the heart of old San Antone'. As one can see from the above postcard, some of the reconstructed buildings still are made of adobe. Some of the 25 structures clustered in the village, like the Cos House, are reserved for special ceremonies, while others, like the Gray-Guilbeau House, are restaurants. The majority of events during Night in Old San Antonio® celebrations do not take place inside these structures but on the streets and patios. In the lower picture, the women making the paper flowers may plan to use the flowers to decorate a Fiesta float or booth.

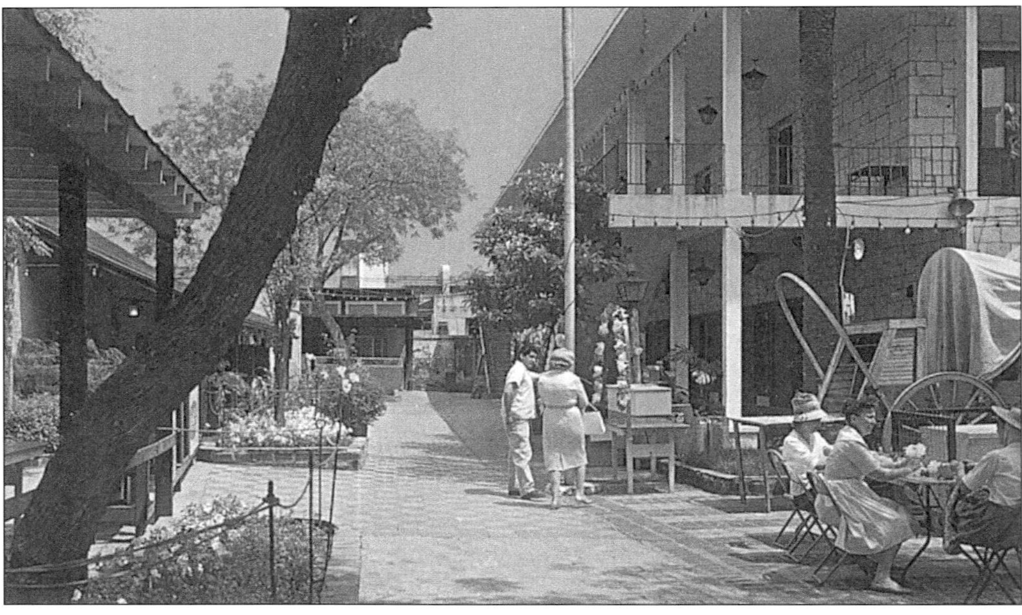

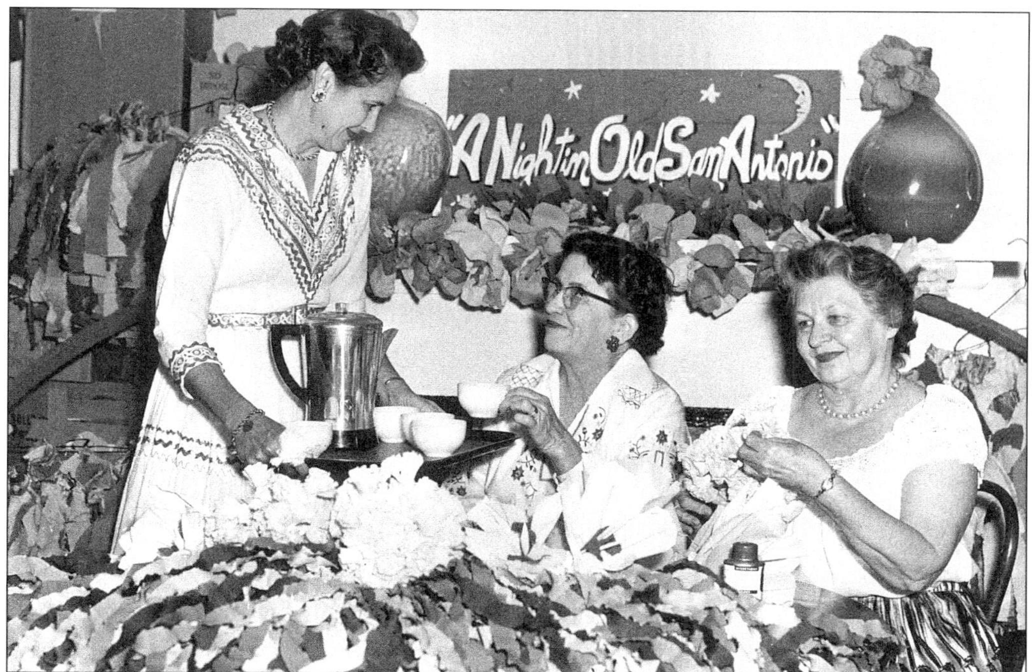

From left to right, Mrs. Rex Martin, Dixie Rees, and Adele Becker, flower fluffers, contemplate taking a break from creating decorative flowers for NIOSA®. Although many of today's flowers are made of paper, in early days, San Antonians used real flowers to decorate their parade floats and horse-drawn carriages. (Courtesy San Antonio Conservation Society Foundation.)

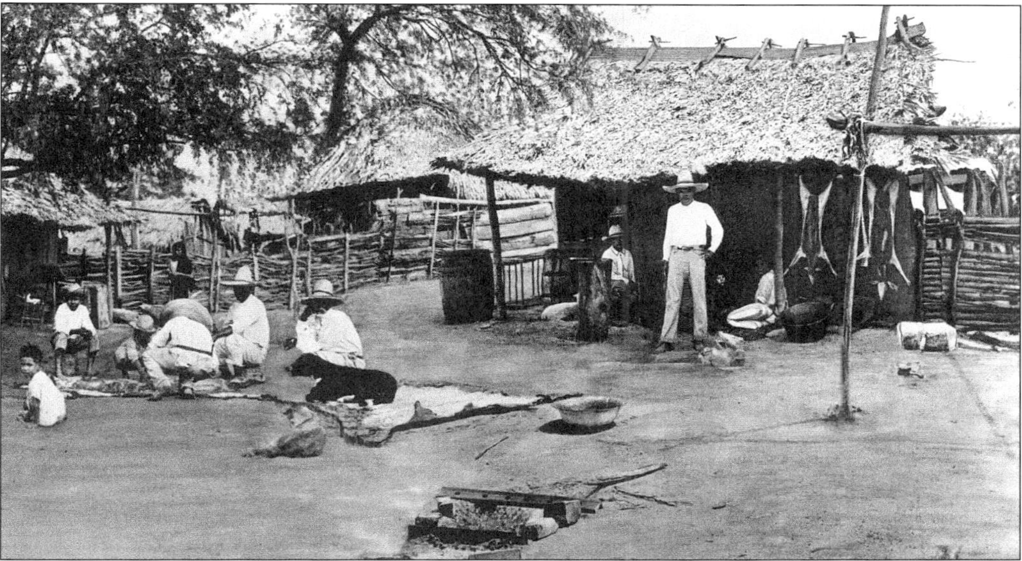

Although one might still find Mexicans working together in rural areas of San Antonio or the surrounding region, I always pictured La Villita's everyday life to appear this way during the time of the conquistadores, when all people, like these Mexicans, skinned and used the hides of animals for warmth or money. (Courtesy Daughters of the Republic of Texas Library, Aniol Collection, 14-1.)

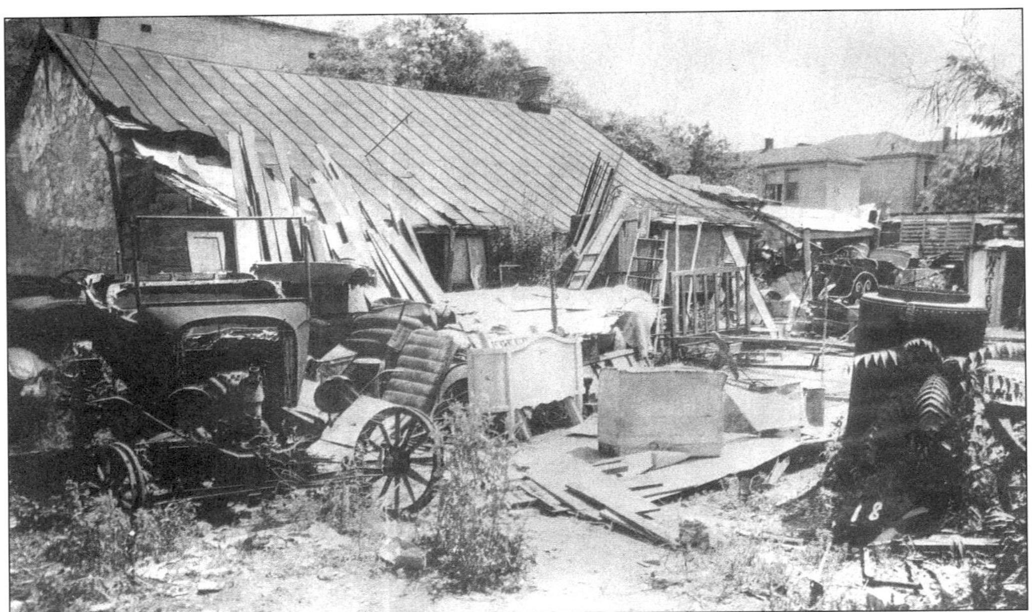

In the late 1930s, the National Youth Administration (WPA) restored the San Martin House, often called the Herrera House, in La Villita. The owner, Rafael Herrera, built the house in the 1850s, but the building is named after Don Jose de San Martin who fought for independence in South America. The society restored several of the buildings in La Villita, some of which have endured floods and neglect. (Courtesy San Antonio Conservation Society Foundation.)

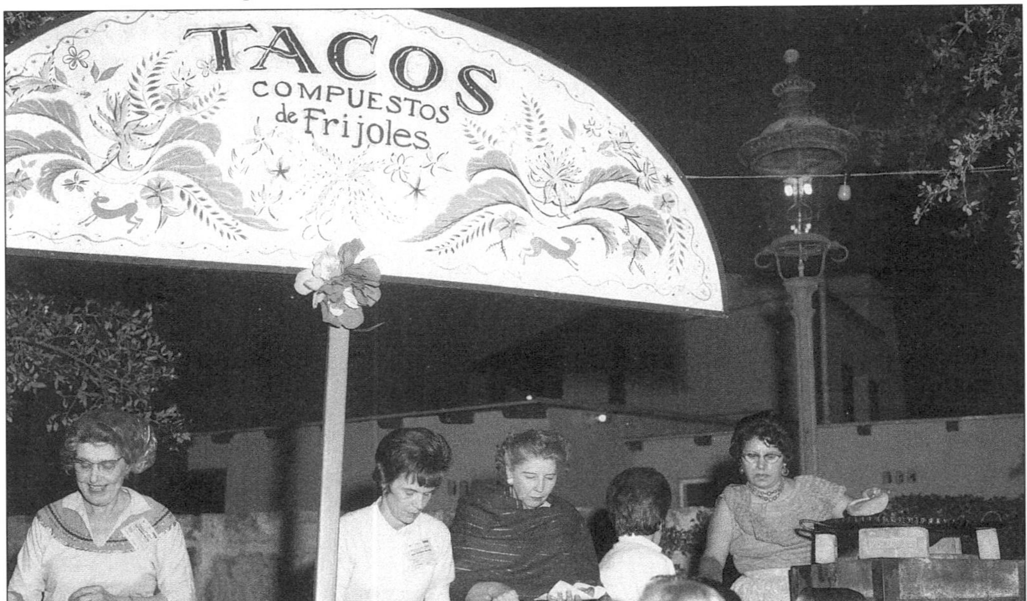

Not only do Night in Old San Antonio® booths offer compuestos de frijoles, or tacos with beans, they also sell fajitas, nachos, and campañadas de pollo, or fried bread stuffed with chicken. NIOSA® lovers consume an amazing quantity of food each year. Cascarones, or colorful confetti-filled eggs, and posters also are sold. Many of the proceeds go directly to the San Antonio Conservation Society, which uses funds to sponsor educational programs or scholarships. (Courtesy Texas Department of Transportation.)

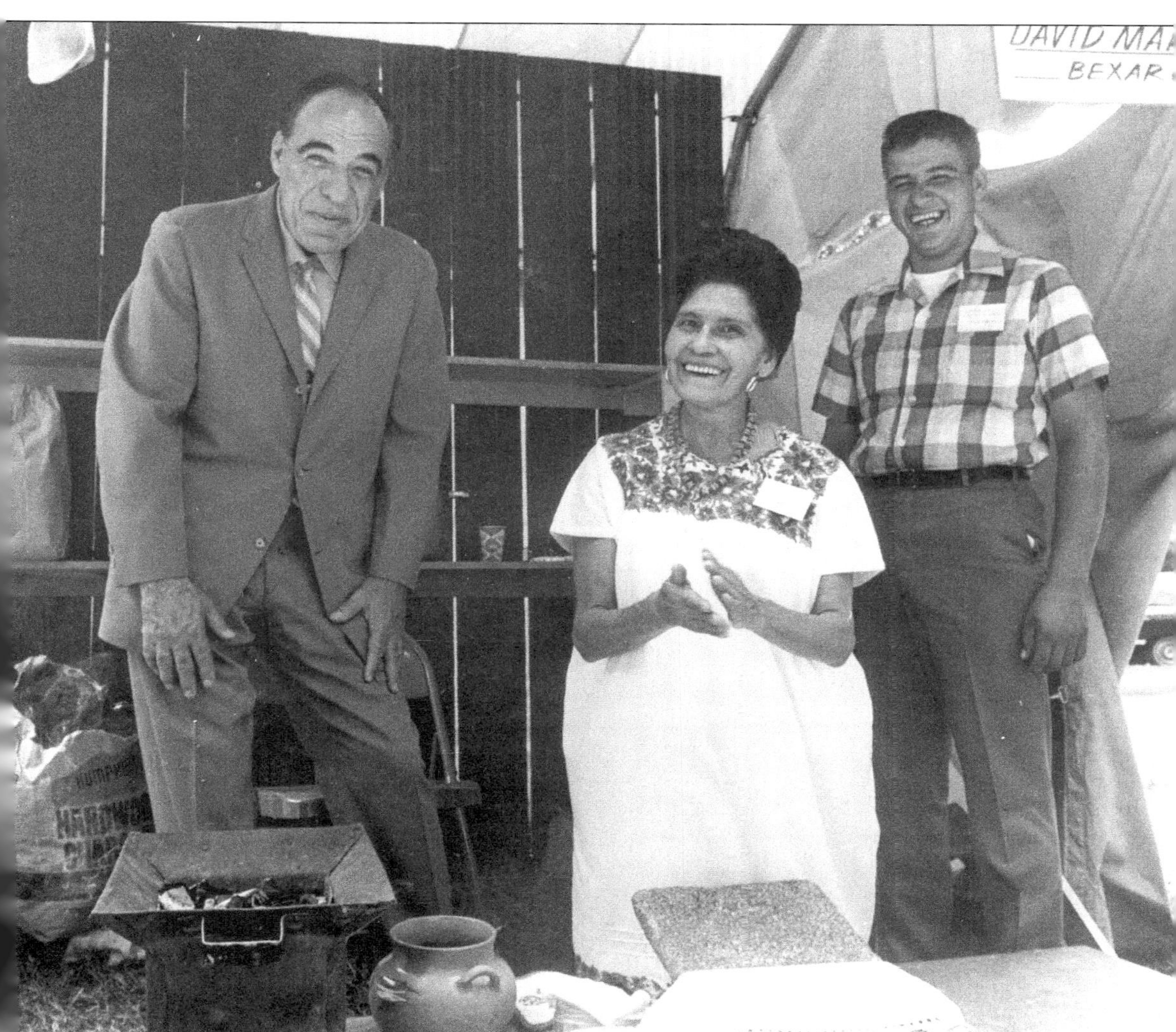

Señora Maria Ochoa, an artistic tortilla patter, worked in the homes of Ethel Harris and Elizabeth Graham, the co-founders of NIOSA®. In the 1950s, the co-founders added "Maria's Tortillas" booth to the Mexican Market area, where Maria and her crew of patters of handmade tortillas became an instant success. Standing on Maria's left is former Congressman Henry B. Gonzalez, and on her right is an unidentified man. (Courtesy San Antonio Conservation Society Foundation.)

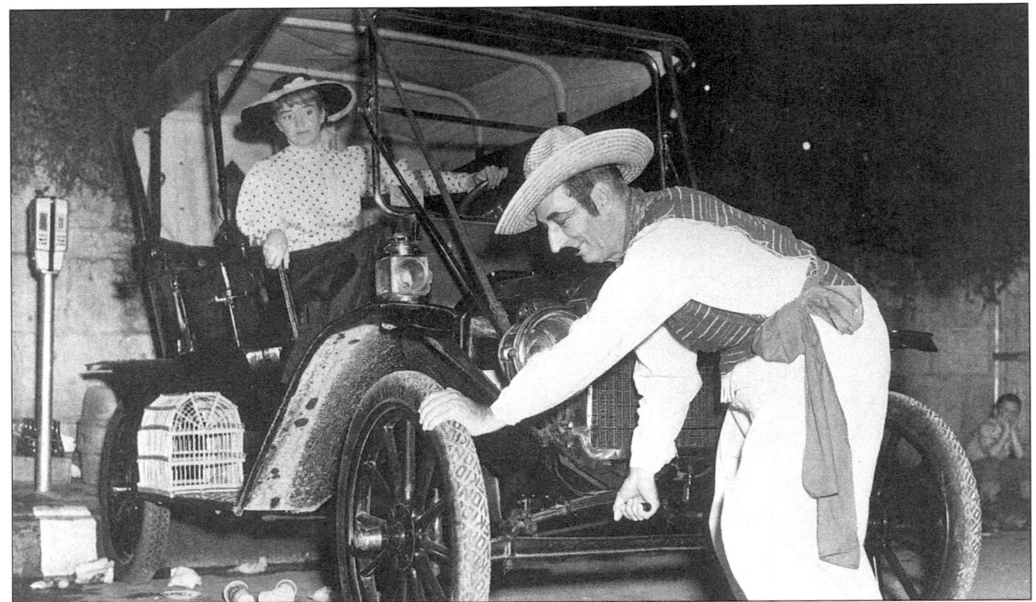

Some interesting characters, such as landscape architect Stewart King, the fellow cranking the car, might appear at NIOSA®. King helped the San Antonio Conservation Society landscape the grounds of their historical 1840 Edmunds-Yturri house. In 1957, when King's picture was taken with this unidentified woman, the procession of antique cars highlighted the opening of a new NIOSA® event. (Courtesy San Antonio Conservation Society Foundation.)

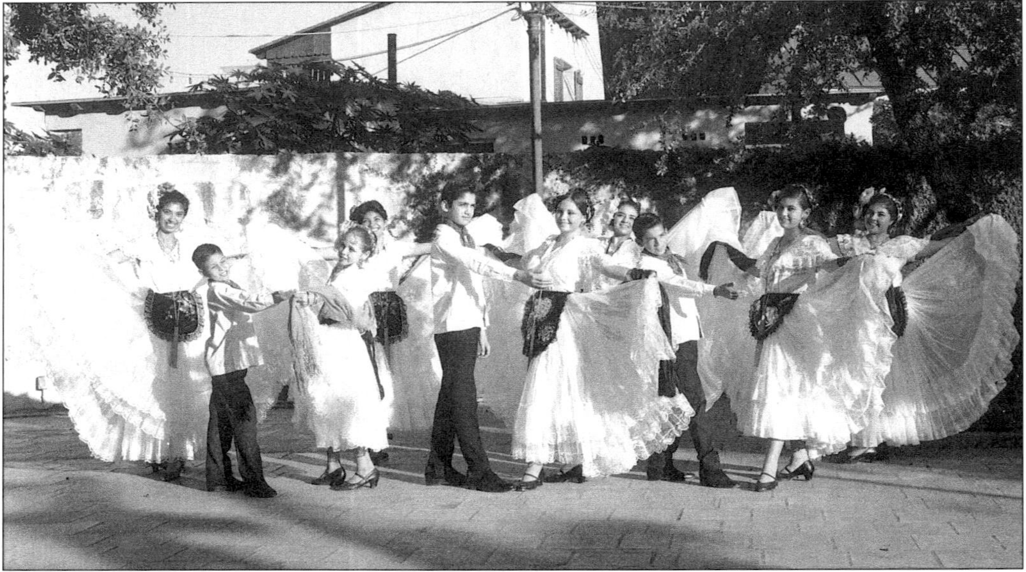

While I eat my tacos and sip my margarita at NIOSA®, I will wander through the crowds, looking for an activity to watch, such as flamenco dancers. These women, who don flowers and demonstrate countless steps and tricks, are fascinating to watch. Although NIOSA® is a four-night event during Fiesta, serious festival-goers can attend the Oyster Bake or Alamo Heights Night to see more dancers and to sample more food, bands, and activities. (Courtesy Texas Department of Transportation.)

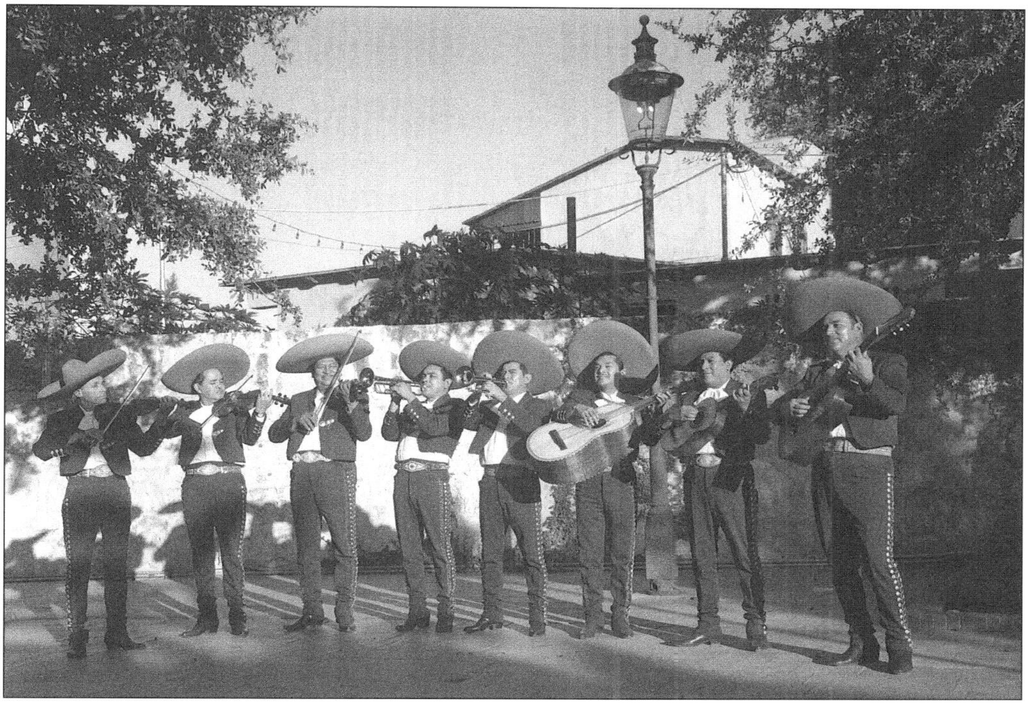

After mariachis play a few Spanish songs to entertain a couple or a festive crowd, they could turn their sombreros over for a tip or two, or they might even follow a couple, asking for more song requests. Mariachis play in Mexican restaurants in La Villita, as well as in other parts of the city. (Courtesy Texas Department of Transportation.)

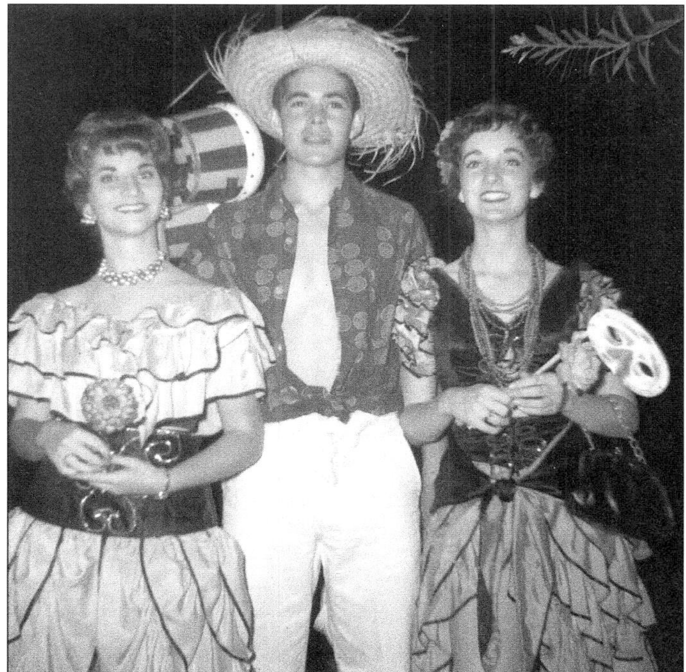

Not only do mariachis and dancers get to wear colorful uniforms, but also parade participants. From left to right, Susan Matthews, and my uncle and aunt, Dick Davenport and Nancy Lambert, don colorful costumes for their River Parade float. (Courtesy Nancy Lambert Davenport.)

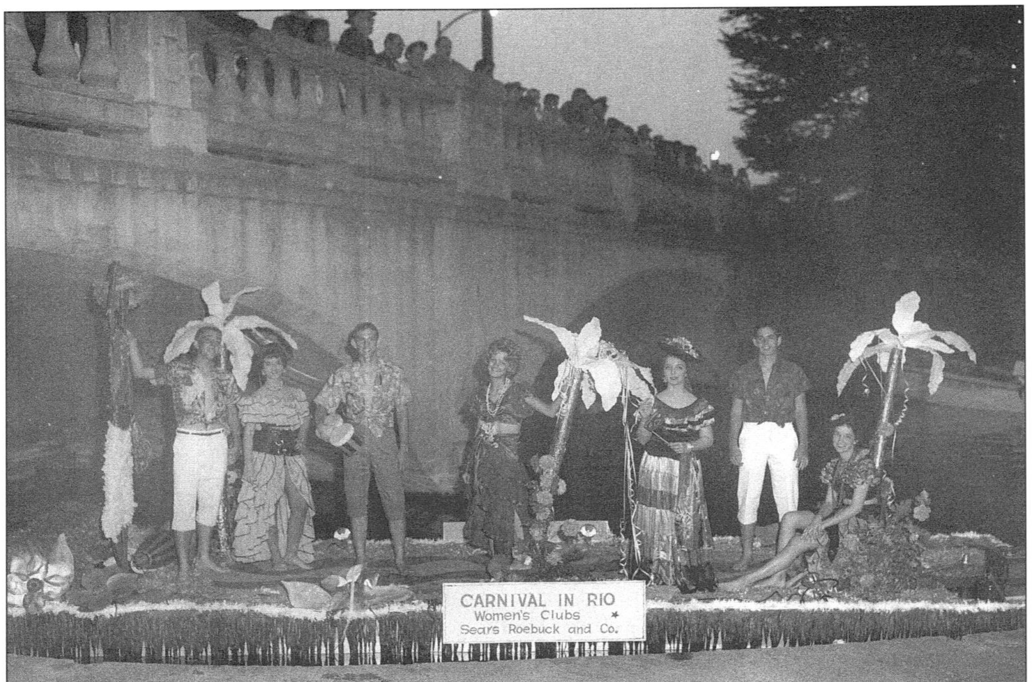

The River Parade, according to some locals, is more exciting and beautiful than the Battle of Flowers Parade, since the floats literally float down the San Antonio River at nighttime as participants wave to enthusiastic crowds. In 1961, my uncle and aunt, pictured on the far right, rode on the "Carnival in Río" float for the Women's Clubs. (Courtesy Thille Lambert Newton.)

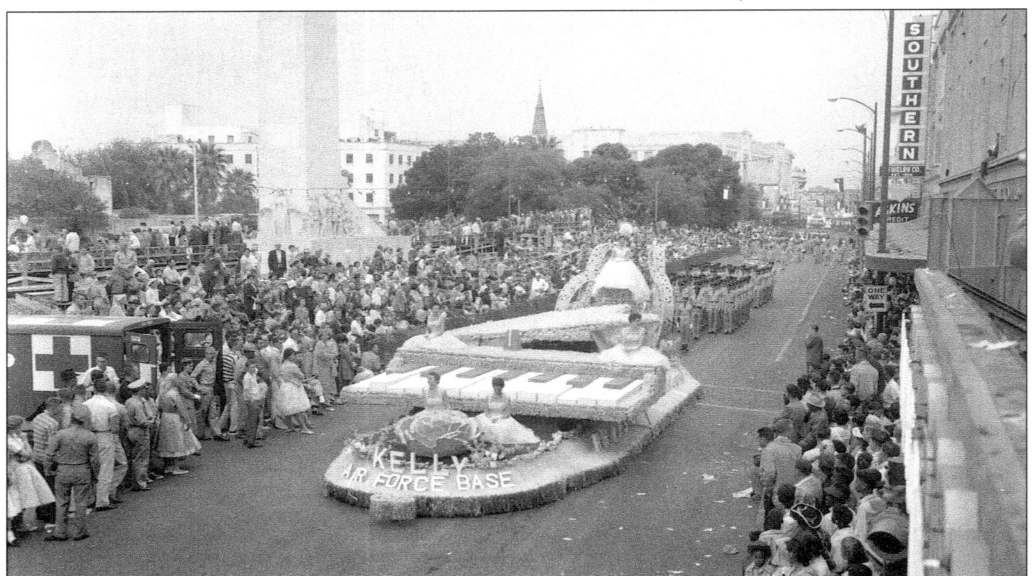

Not only do church groups, schools, and local bands ride or march in the parades, but military soldiers do, too. Kelly Air Force Base is no exception. Themes for groups and their floats vary; some groups invite members to walk behind the floats or skip the float altogether and ride on horses. (Courtesy Texas Department of Transportation.)

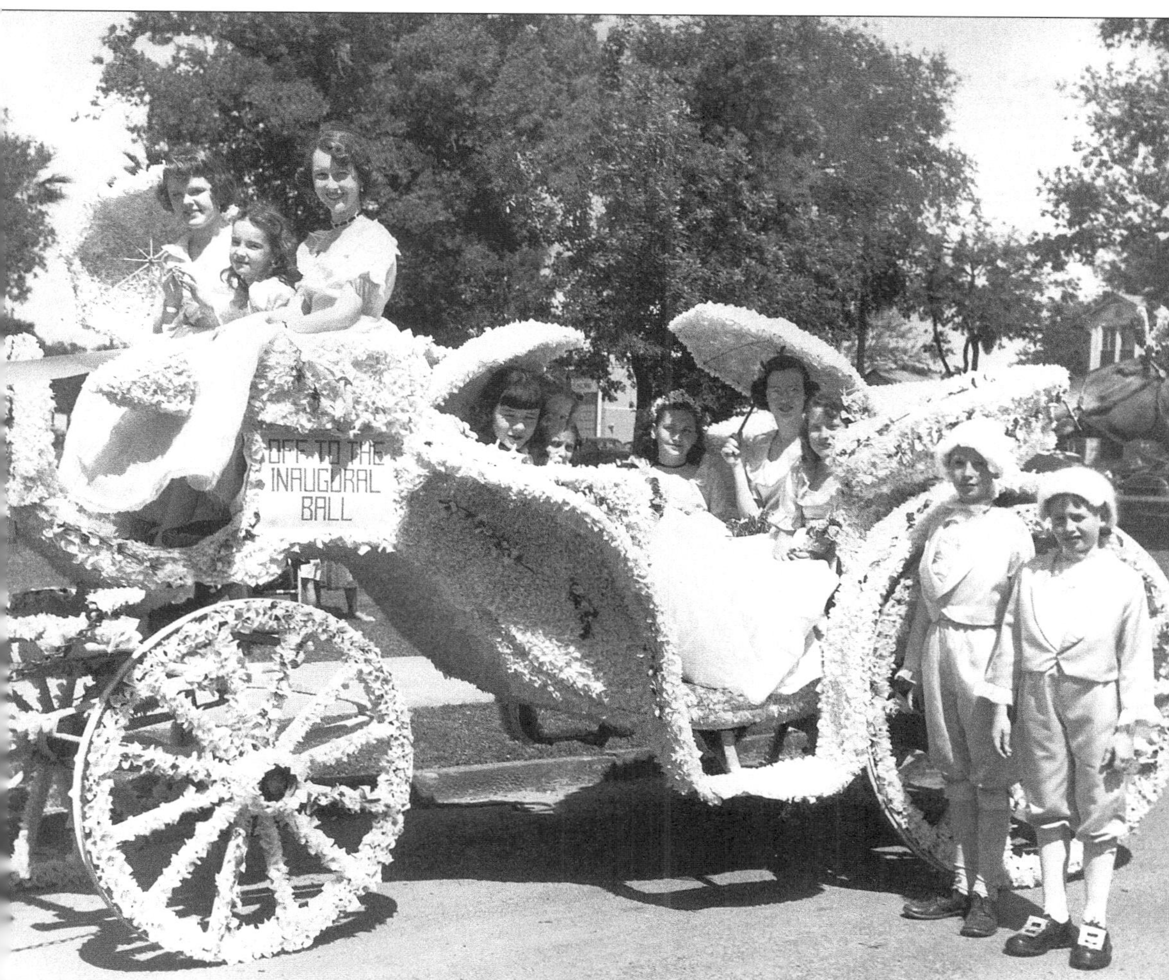

Schools close, volunteers decorate floats with colorful paper flowers, and children don their gayest apparel during the annual Battle of San Jacinto parade, otherwise known as the Battle of Flowers Parade. Participants from local churches, schools, and organizations such as the Children of the American Revolution ride or march through the streets of old San Antonio. In this prize-winning 1952 float, named "Off to the Inaugural Ball," my mother, Thille Lambert, and my aunt, Nancy Lambert, sit in the two right-hand side front seats; my uncle, Joseph B. Lambert, the taller fellow, stands next to the back wheel. (Courtesy Thille Lambert Newton.)

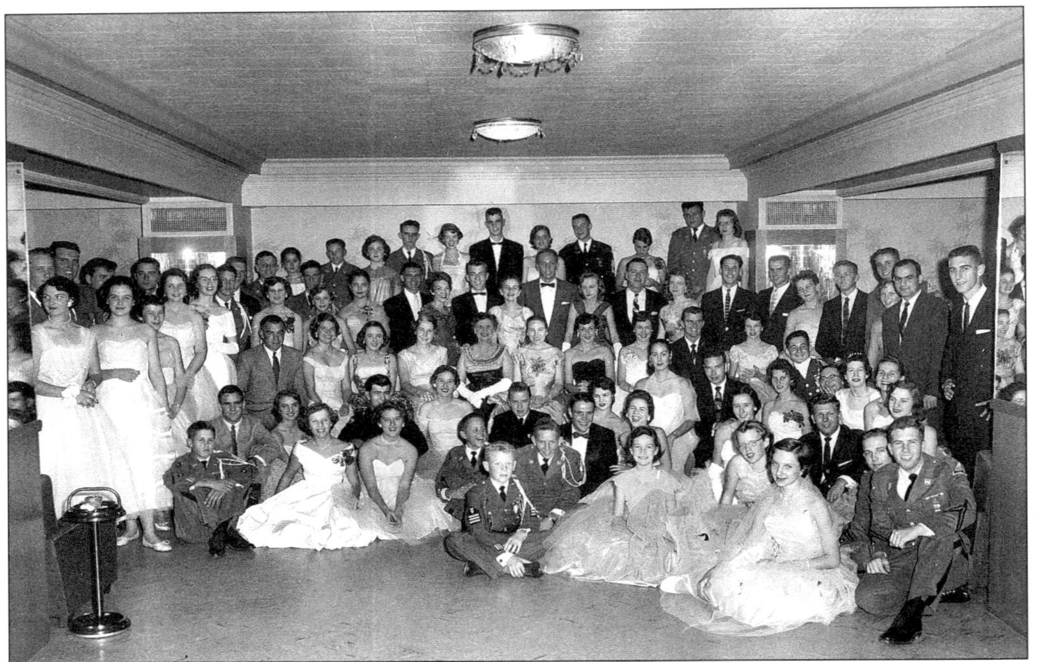

Other ongoing festivities, such as the Pages' Ball for the United Daughters of the Confederacy during the San Antonio Convention of 1955, not only allow Texans to raise money for Fiesta events and related benefits, but also demonstrate their strong support for diverse causes and organizations. During the convention, the pages took messages and ran errands, but at the ball, they enjoyed themselves. (Courtesy Nancy Lambert Davenport.)

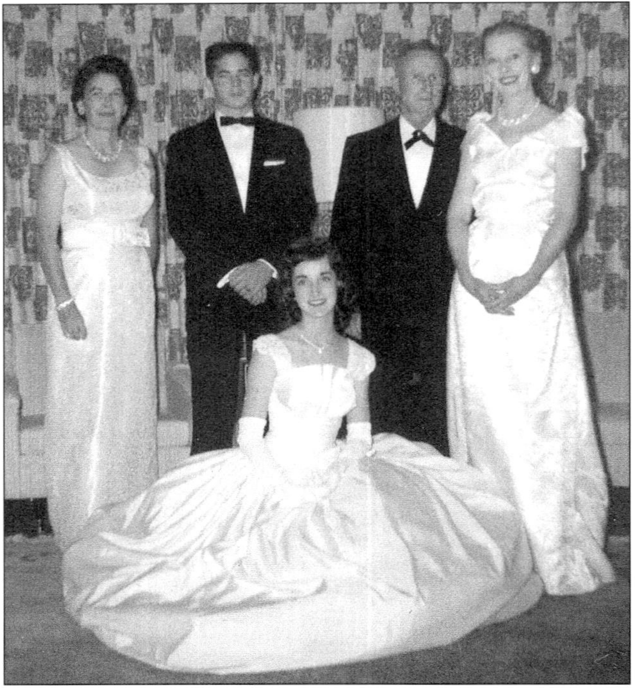

Standing from left to right are the following: Maxine Irwin Davenport, Dick Davenport, Joseph Idus Lambert, and Elizabeth Kirwan Lambert; seated is Nancy Lambert. Nancy was a princess in the International Black and White Ball in 1960. In hopes of providing Mexican-American and Anglo-American cultures with the opportunity to establish stronger relations, young women and their families enjoyed a season of social gatherings. (Courtesy Nancy Lambert Davenport.)

Six

DEEP INSIDE '09 TERRITORY:

ALAMO HEIGHTS

The zip code for Alamo Heights is 78209, and those who live there are called '09ers. Situated on the northeast side of San Antonio, Alamo Heights has its own festivities, traditions, and spirit. Three generations of my family have lived in and attended schools in '09. We have marched—and still do—in the Howdy Night parades as members of the band and dance teams. After parades, games, or parties, '09ers frequent places along the street of Broadway, including Broadway 50-50, Alamo Heights's only bar, or Earl Abel's restaurant. Since '09ers also maintain high standards for academic excellence, dedication to the quality of education plays a significant role in their everyday lives. The roots for Alamo Heights's school district began in the early 1900s and continue to grow along with the community.

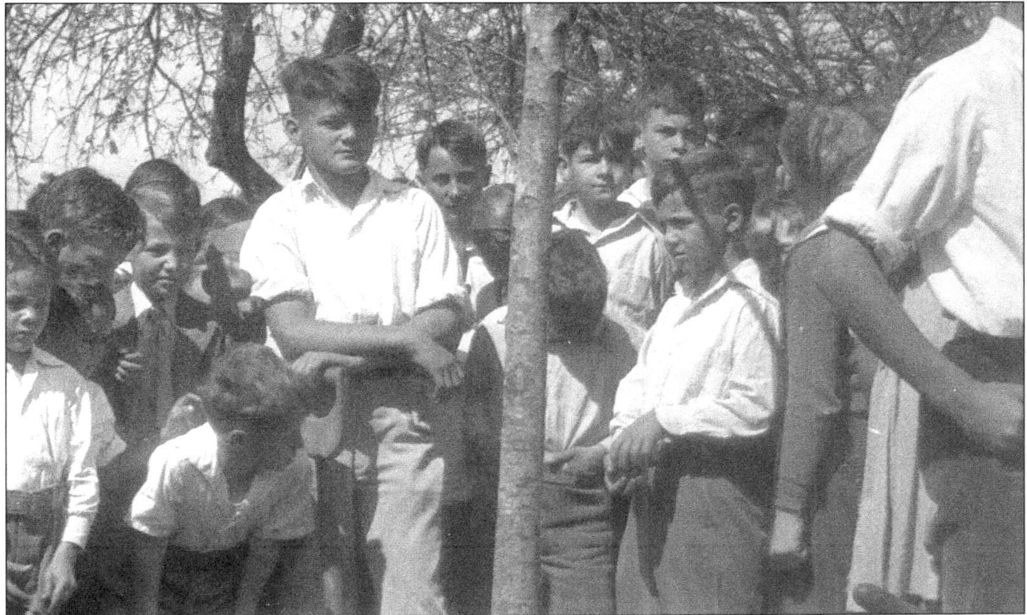

Alamo Heights is a tightly knit community, and here, students of all ages watch solemnly as a tree is planted on the campus of the current elementary school, Cambridge. (Courtesy Harry Orem.)

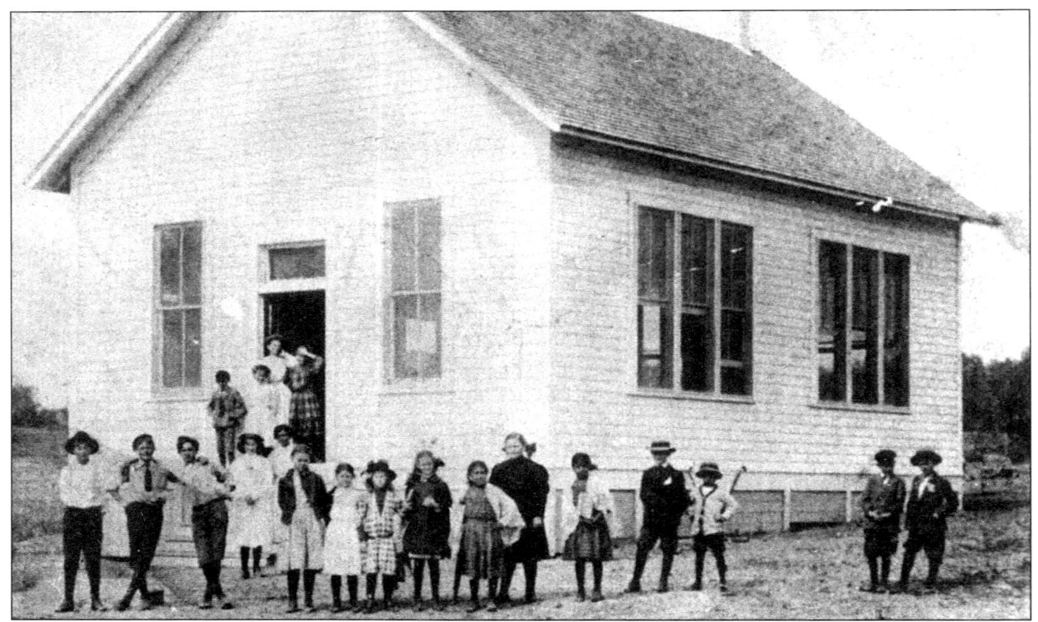

Built in 1909, the first Alamo Heights school, once situated on Townsend between Abiso and Ogden Lane, was one of many built in years to come. Today, '09ers attend two elementary schools, Cambridge and Woodridge, one early childhood learning center for kindergartners, Howard, and the junior and senior high schools. Robbins, a third elementary school, closed a number of years ago but still is owned by the school district. (Courtesy Broadway 50-50 and Louis M. LaRocco and Frank R. Little.)

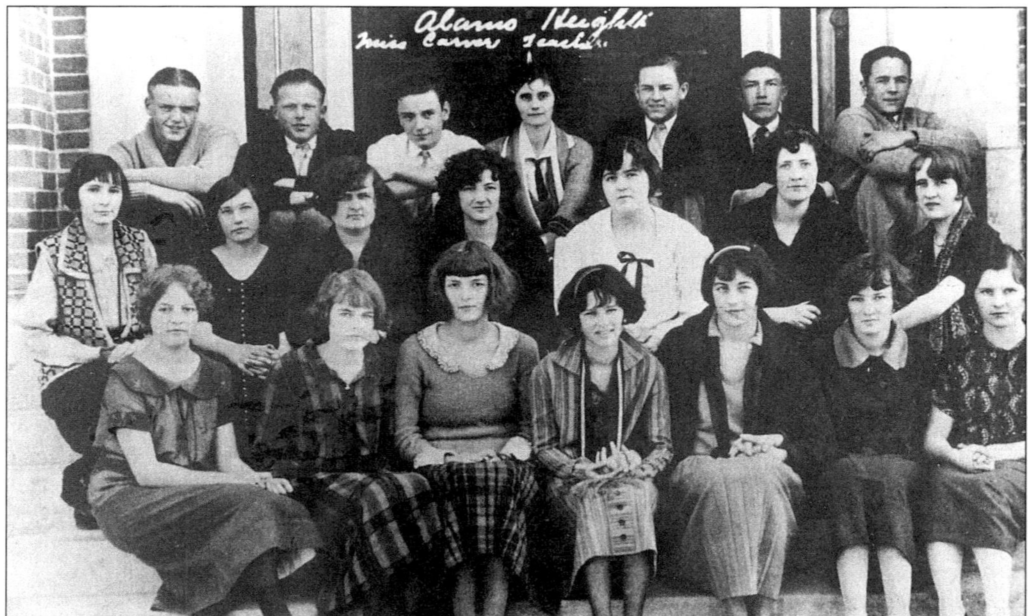

The Class of 1925 was the first graduating class of Alamo Heights High School. Miss Mary Carver taught this class of approximately 20 students. Today, nearly 200 students graduate per year. (Courtesy Broadway 50-50 and Louis M. LaRocco and Frank R. Little.)

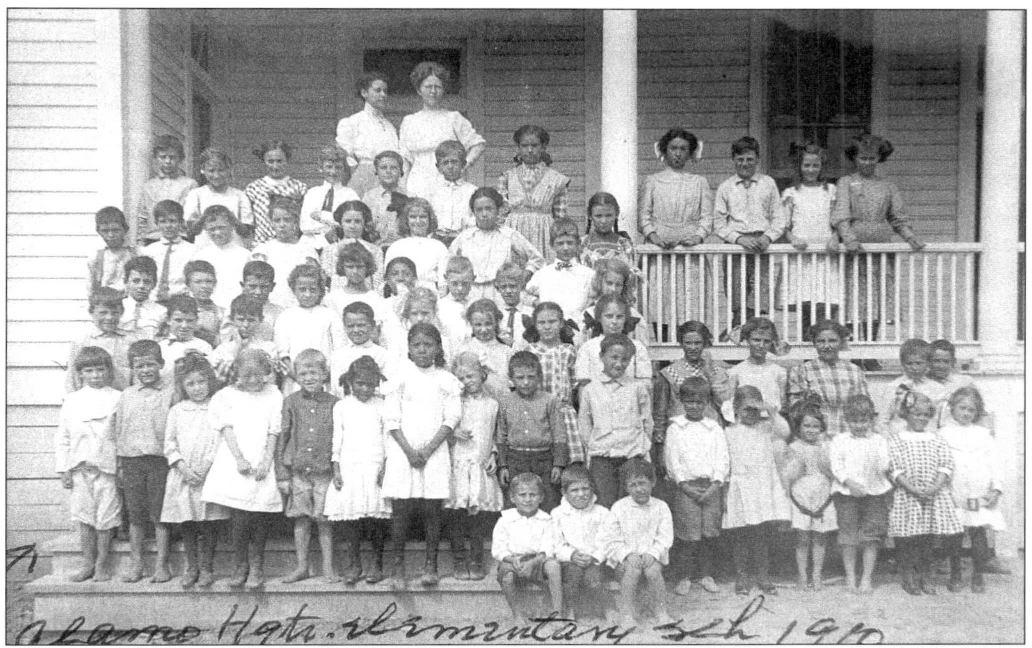

The second Alamo Heights school was built in 1910. This two-room schoolhouse was located on Ogden Lane between Townsend and Columbine. The teachers were Miss Ella Sackmann and Miss Mary Peel. Notice that some of the children are barefoot; the rooms in those pre-air-conditioning days must have been extraordinarily hot. (Courtesy Harry Orem.)

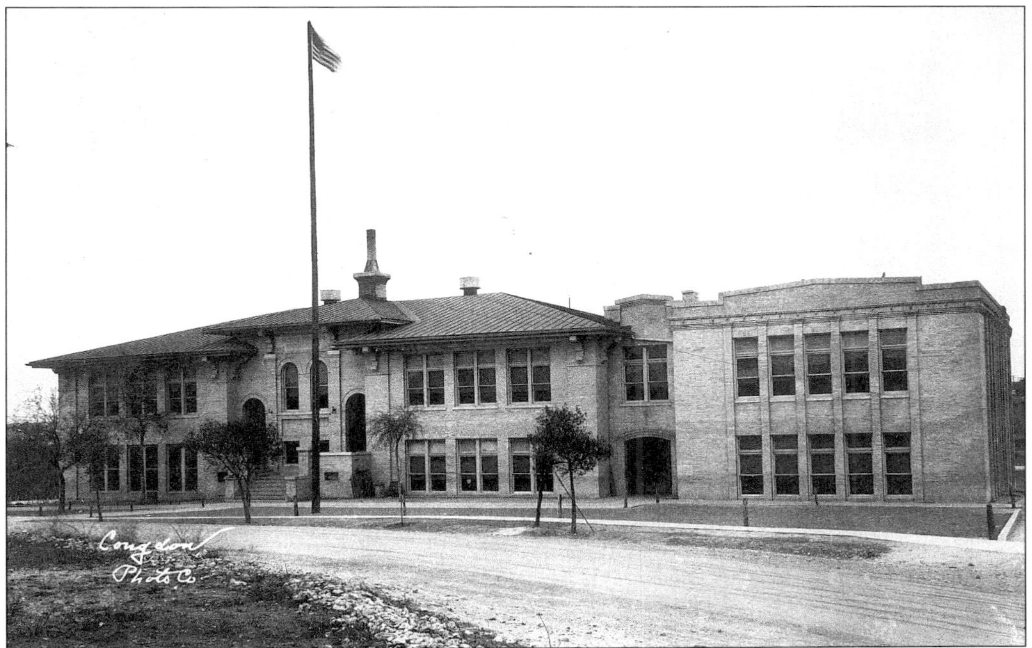

Students attended classes in six rooms in this school constructed on Cambridge Oval in 1912. The school district demolished this building in 1928 to make way for larger additional sections. (Courtesy Harry Orem.)

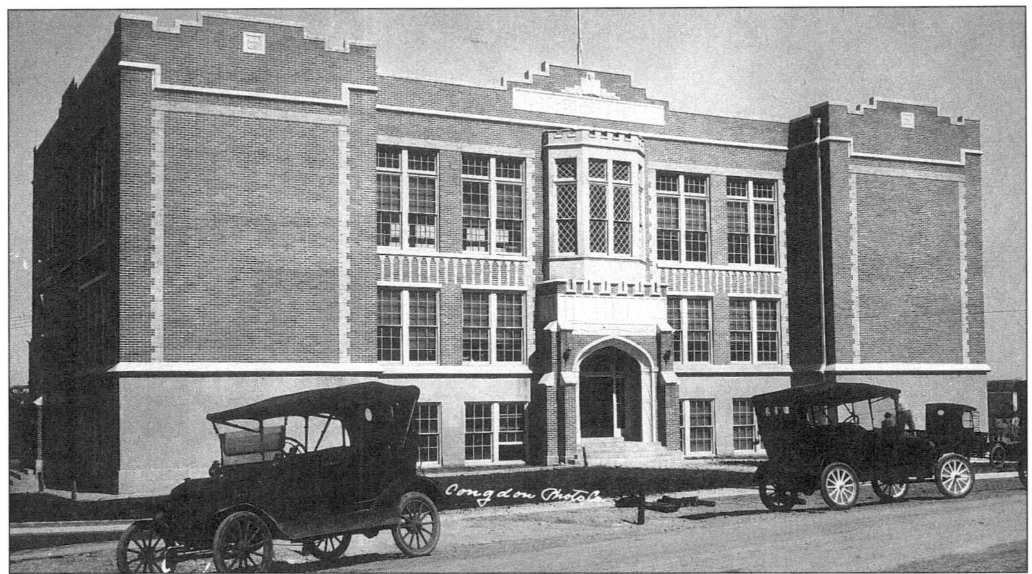

Upon its completion in 1922, Building III, originally called Alamo Heights High School, was the first of three structures that became the current elementary school. When my mother attended Alamo Heights in 1950, Building III was the junior school, and in 1981, I attended second grade here. Sometimes we played games on the empty top floor, which was the auditorium in the 1920s. (Courtesy Harry Orem.)

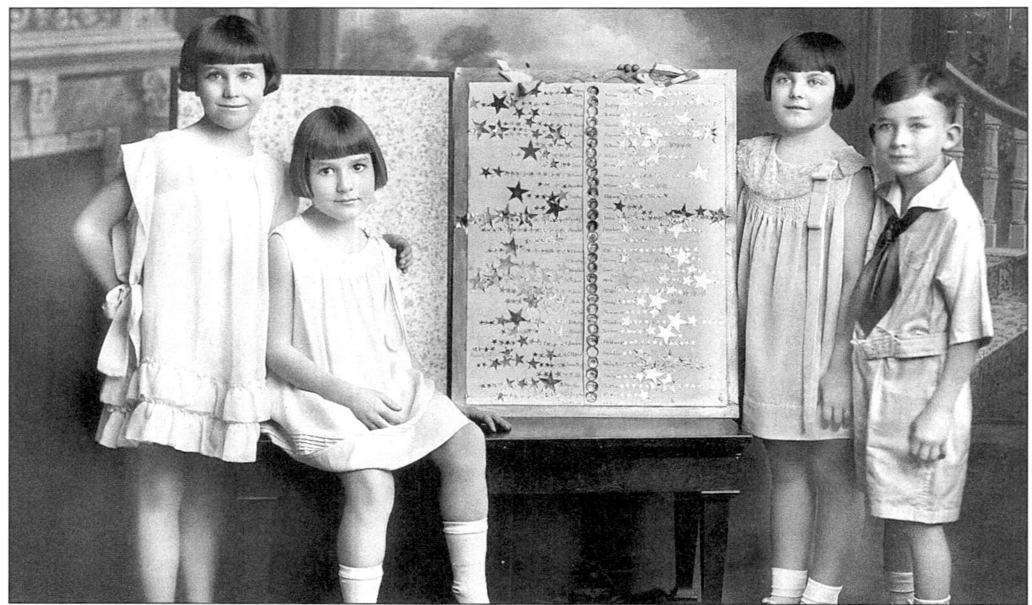

Holding what might be an honor-roll poster, four students stand inside of what is now Cambridge. During my elementary school years, the principal, Mr. Rode, always recognized the honor students, but he knew every student by name. He also kicked off each school year with a theme, and he greeted students with a pun from that theme. In the year of the bear, every morning, he announced over the loudspeakers, "Have a beary good day!" (Courtesy Harry Orem.)

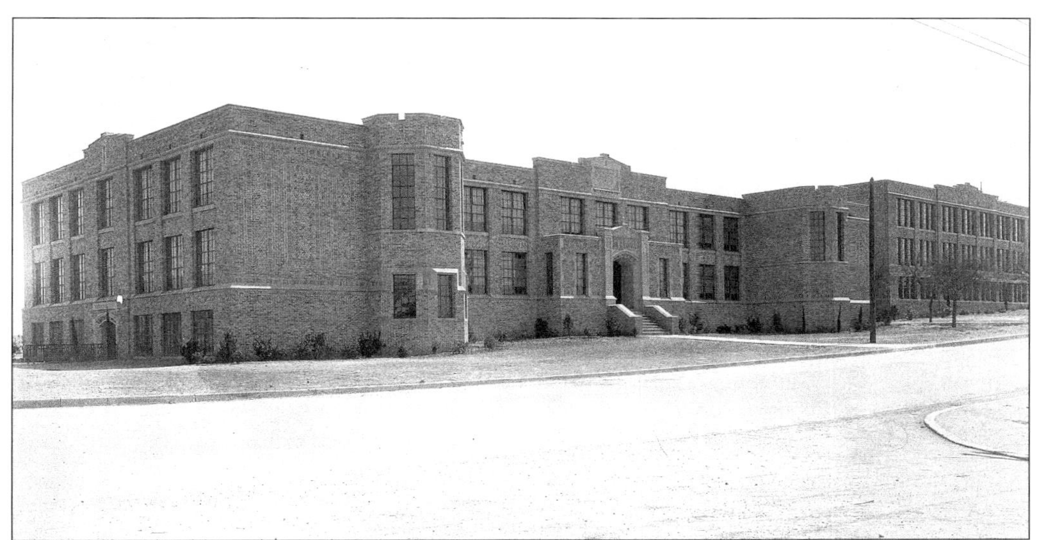

Construction for Buildings I and II, located to the left of Building III, began around 1928. The junior school stood on the left, and the elementary school stood in the middle. Today, Cambridge's elementary school students attend classes in all three buildings. (Courtesy Harry Orem.)

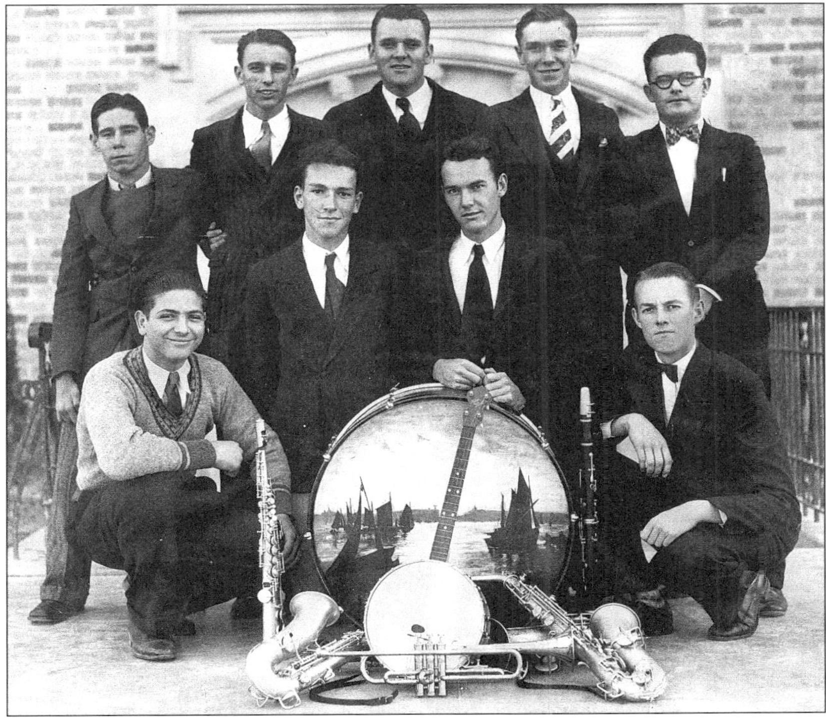

Alamo Heights's first jazz band, the Heights Hoodlums, banded together in the late 1920s. Although the order of people is not noted, several members signed the picture on the back as follows: "Jack Reid Hill, Dir.; Ben Freeman, alto sax, Bernard Pomerantz, violin and clarinet, John Hagy, drums, Bill Muegge, sax, Bill Ellington, banjo, Dan Castles, sax, and Alvin St. John, sax." The Hoodlums gave the picture to Superintendent J.F. Howard in 1929. (Courtesy Harry Orem.)

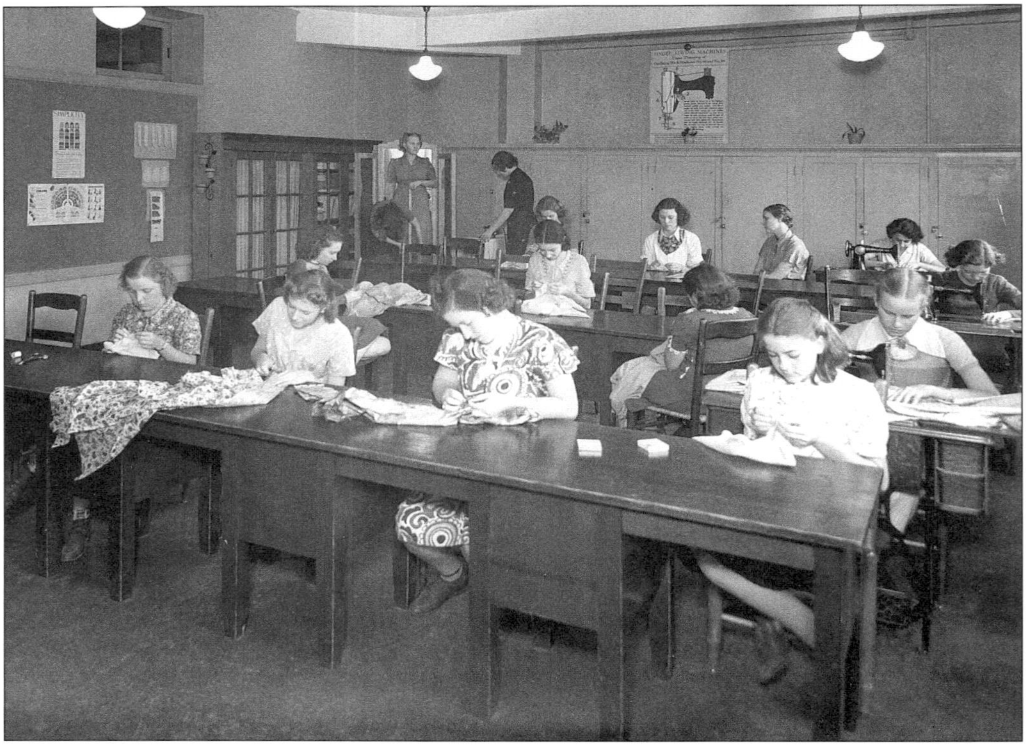

In 1937, the basement of Building III, or the former high school, hosted homemaking classes for the girls. Above, girls practice sewing with machines or basting by hand. Below, a cooking class engages in all processes of preparing a meal, from mixing ingredients to sitting down to sample the food. After the war, some girls still chose to take homemaking as an elective. (Both courtesy Harry Orem.)

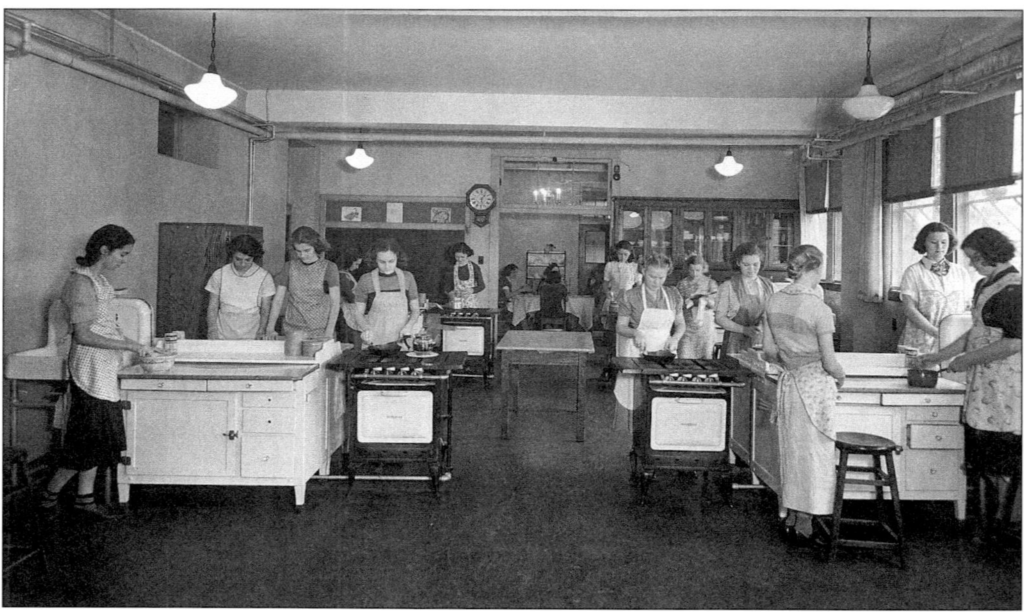

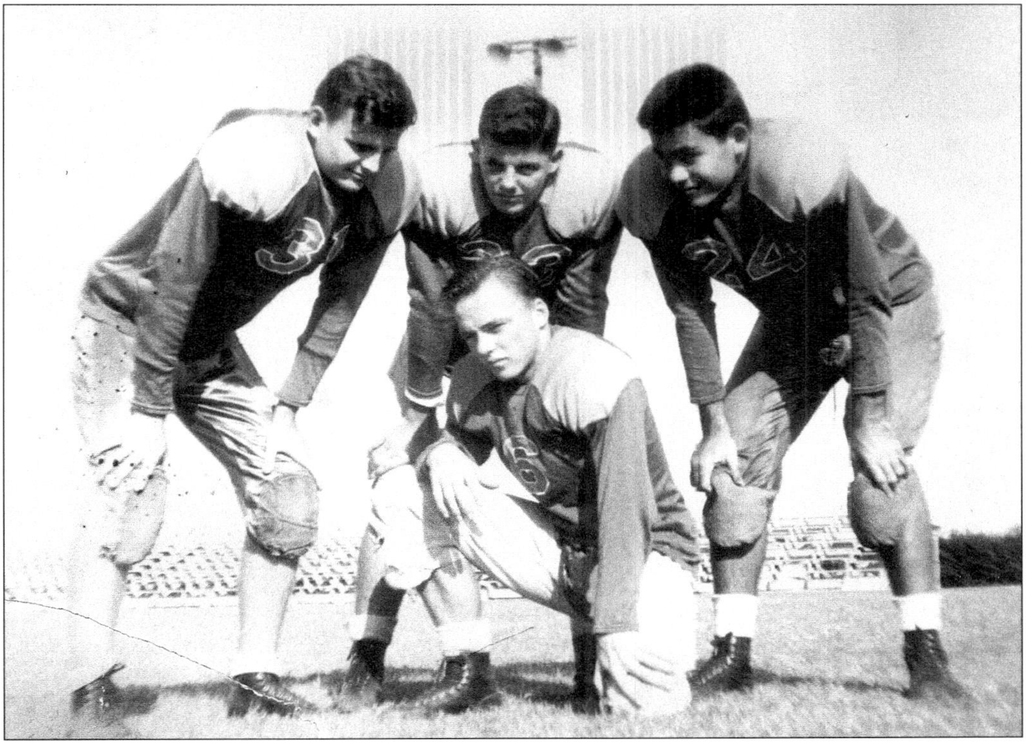

These proud 1943 district championship football players are, from left to right, as follows: (standing) Malcolm McDaniels, Albert Harris, John Hunt; and (kneeling) Robert Melland. The school won district again in 1954, when my mother attended Alamo Heights High School, and in 1991, my senior year. (Courtesy Harry Orem.)

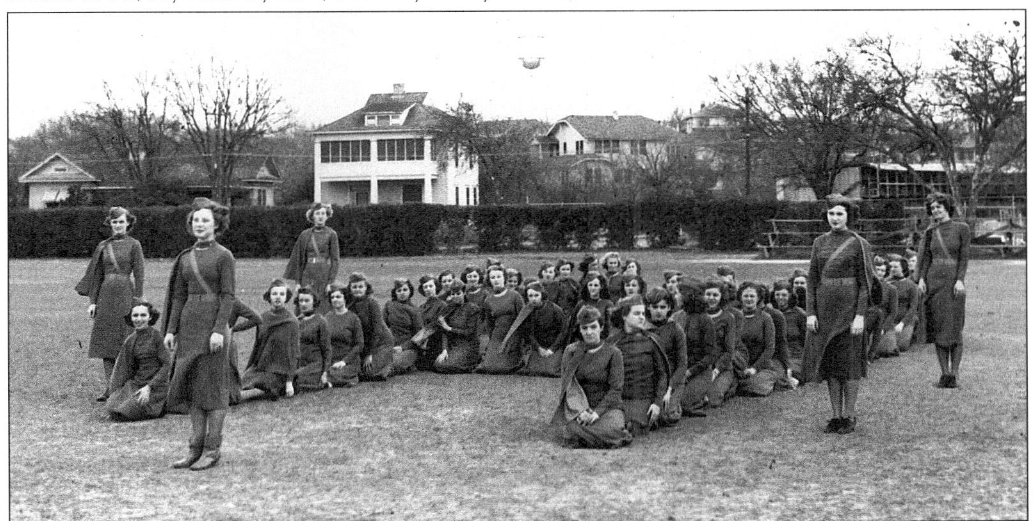

San Antonio has two teams named the Spurs: the San Antonio Spurs, the professional basketball team, and the Alamo Heights Spurs, the dance team. In the 1950s, my mother was a Alamo Heights Spur, and she marched with the band during parades and performed during halftime shows at football games. Go, Spurs, go! (Courtesy Harry Orem.)

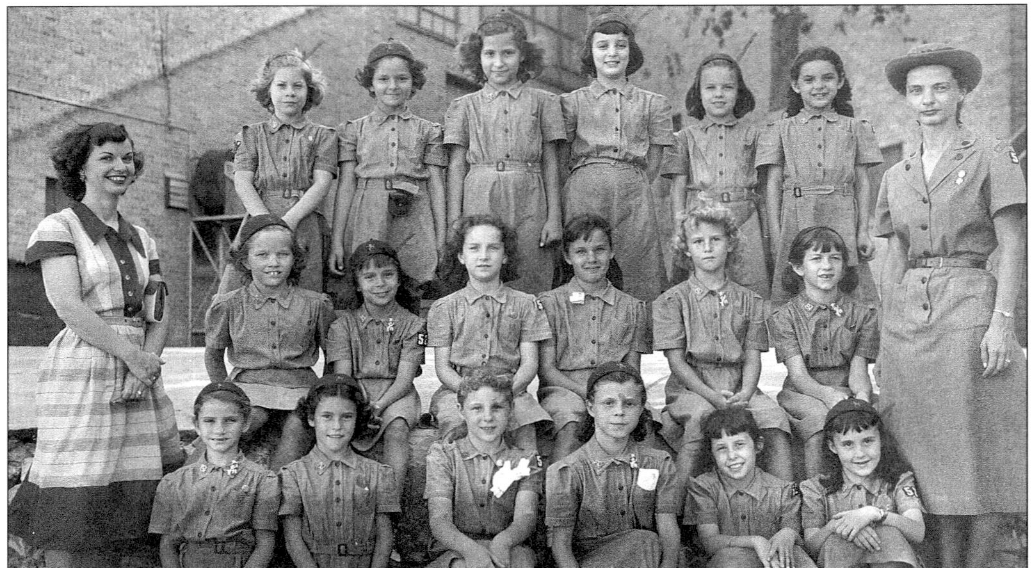

In 1952, the 52nd Brownie troop posed for a picture by what is now Cambridge Elementary School. From left to right are as follows: (front row) Susan Matthews, unidentified, Sue Nitchke, unidentified, Diana Serur, and Mary Katheryn Behrer; (second row) Mrs. Wallace, unidentified, unidentified, Nancy Lambert, Lindsey Dinkens, Terry Folbre, Penny Hight, and Mrs. Landers; (back row) Juliet Carnahan, unidentified, unidentified, Candy Katz, Katheryn Lateer, and Carolyn Wallace. (Courtesy Nancy Lambert Davenport.)

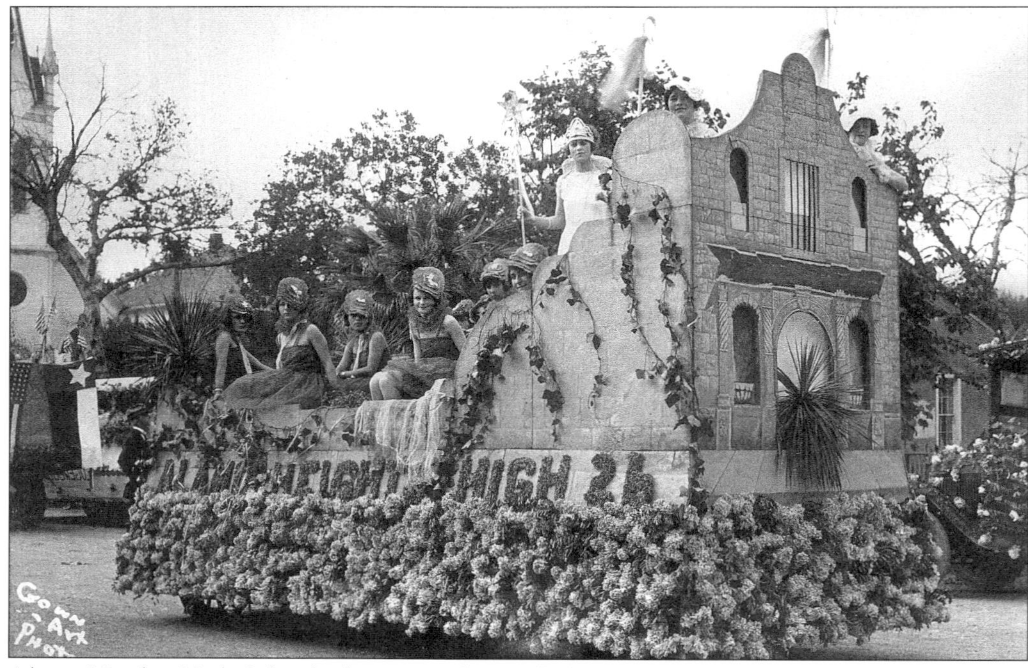

Alamo Heights High School's first Fiesta float rolled down the streets in 1926. For many years, the students of Alamo Heights also served as the "Super Scoopers." They walked down the streets with shovels and trash cans and cleaned up after the horses. (Courtesy Harry Orem.)

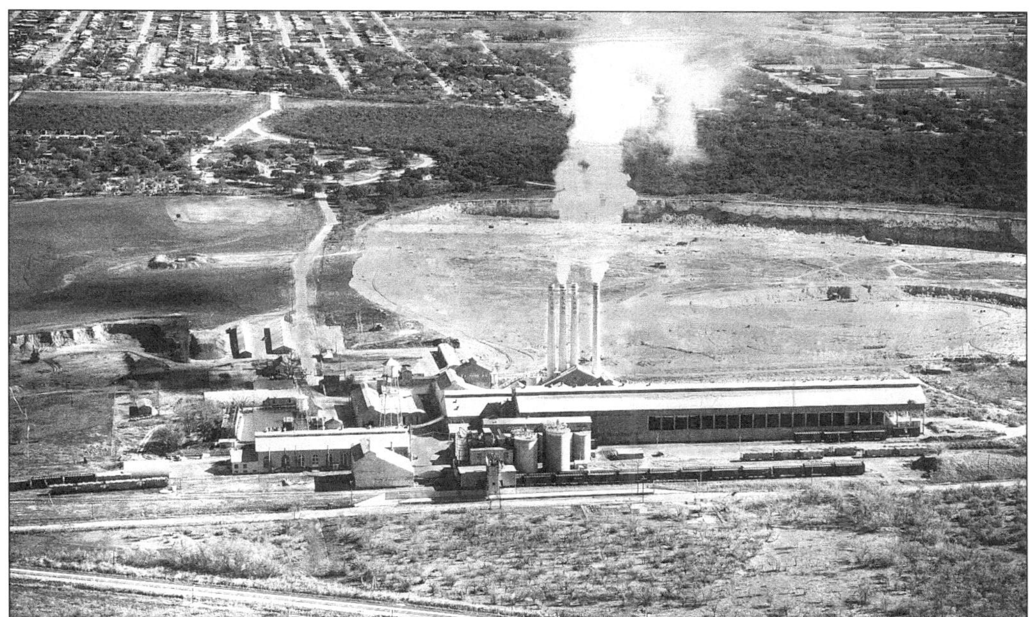

Now known to many San Antonians as Lincoln Heights, Cementville was out in the country when it was built from 1907 to1909. This aerial view looks east; the plant and smokestacks are in the foreground. San Antonio is in the upper left corner, and the current Alamo Heights High School is in the upper right corner. Today, the quarry is a golf course, and around the rim of the quarry are houses and apartments. The main quarry building is a movie theatre, and although the smokestacks remain, shops, bars, and restaurants now surround the old site of Cementville. (Courtesy Stanley Schmidt.)

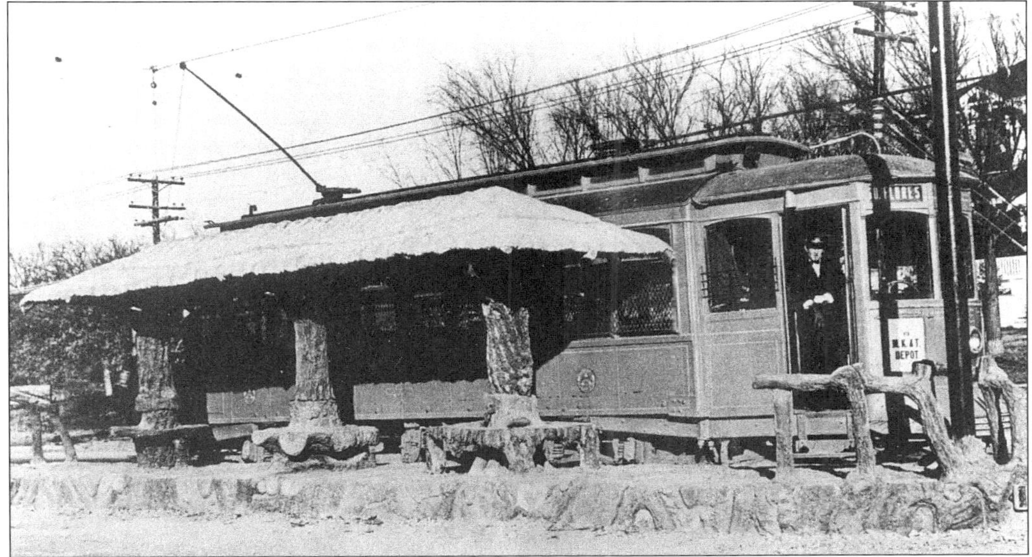

In the early 1900s, Cementville's employees who relied on public transportation disembarked at this trolley stop, built by Dionicio Rodriguez on Broadway at Patterson (which later became a bus stop). They walked 3 miles to the factory. (Courtesy Broadway 50-50 and Louis M. LaRocco and Frank R. Little.)

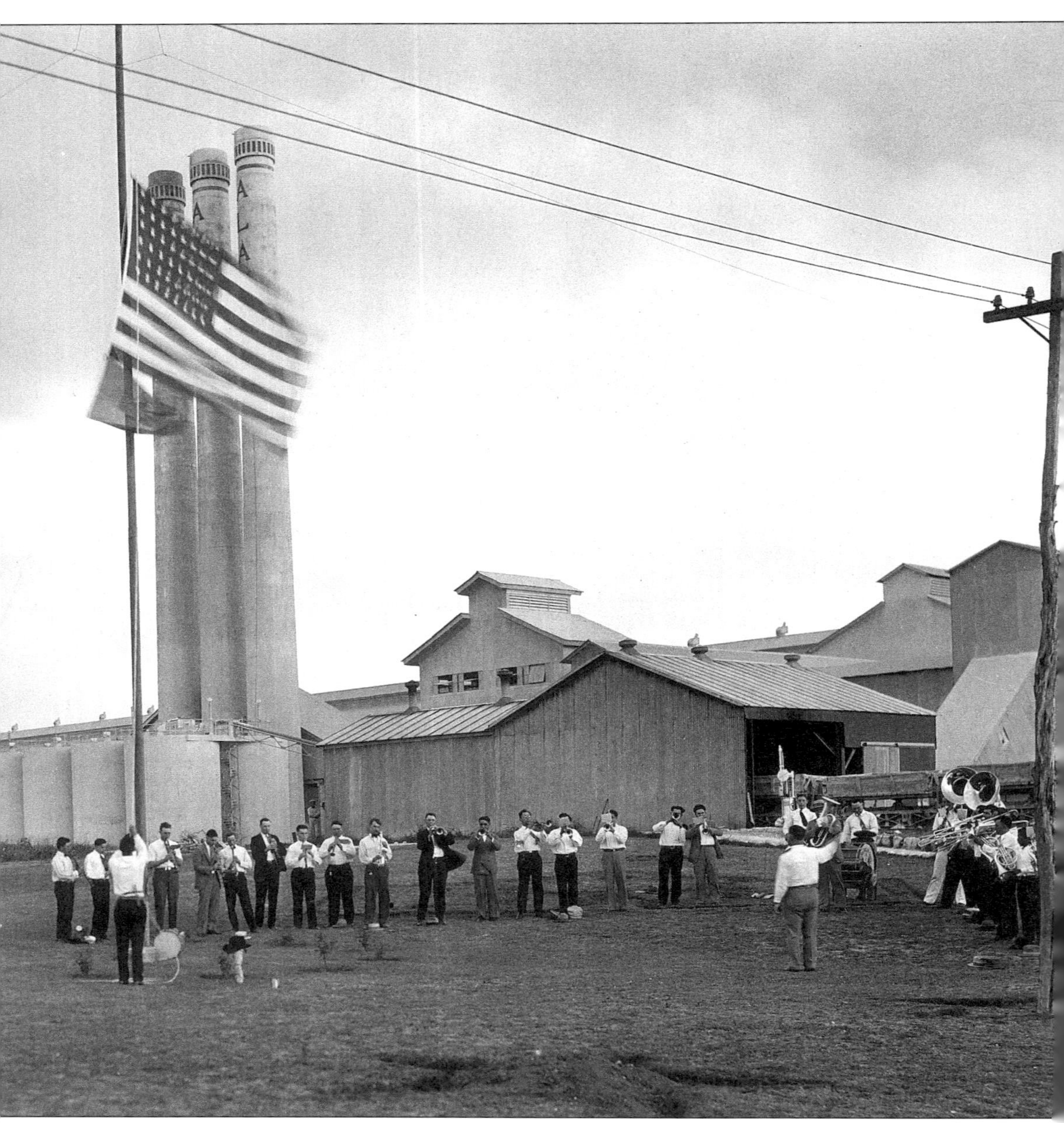

Cementville was not just a factory; many workers and their families called it home. The walk from the end of the street car line on Broadway at Patterson was over 2 miles, and in emergencies, the president, Mr. Charles Baumberger Sr., picked up workers in his buggy or automobile to get them to the plant. When he moved two important employees and their families to old farmhouses at the plant, the idea worked so well that he decided to build a village on the plant. Rent cost only $1 to $3 per week and was based on electrical outlets in the houses. The employees enjoyed electricity in their homes many, many years before some other residents in San Antonio. The workers enjoyed one another's company during picnics and other festivities hosted by the plant. In this 1922 image, the Cementville Band plays the National Anthem as the flag is raised during a ceremony. (Courtesy Stanley Schmidt.)

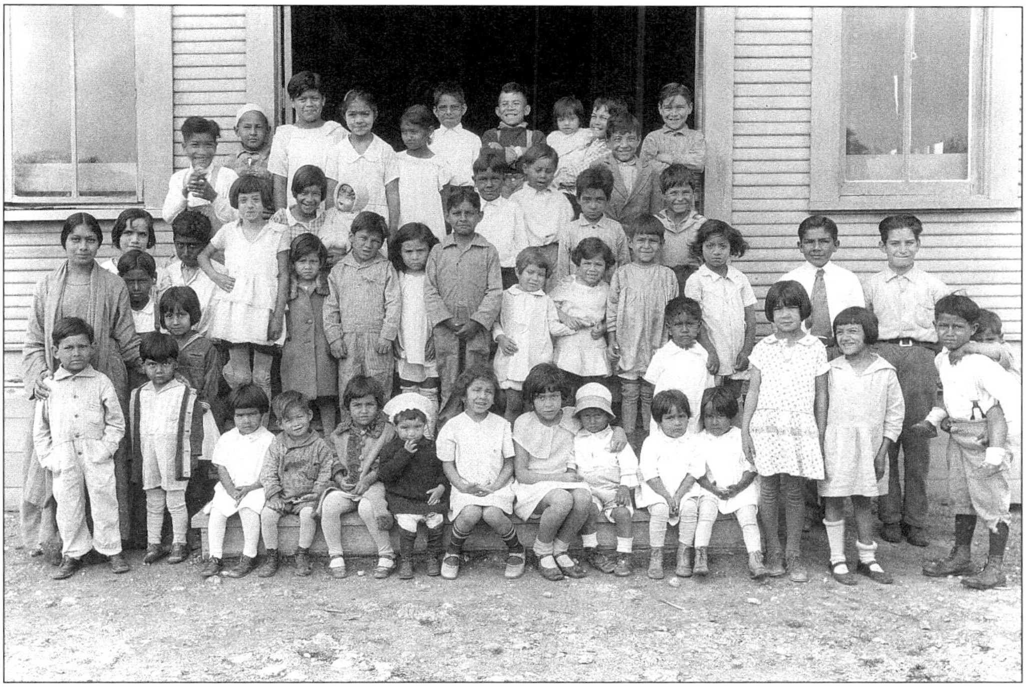

Children at Cementville attended a four-room schoolhouse located on the plant grounds for many years. Teachers from Alamo Heights Independent School District taught the children. Above, the Cementville children stand outside of their schoolhouse in 1928, and below, they stand on the grounds near the village, which was covered in bluebonnets. The bluebonnets are now gone, replaced by Lincoln Heights houses and shops. (Courtesy Harry Orem.)

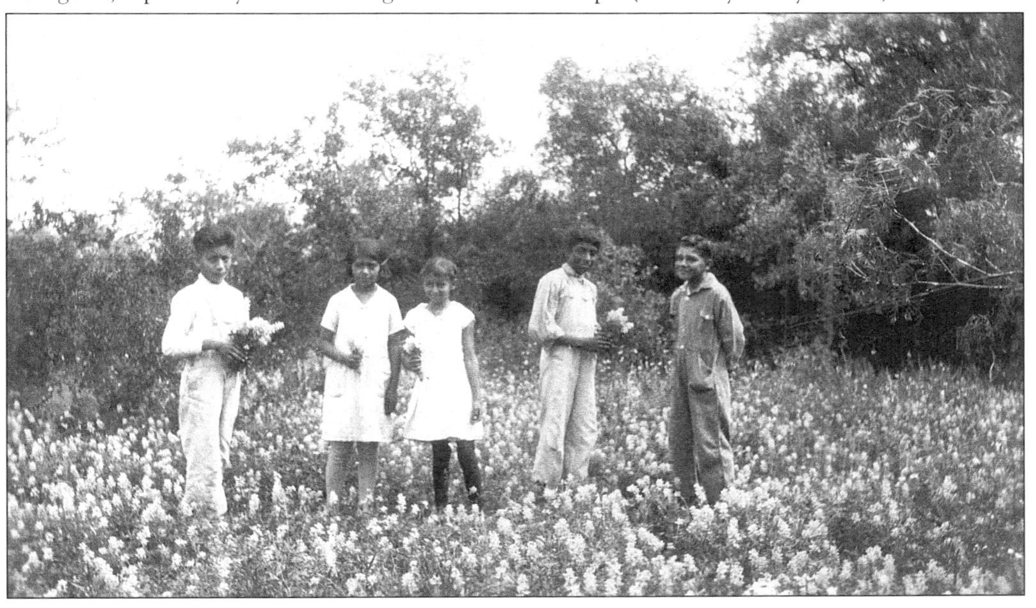

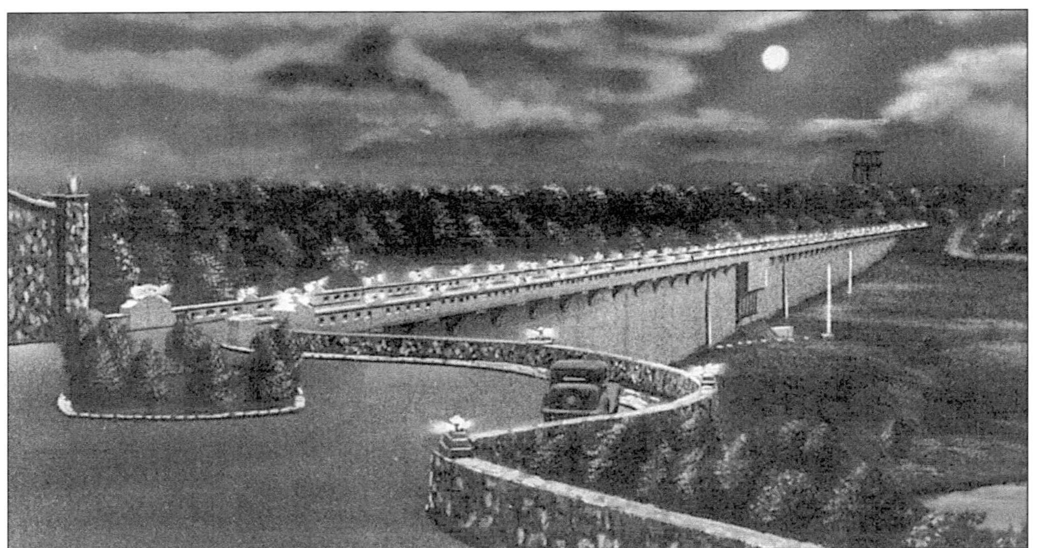

Formed "at a cost of $1,500,000," the Olmos Dam, located near Alamo Heights, stretches "across a dry channel which drains the rainfall from a wide area of hilly country." Although cars do not drive directly across the top of the dam anymore, people still park to look at the land surrounding it. Although today's dam is sturdy, flood waters that collect in the basin still can flow into Alamo Heights, as they did in 1998.

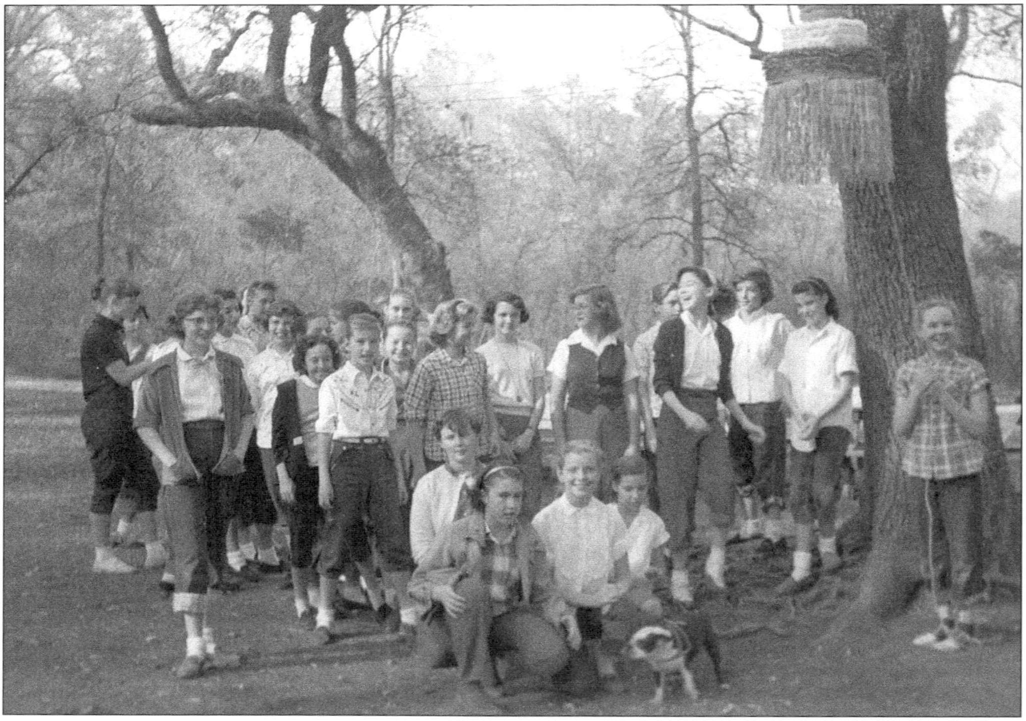

During dry times, people drive through Olmos Basin and stop in a shady area for a picnic or party. During a warm winter day in January of 1956, Carlita Hughes, who holds the rope of a piñata, celebrated her 12th birthday with friends in the basin. (Courtesy Carlita Hughes Kosty.)

In the early 1950s, Alamo Heights's band uniforms were made of 100% wool; my uncle, Joseph B. Lambert, models one of these uniforms. During parades and other events, volunteers squirted water into band members' mouths to keep them cool, but despite volunteers' efforts, many players fainted (and still do) during unusually warm days or long marches. (Courtesy Thille Lambert Newton.)

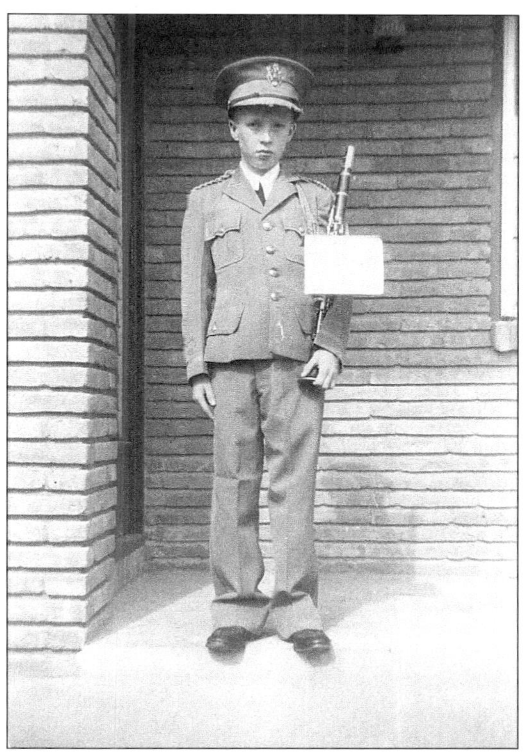

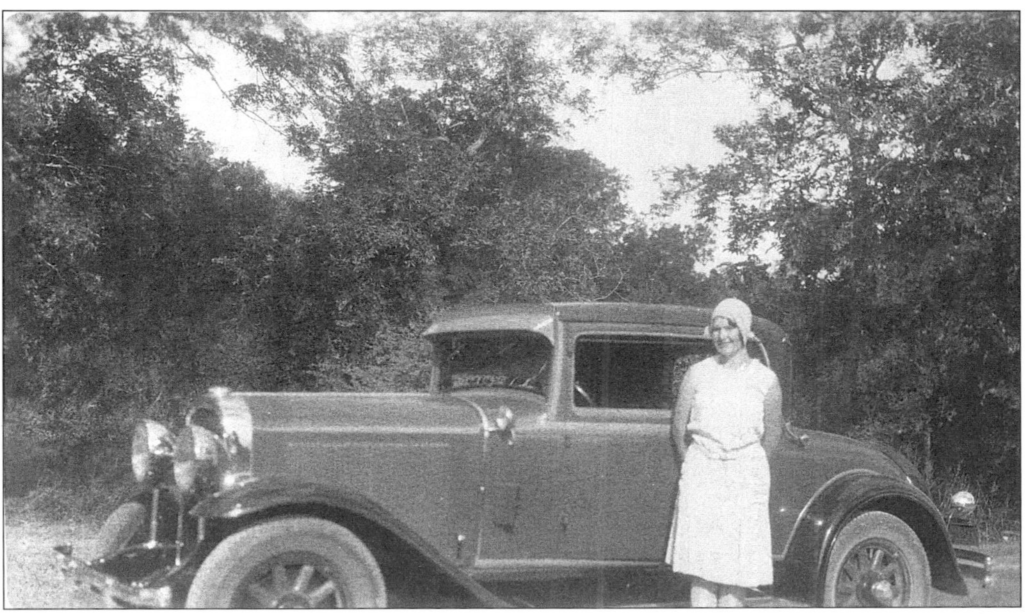

Maxine Irwin loved to drive her Ford roadster around the streets of Alamo Heights. Her dress and hat represent the clothing that flappers wore in the Roaring Twenties. (Courtesy Cynthia Davenport Woodland.)

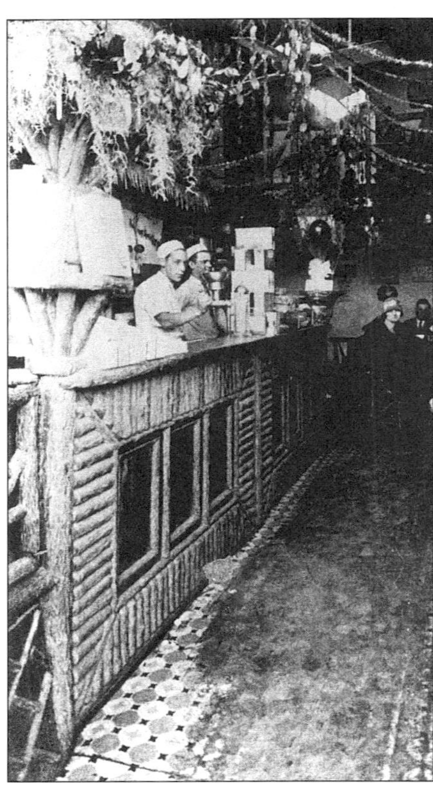

When I'm ready for a beer and some company, I'll head to Broadway 50-50. Formerly referred to as Montanio's 50-50, this bar has drawn locals of all ages back to its rooms again and again. In 1998, my family and I celebrated St. Patrick's Day here. (Courtesy Broadway 50-50 and Louis M. LaRocco and Frank R. Little.)

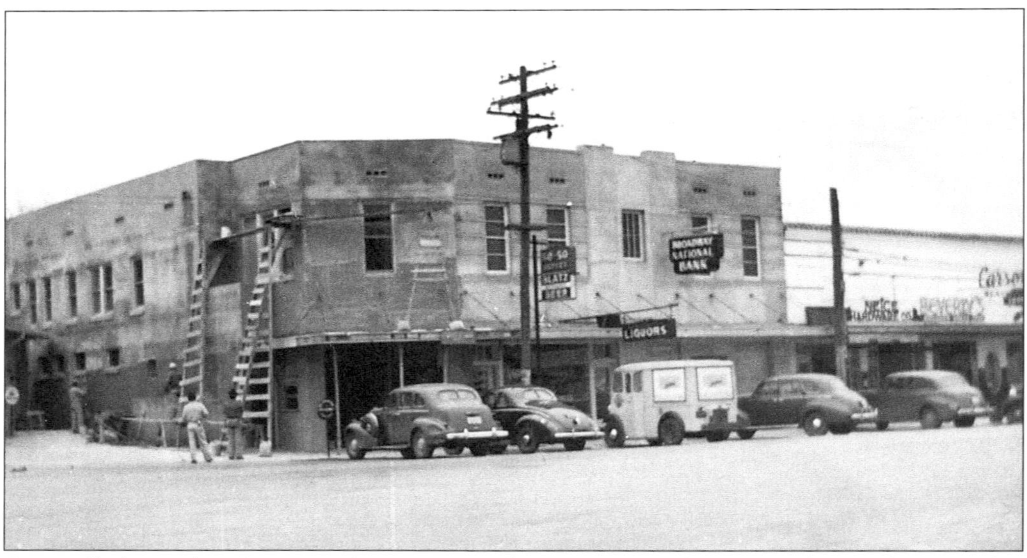

Originally located at 5044 Broadway, next to the present Broadway 50-50 bar as shown in this picture, the Broadway National Bank drew support from Alamo Heights residents in its early days. Although the bank has grown over the years, during World War II, the founders, Colonel Charles E. Cheever Sr. and his wife, Betty Cheever, struggled to keep the bank on its feet. Today, Broadway National Bank is the largest independently-owned bank headquartered in San Antonio. (Courtesy Broadway National Bank.)

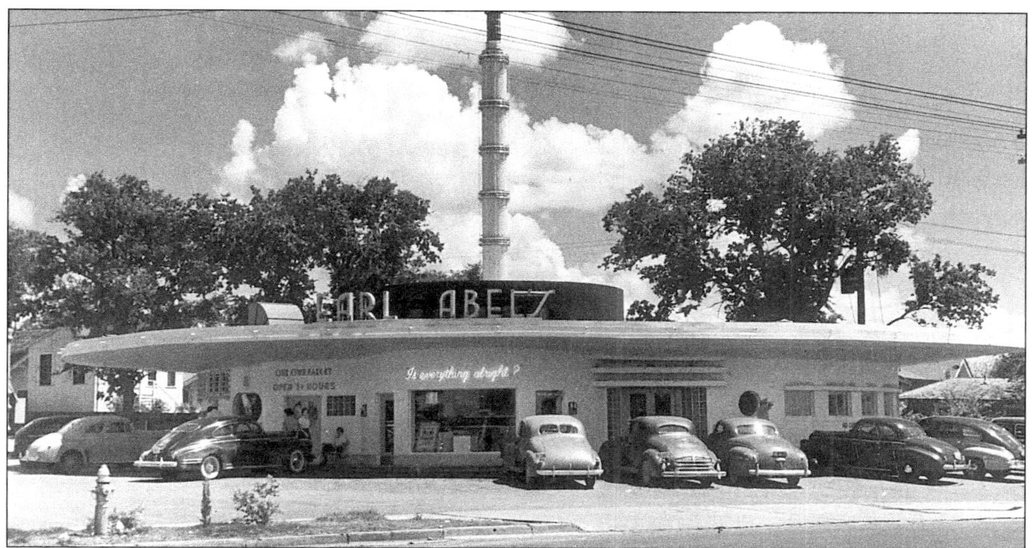

Earl Abel's, a restaurant located on Broadway near the University of the Incarnate Word, has drawn San Antonians to its doors for years. After a formal dance in high school, a group of friends and I drove to Earl Abel's for a late-night snack. The Gothic-like atmosphere of the restaurant, as well as its sign that reads, "Eat Here, Diet Home," adds to its appeal. (Courtesy Jerry Abel.)

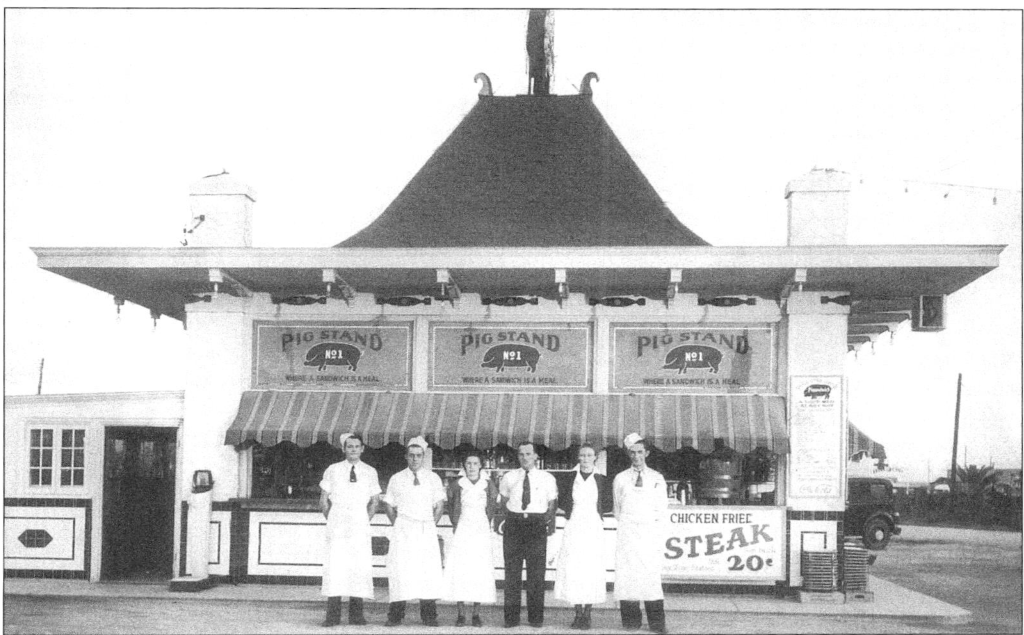

After games in the 1950s, '09ers flocked to Pig Stand™ on Broadway just outside of Alamo Heights for a Coke or an original Pig Sandwich™, which consists of barbequed pork, relish, and sauce. In the 1920s, Pig Stand was the original drive-in, and today, locations exist in Beaumont, Houston, and Lytle in addition to San Antonio. Royce Hailey started working at Pig Stand as a car hop, and now his son, Richard Hailey, continues the Pig Stand tradition. (Courtesy Pig Stand.)

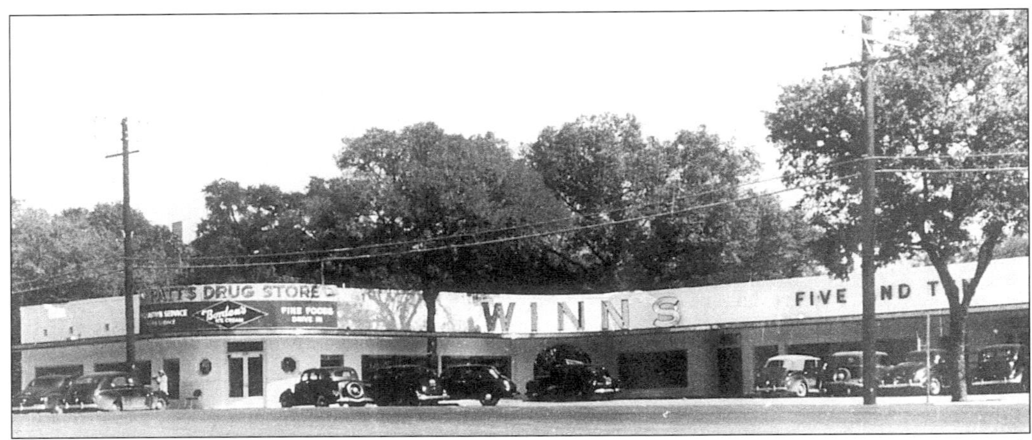

My mother worked at Winn's for one summer in the mid-1950s for 35¢ an hour. Pleased with her work, Winn's invited her to continue working at that salary, but upon her graduation from high school, my mother chose to attend college. Although this Winn's closed a few years ago, Patt's Drug Store still stands on this corner on Broadway. (Courtesy Broadway 50-50 and Louis M. LaRocco and Frank R. Little.)

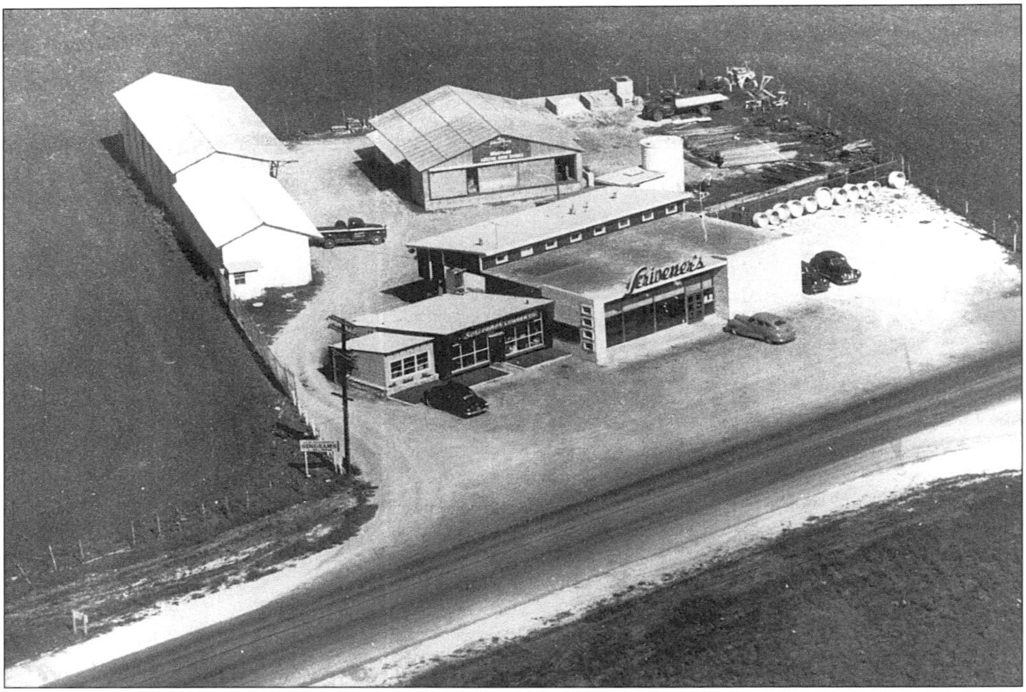

Turning a lumberyard into a department store sounds like an unusual feat, but the Scrivener family managed it. Scrivener's opened in 1946 as a lumber store, but by adding new merchandise such as fabrics for dresses, it became a popular store for San Antonians and visitors. Today, the store still stands on its original site on Broadway, although it now is surrounded by a highway and numerous buildings. Ernest Scrivener Sr. built the first Alamo Heights school. (Courtesy Ernest Scrivener Jr.)

John LaRoche, Mimi Cavender, and Michael Lamm (pictured from left to right) stroll along the Riverwalk, a popular place for Alamo Heights students to go on weekends. (Courtesy Carlita Hughes Kosty.)

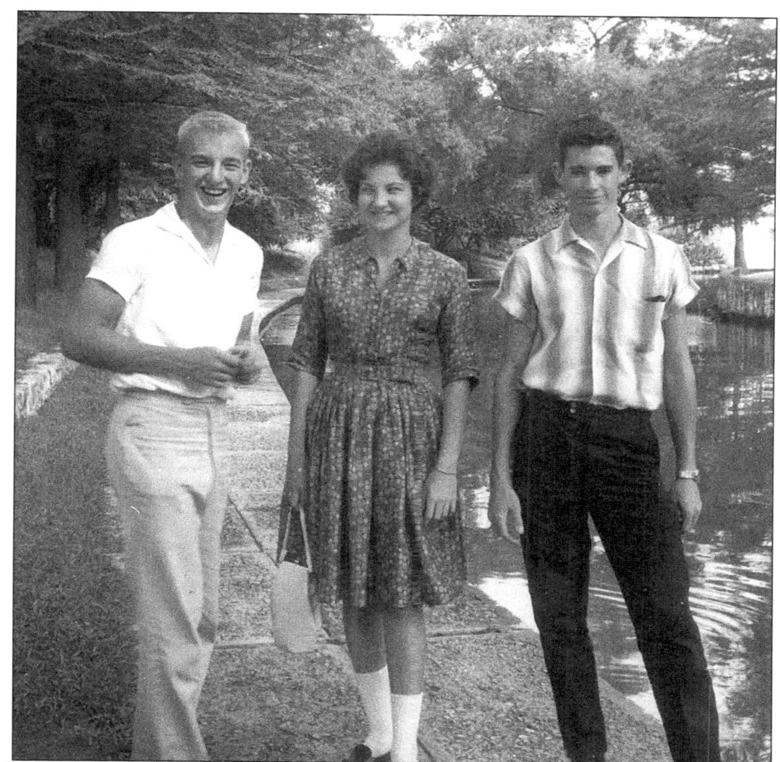

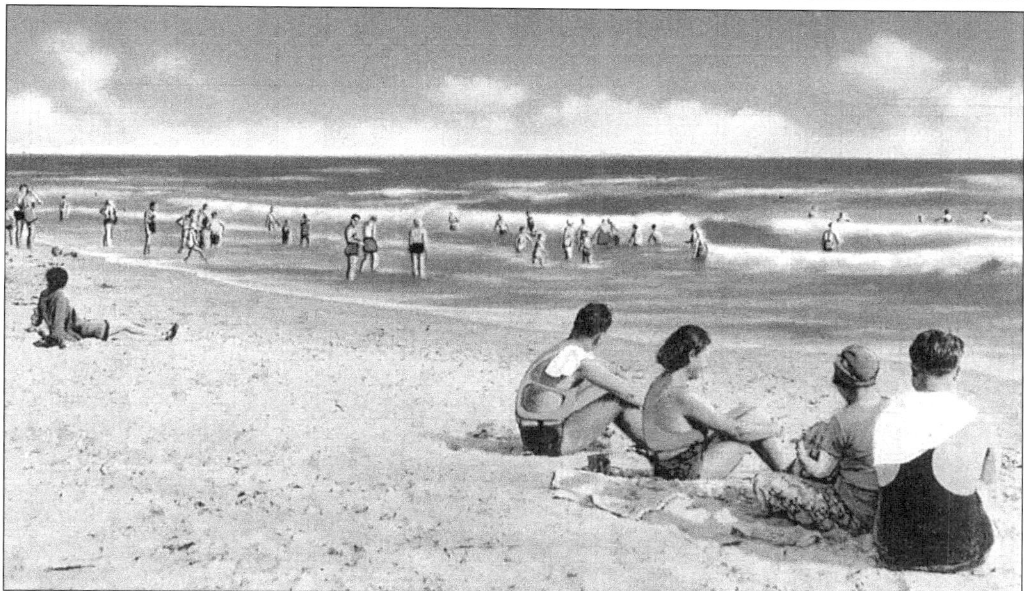

During spring and summer breaks, '09ers pile into their cars after decorating them in shoe polish with word's such as "South Padre or Bust!" Nearly every year until I left for college, I spent at least one week on the Gulf of Mexico, whether at Rockport, Port Aransas, or South Padre. After a few long days at the beach, my friends and I would then head to Mexico for an afternoon of shopping or an evening of dancing.

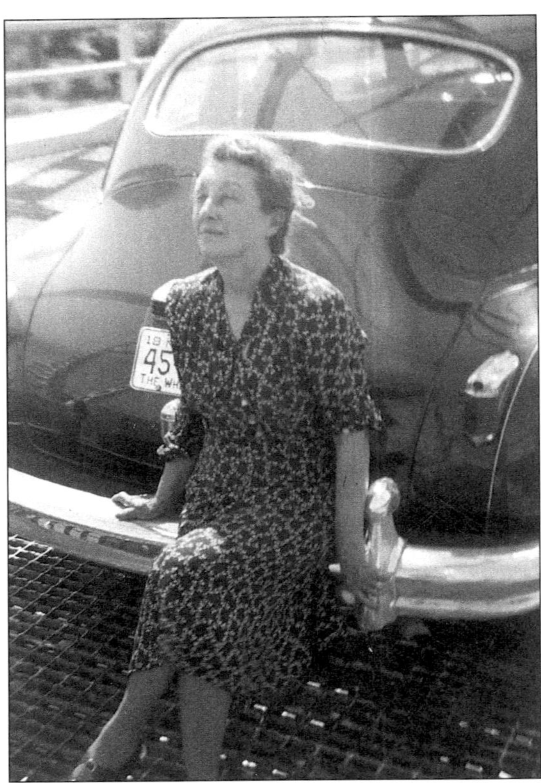

Emma Thille Kirwan Rochford, my great-grandmother, sits on her Chrysler, dreaming of Mexico before heading south of the border. My aunt Nancy recalls going for "long, hot, dusty Sunday afternoon rides in the back of the car." Although Texans love Texas, Mexico beckons to them. Nearly every year, my family and I fill our coolers with Cokes and drive down to either Laredo or to Matamoros. Although the road is flat and dirty the entire way, drinking a margarita while bargaining for silver jewelry in Laredo's shops is thrilling. (Courtesy Nancy Lambert Davenport.)

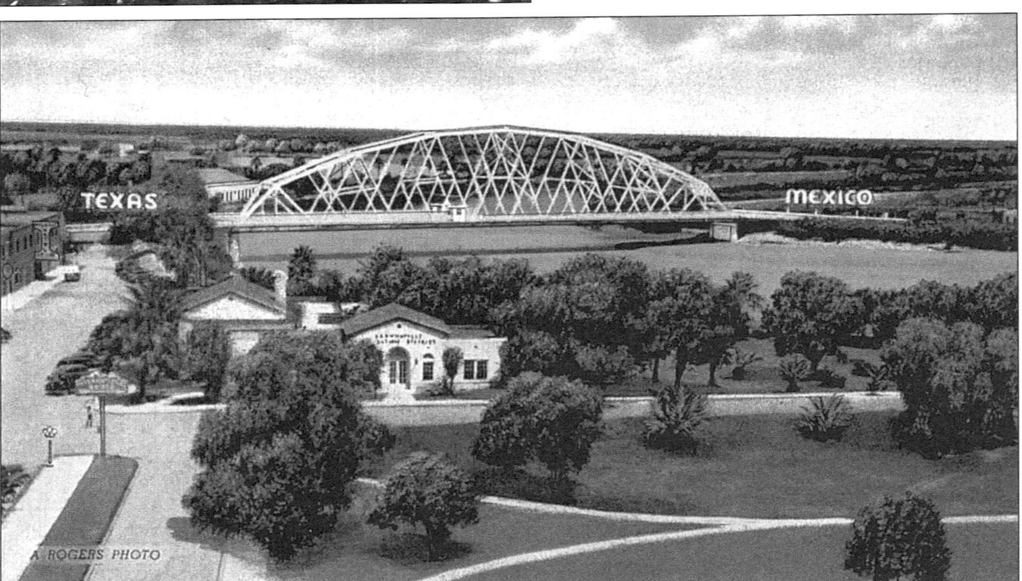

I always cross the bridge from Texas to Mexico empty-handed, but return laden with blankets, silver earrings, piñatas, and tequila. I can do most of my shopping south of the border, but I've had trouble getting back. One especially hot day in August, after a busy day at the mercado (or market), a friend of mine and I got lost. Whenever we asked a Mexican, "How do we get back to Texas?" they pointed south, west, or east, but never north, where Texas really was.

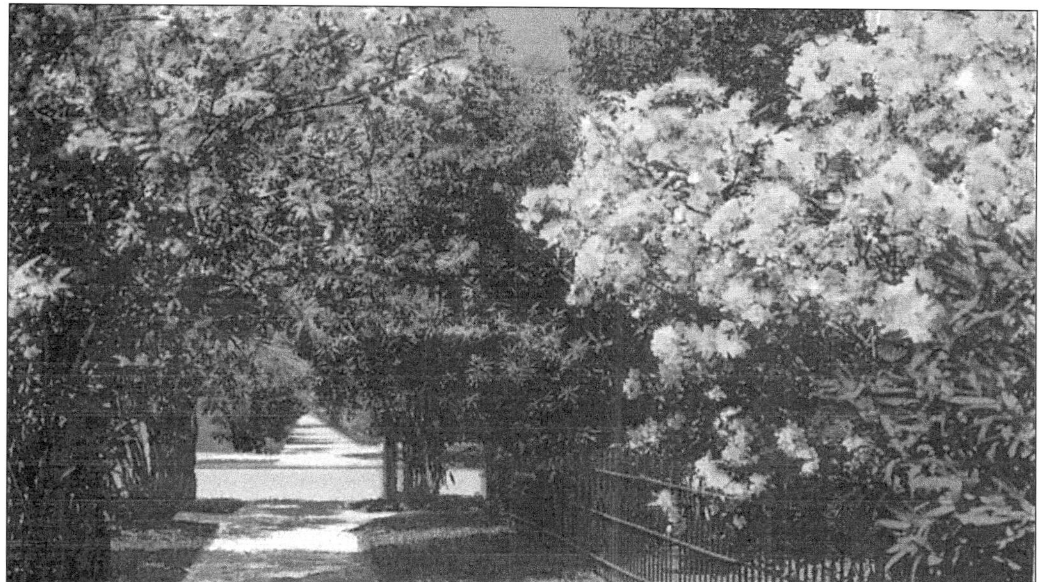

At my parents' house in San Antonio, we have fig and banana trees, but the crepe myrtle trees are the most beautiful ones. Whenever I see crepe myrtle, I think of home. In the summertime, along the Riverwalk and the streets of San Antonio, crepe myrtle trees, which need little water and lots of sun, bloom in shades of white, pink, and purple.

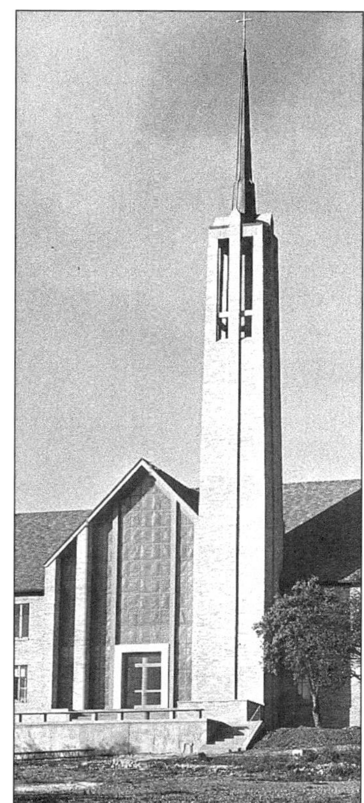

Not too long after settling in San Antonio, my grandfather joined St. Luke's Episcopal Church in Alamo Heights. He sang in the choir for a number of years. The current church building, built in the 1950s, is located on St. Luke's Lane near the old Texas Military Institute school, but the first St. Luke's was established around the turn of the 20th century. (Courtesy The Episcopal Diocese of West Texas.)

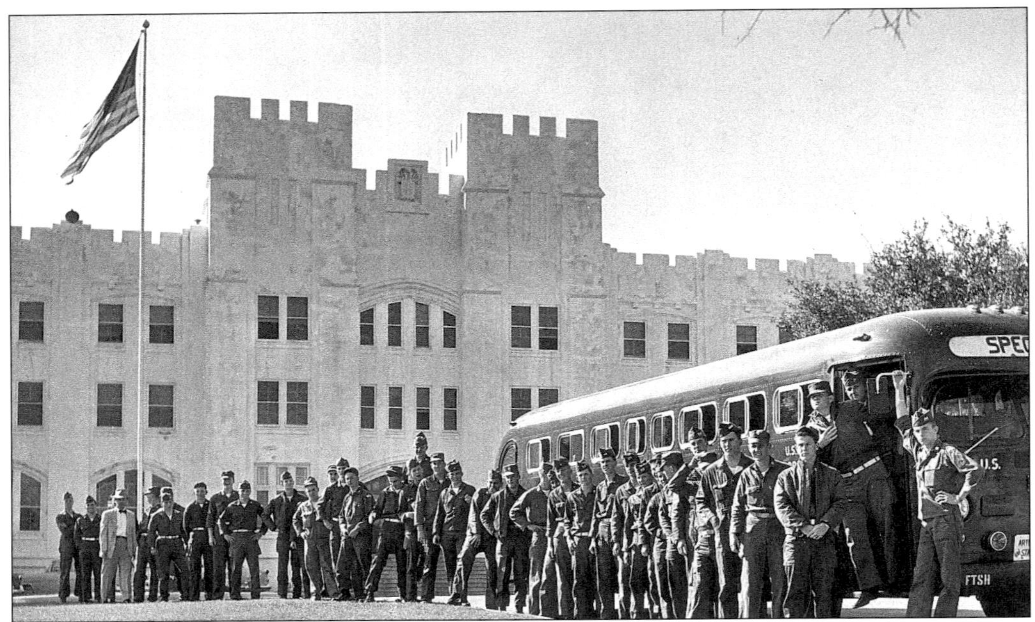

Students from West Texas Military Academy, later renamed Texas Military Academy, stand in front of "Old Main" before boarding buses bound to Camp Bullis for training exercises. "Old Main," a pre-cast, tilt-up structure built in the 1910s by alumni Willard and Guy Simpson, housed classrooms, a dormitory, and a library. Although the board of trustees decided to make the school's JROTC program optional in 1974 and construction for a new school on the outskirts of San Antonio began in the 1980s, Texas Military Academy continues to uphold its mission "to provide an excellent educational community, . . . challenging motivated students to develop their full potential in service and leadership." (Courtesy Texas Military Institute.)

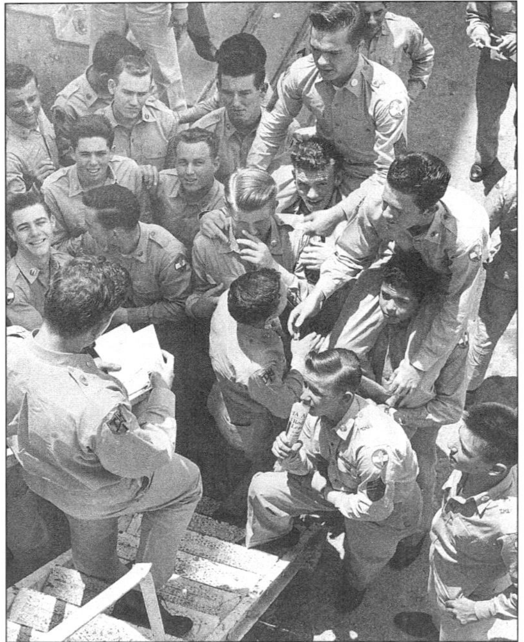

In this 1950s shot, a group of Texas Military Institute boarding students hope for letters during mail call. Girls did not attend the school until the 1970s, when the board decided to allow females to enroll as day students. (Courtesy Texas Military Institute.)

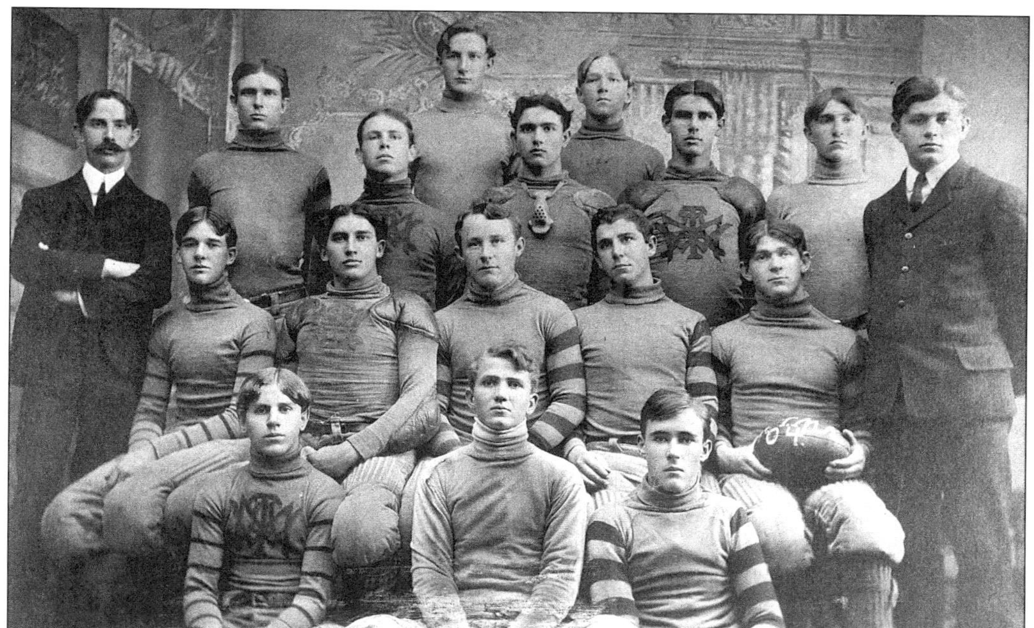

This shot of West Texas Military Academy's football players was taken in 1904, the 11th year of the Academy's existence. When the Academy first opened, admitting 12 students and 10 teachers, the founder, the Right Reverend James Steptoe Johnston, the Bishop of the Diocese of West Texas, wished the school to provide "the best intellectual, moral, and physical training" to young boys in Texas. (Courtesy Texas Military Institute.)

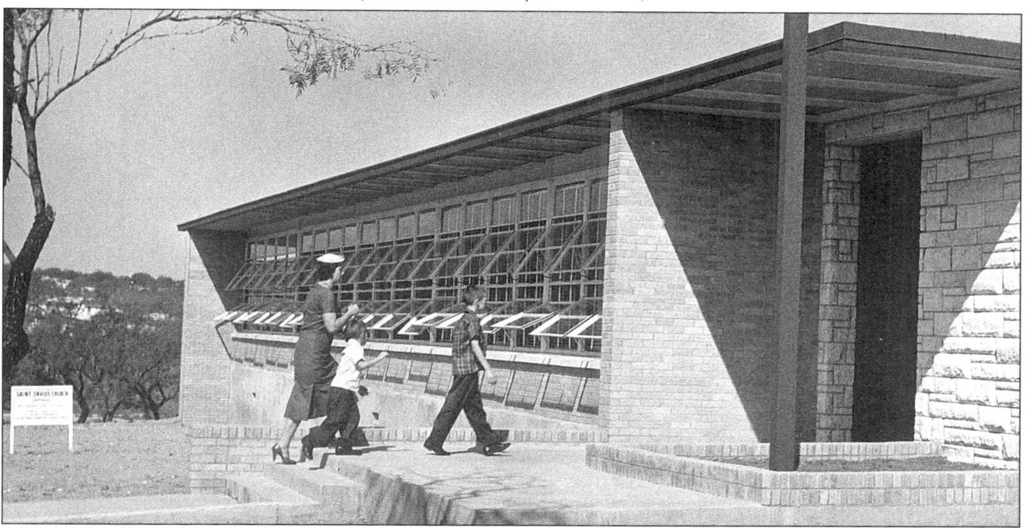

In his later years, my grandfather attended St. David's Episcopal Church, often referred to as "the only church in Terrell Hills," since it was closer to his house. The church has expanded greatly since this picture was taken in 1952, the year the church was founded; since then, my family has watched the expansion of the church and participated in numerous youth and adult group activities. Today, the church stands near the left side of this structure, which now houses classrooms for preschool and elementary school children. (Courtesy The Episcopal Diocese of West Texas.)

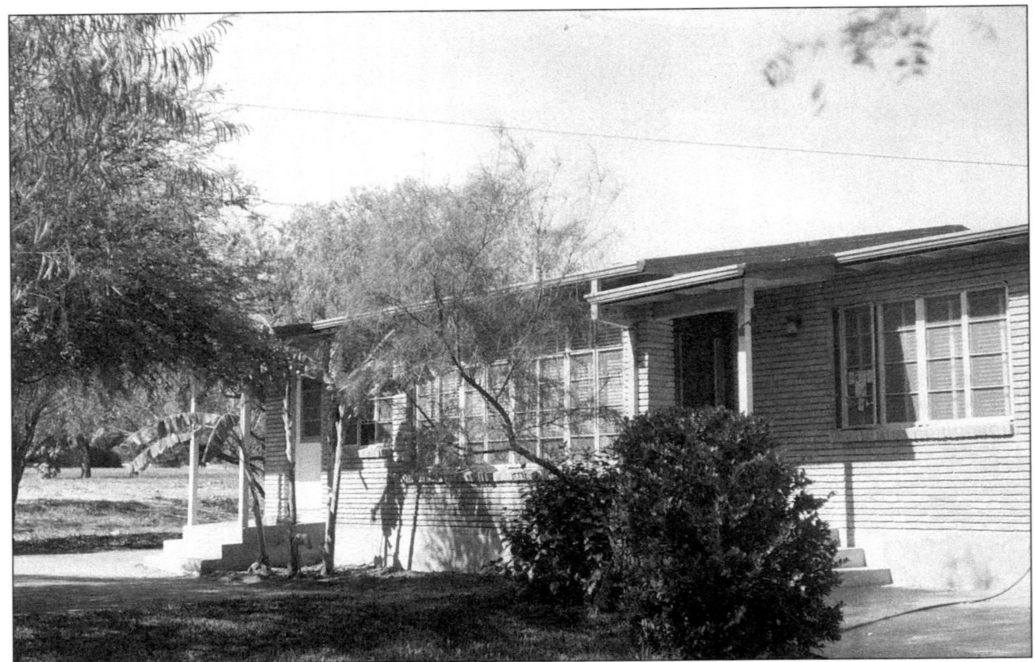

In 1951, my grandparents and their three children moved into 536 Terrell Road near Alamo Heights. This house now exists as one of few one-story houses in the area, and my cousins and I spent many childhood days together in the house and yard, making pralines, hunting for snails, or plucking figs. (Courtesy Thille Lambert Newton.)

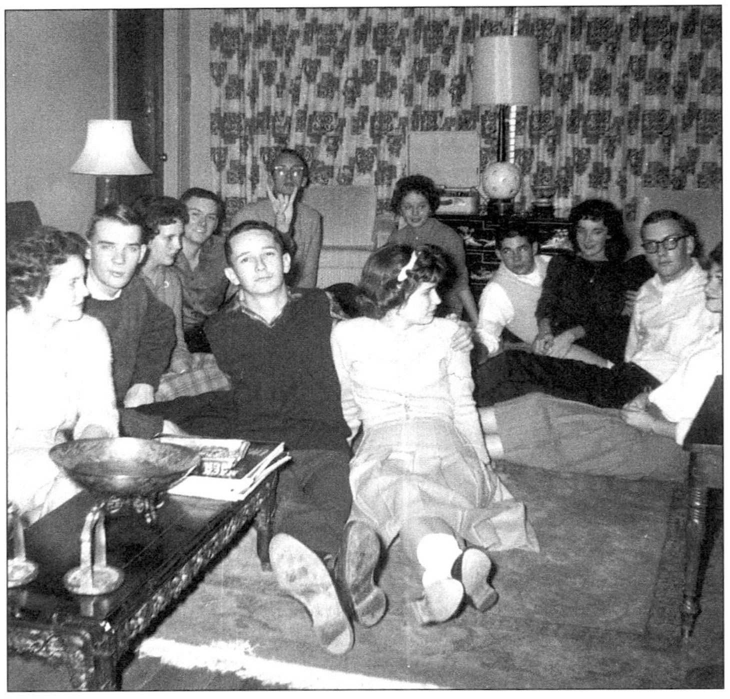

At a New Year's Eve party c. 1960, future state senator Jeffrey Wentworth (sitting in the midst of his friends and next to Bobby Ann Harper) rings in the new year at my grandparents' house on Terrell Road. Seated behind Wentworth and Harper are as follows, from left to right: Laurie Hargis, Bill Jordan, Helen Ruck, Charles Palm, Joseph B. Lambert, Donna Carlson, Dick Davenport, Nancy Lambert, Richard Ellington, and Susan Matthews. (Courtesy Nancy Lambert Davenport.)

Seven

DEEP-SEATED PATRIOTISM:
AIR FORCE BASES AND ARMY POSTS

Every generation of my family, up until mine, has boasted a soldier or two. As children, my brothers, cousins, and I often watched army polo matches and frequented the officers' clubs, and our elders donated nylon stockings for parachutes or fought against European or Mexican soldiers.

Military life has always played a large role in my family's history, as well as in the history of San Antonio. The city is home to four air force bases—Kelly, Brooks, Lackland, and Randolph—and to one army post—Fort Sam Houston. During times of war and peace, San Antonians, whether soldiers or civilians, contribute a significant amount of time and energy to support the bases.

In this chapter, I include a special coverage of Randolph in order to portray different dimensions of military life in San Antonio. I also introduce one western post, Fort Clark, where my grandfather and the other members of Troop D, 13th Cavalry, were stationed in the 1910s. He migrated from Fort Clark to other posts in Illinois, Georgia, and Kansas until Fort Sam Houston became his final stop.

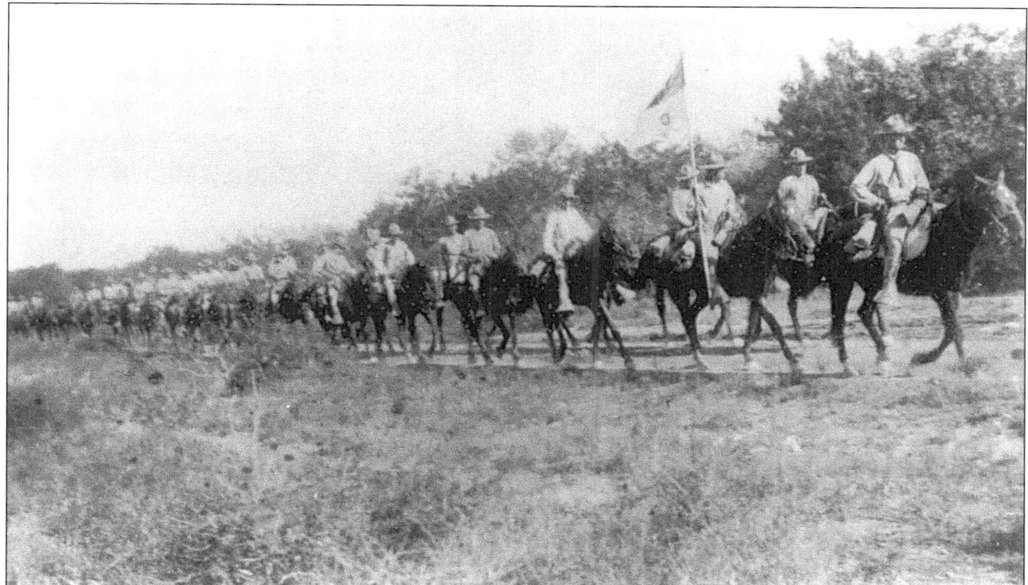

As captain, Joseph Idus commanded Troop D, 13th Cavalry, as it traveled from Fort Clark to the headwaters of the Nueces River in the 1910s. (Courtesy Joseph B. Newton.)

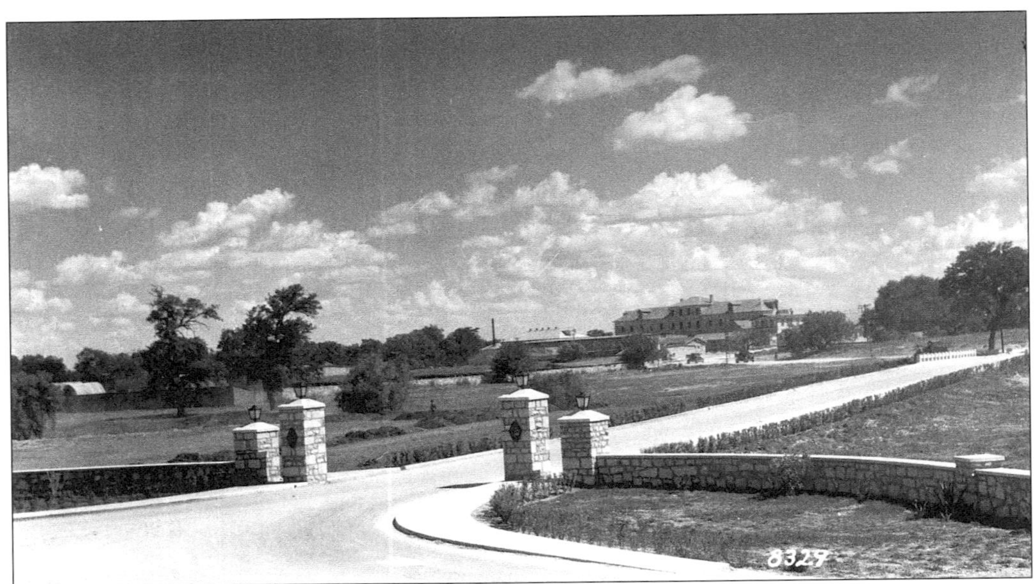

In 1918, Joseph Idus and his regiment, Troop D, 13th Cavalry, "received War Department orders to [move] to Fort Clark, Kinney County, Texas, near the town of Brackettville," as he noted in his memoirs. During the march, "a message arrived on November 11, 1918, telling [the troop] the armistice was signed and the war was over," but my grandfather said, "This news . . . did not alter our plans." (Courtesy Daughters of the Republic of Texas Library, Ekmark Collection, FC8329.)

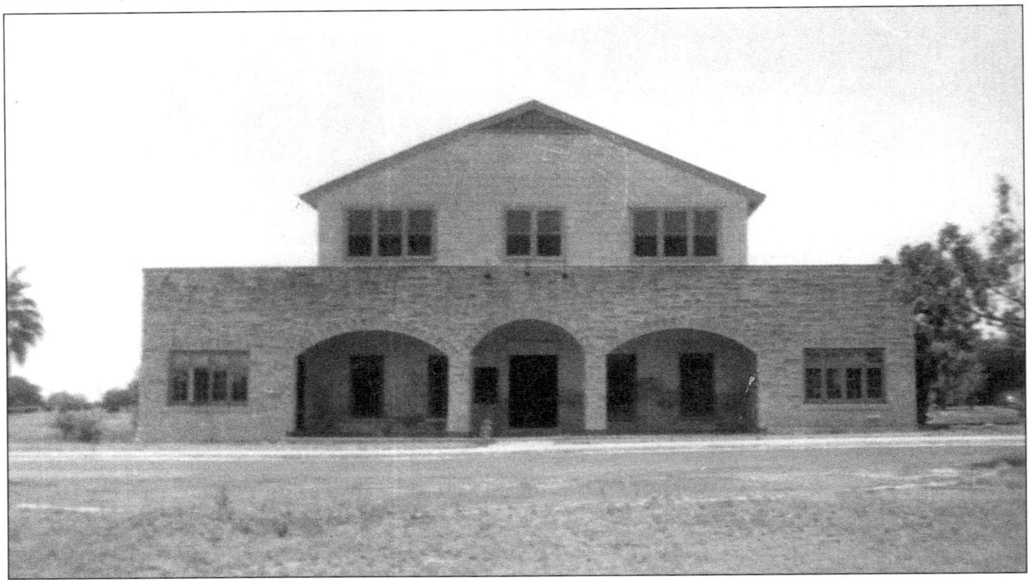

According to Joseph Idus's memoirs, Fort Clark "army post was built immediately after the Mexican War (along with several others) as a protection to our new international border, and was about thirty miles from the Rio Grande. . . An outstanding natural feature which finally probably decided the exact location . . . was Las Moras Springs and Creek which provided a great quantity of water." In 1952, he returned to Fort Clark to take this picture of the post headquarters. (Courtesy Thille Lambert Newton.)

In his memoirs, Joseph Idus wrote, "In May, 1916, [t]roops headed by General John J. Pershing were . . . searching for the bandit, Pancho Villa, in northern Mexico." In 1917, "Black Jack" Pershing commanded the Punitive Expedition in Mexico, and military officials worried that Pancho Villa would attack the border towns. My grandfather felt ready to confront any bandits: "We are no longer allowed to go swimming in the Rio Grande, because there is danger of being attacked . . . I should rather take chance of a few 'Greasers' bullets than leave off bathing." (Courtesy Fort Sam Houston Museum.)

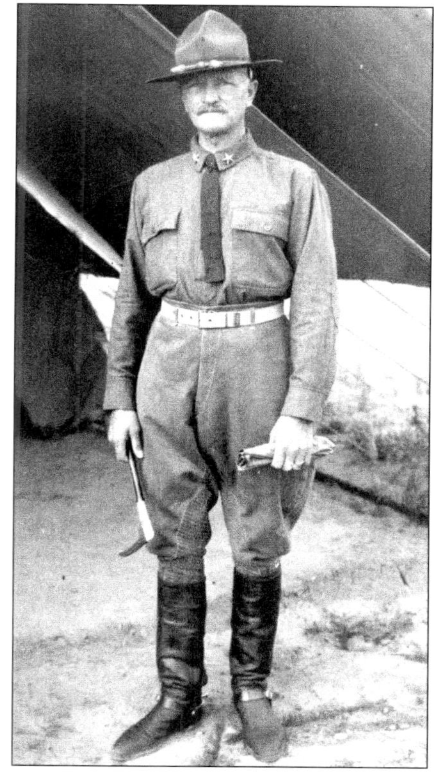

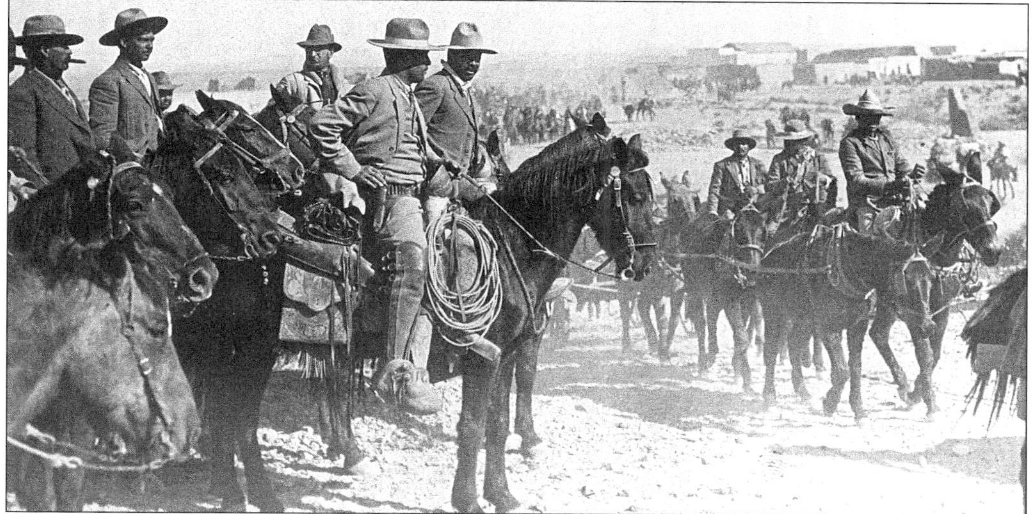

Pancho Villa, the man with the pistol, and his men stepped over the Mexican border and attacked a few United States towns in the 1910s, right about the same time my grandfather enlisted in the Texas National Guard. According to my grandfather, "Villa attacked Columbus, New Mexico and killed several American people. . . there was strong feeling between the people of the United States and Mexico, even the possibility of war. The [Texas] National Guard was federalized, and . . . sent to the Mexican border, to watch and wait . . ." (Courtesy Charlie Shoup, ChampionStuff.)

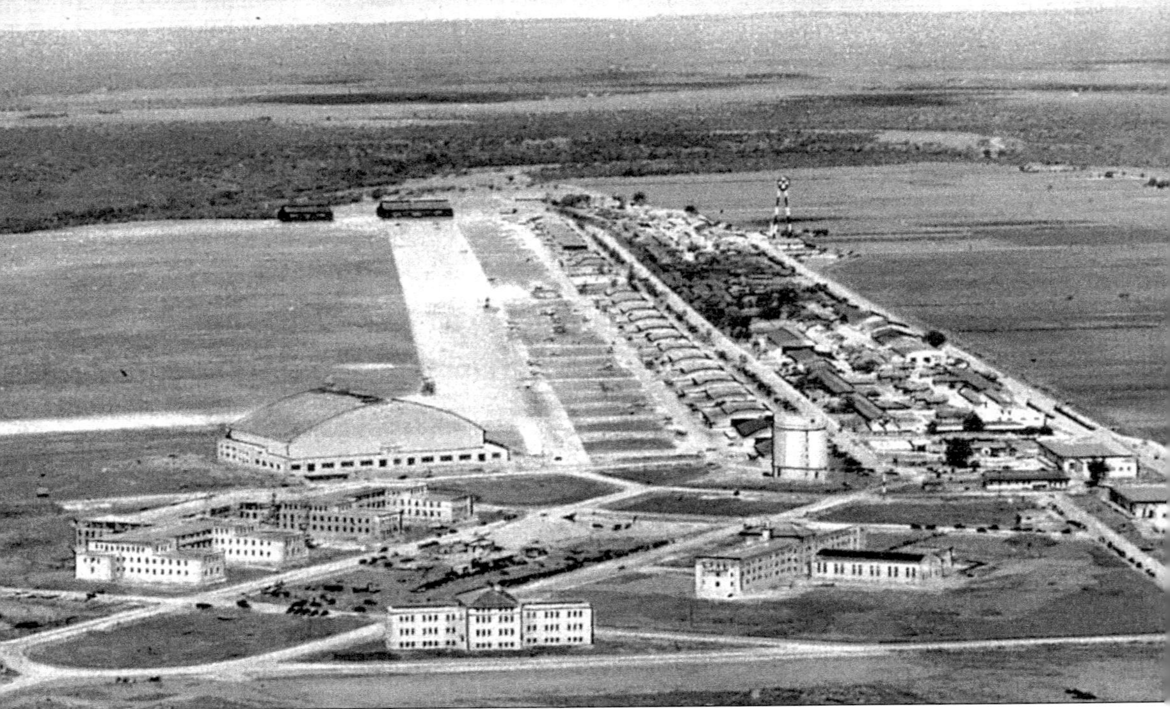

This aerial view of Kelly Air Force Base depicts the length of the flight line. Although some of the structures pictured here still stand today, the land around the base is filled with roads and buildings. Kelly will close July 13, 2001, after over 80 years of faithful service to the United States and to San Antonio.

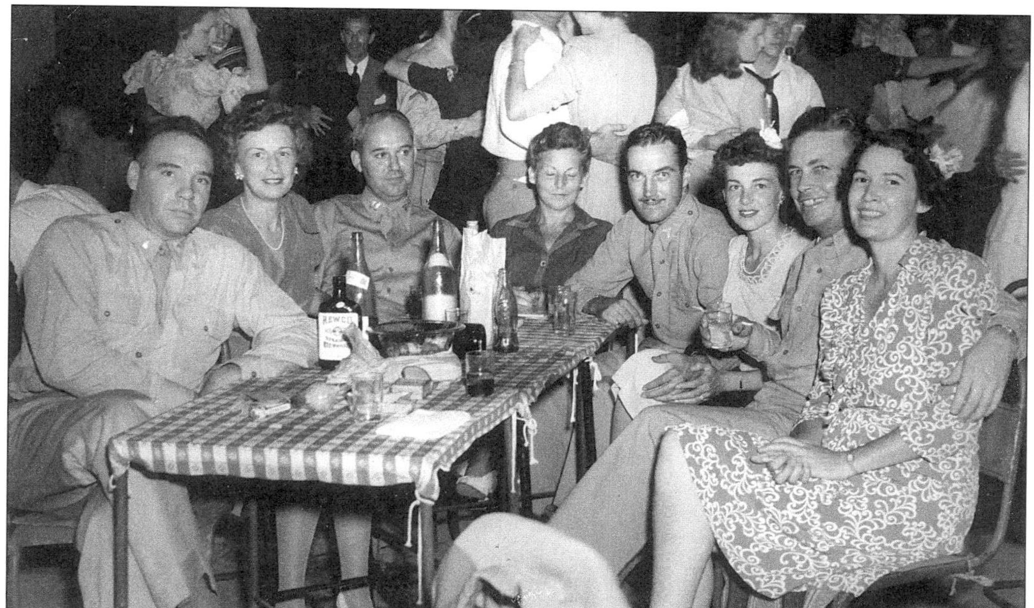

During World War II, Howard and Maxine Davenport, pictured on the far right, gather with a group of unidentified friends at Seven Oaks Night Club. Howard and his friends worked together at Kelly during the war and relaxed together after work at Seven Oaks, a nightclub located on the 5000 block of Broadway in Alamo Heights in the early 1940s. (Courtesy Cynthia Davenport Woodland.)

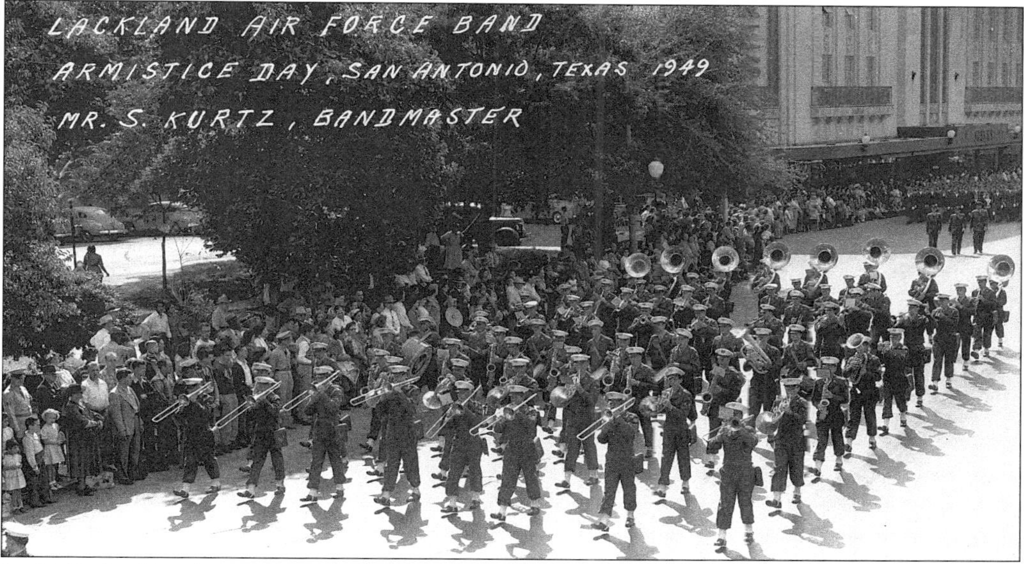

In 1949, Lackland Air Force Base participated in the Armistice Day Parade in San Antonio. Lackland, originally called the San Antonio Aviation Cadet Center, came into existence in 1942 when the War Department divided part of Kelly's property. Brigadier General Frank D. Lackland, after whom the base is named, initiated the idea to found an aviation cadet reception and training center. (Courtesy Daughters of the Republic of Texas Library, Ekmark Collection, CP22135.)

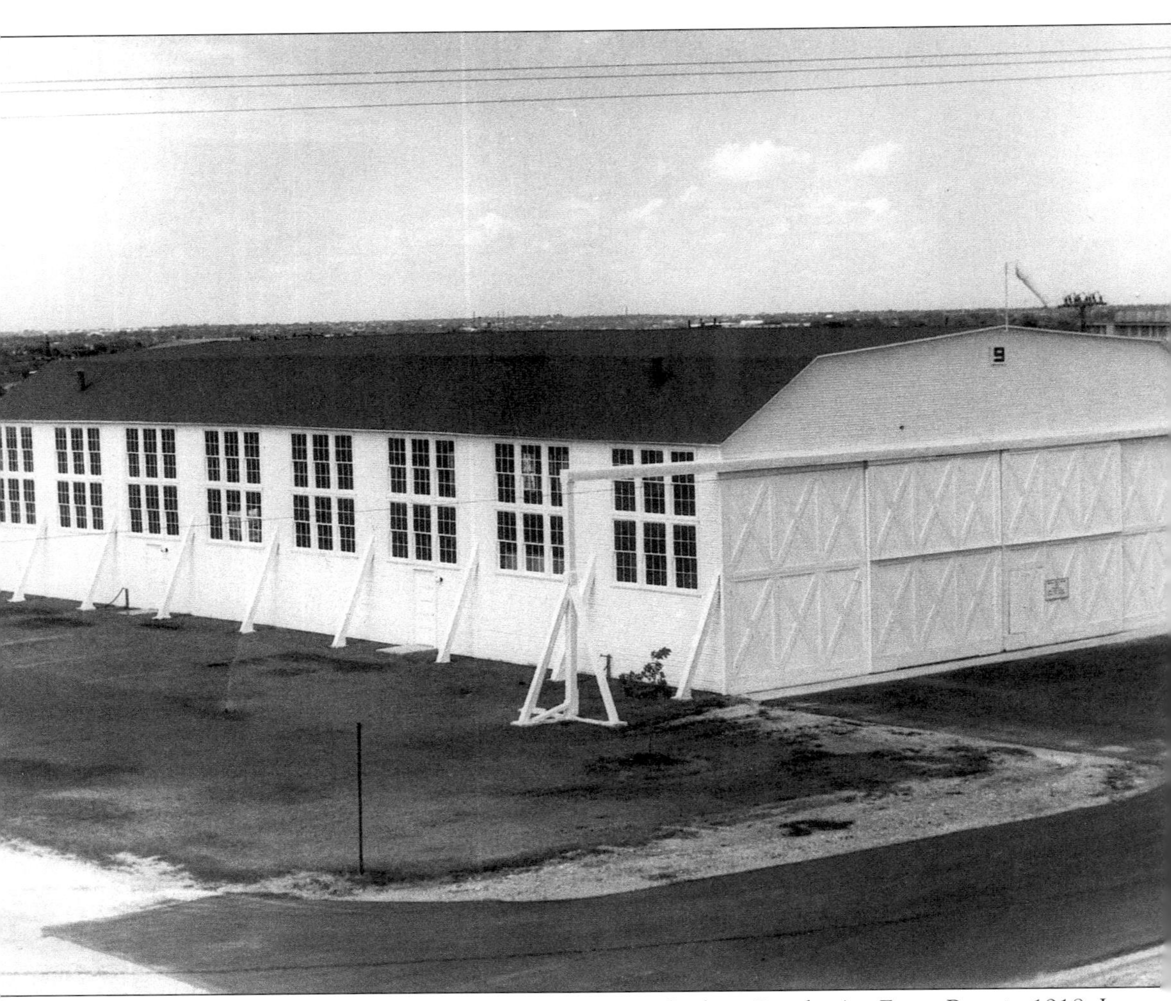

This Texas Historical Landmark, Hangar Nine, was built at Brooks Air Force Base in 1918. In 1969, it was renovated and became the Edward H. White II Memorial Museum. Brooks Air Force Base, once called Kelly Field #5, was formally named Brooks Field in 1918 after Cadet Sidney Brooks Jr., who died when his plane crashed during a landing attempt. (Courtesy Brooks Air Force Base.)

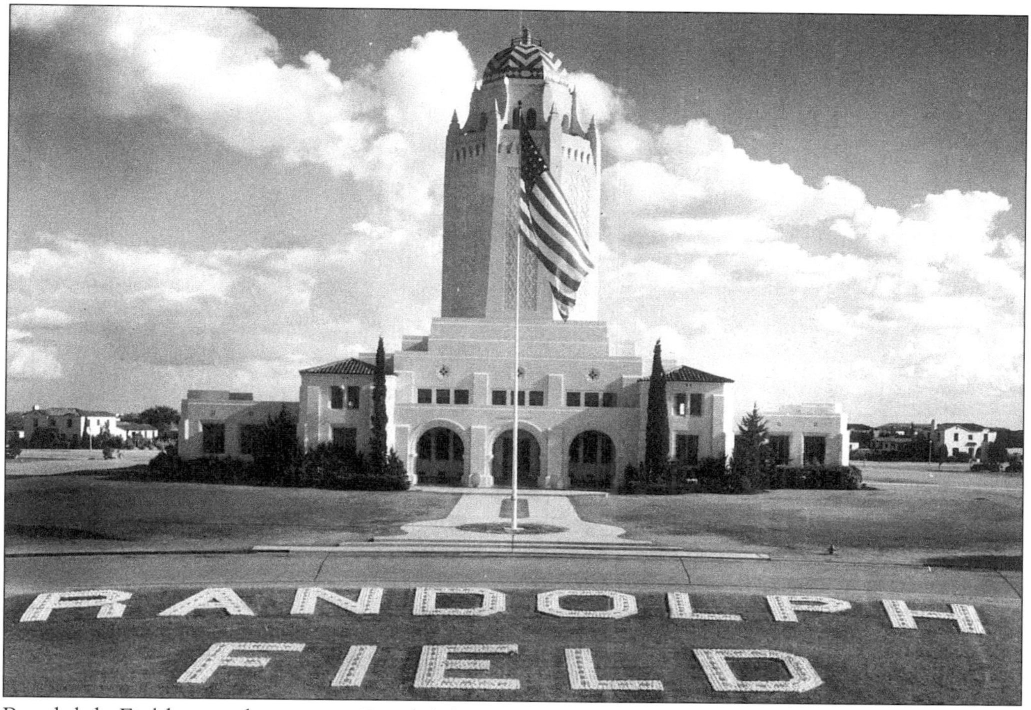

Randolph Field, now known as Randolph Air Force Base, was dedicated in 1930. The base appears tranquil and quiet in this December 1944 shot, when pilots were fighting in World War II. The Taj Mahal water tower stands 170 feet tall. (Courtesy Brice Woods and family.)

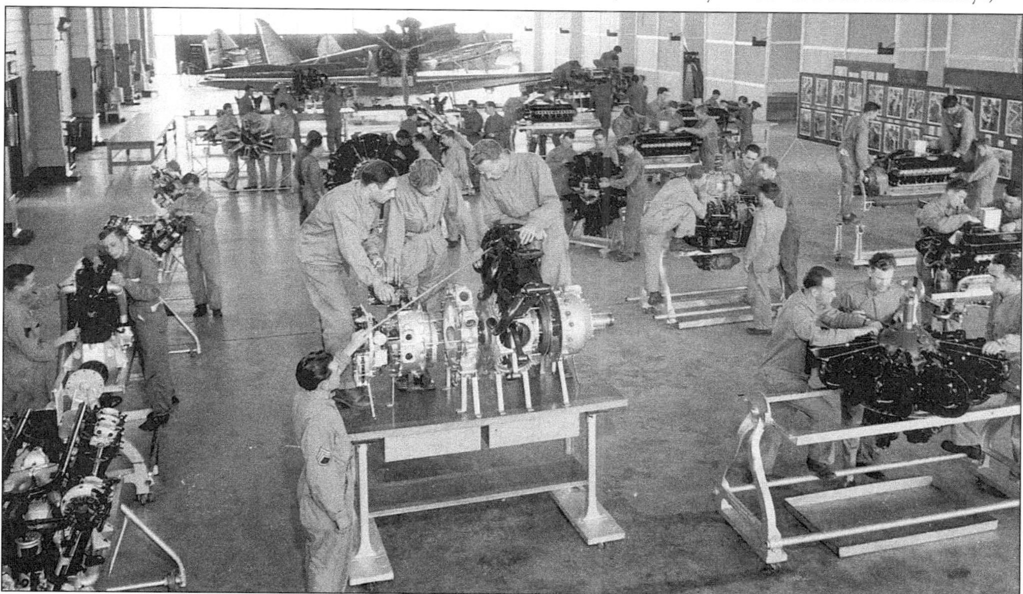

A group of mechanical students examines different plane parts at Randolph. In the 1930s, cadets received extensive instruction on airplane engines and maintenance and studied the art of navigation as well. (Courtesy 12th Flying Training Wing, History Office, Randolph Air Force Base.)

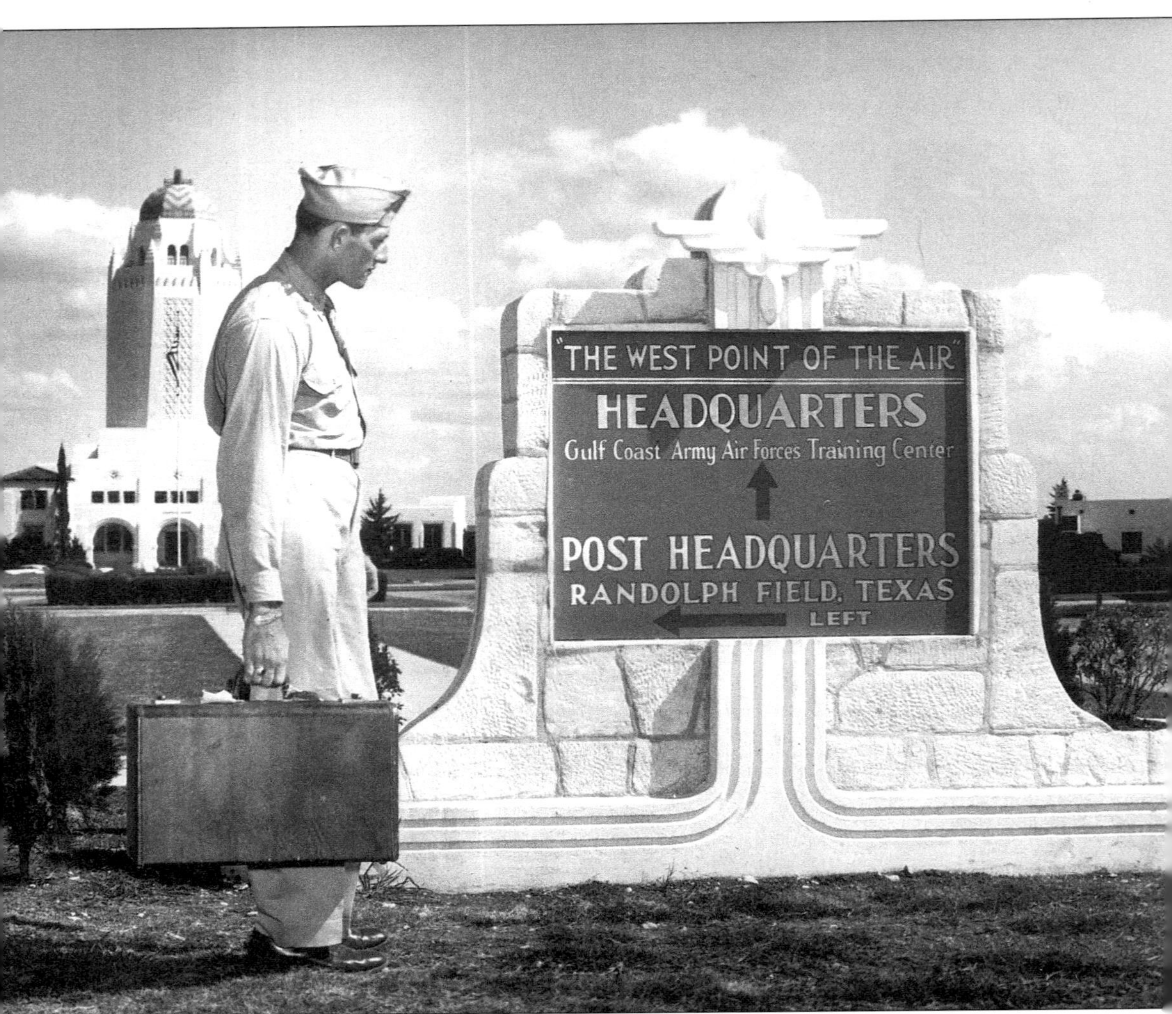

An unidentified man looks at this sign for Randolph, once known as "The West Point of the Air." When Randolph first opened, cadets studied the basic and primary phases of flying instruction before moving to Kelly for advanced training. The base is named after a native Texan, Captain William M. Randolph, whose AT-4 plane crashed in 1928. (Courtesy 12th Flying Training Wing, History Office, Randolph Air Force Base.)

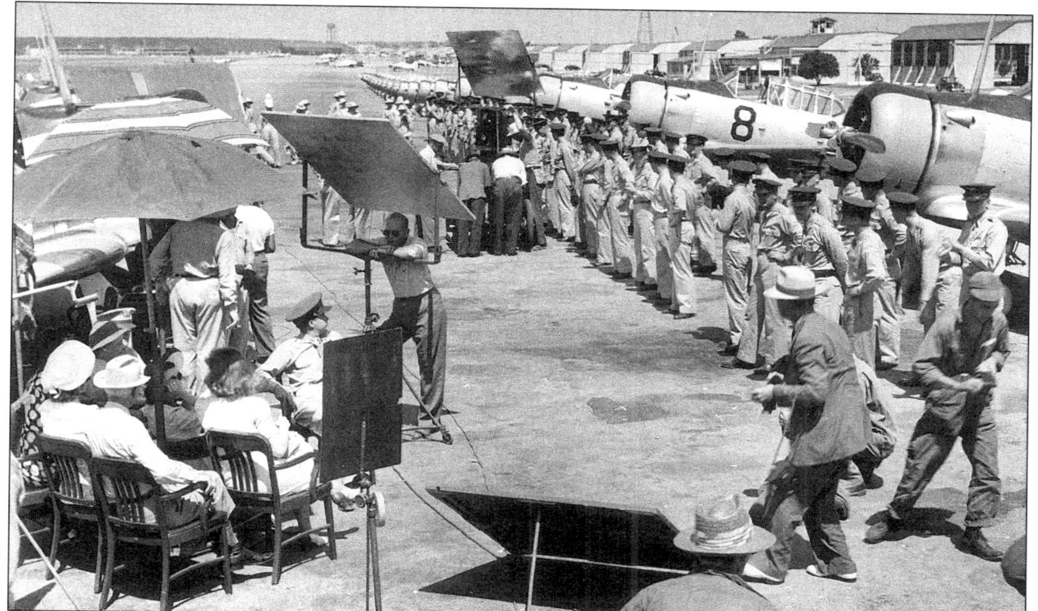

In the early 1940s, moviemakers arrived at Randolph to film *I Wanted Wings*. The movie was directed by Mitchell Leisen and included actors William Holden and Veronica Lake. In the lower photo, the shadow of the filmmaking crew appears in the lower right-hand corner, and the base operations building is located in the center. (Both courtesy 12th Flying Training Wing, History Office, Randolph Air Force Base.)

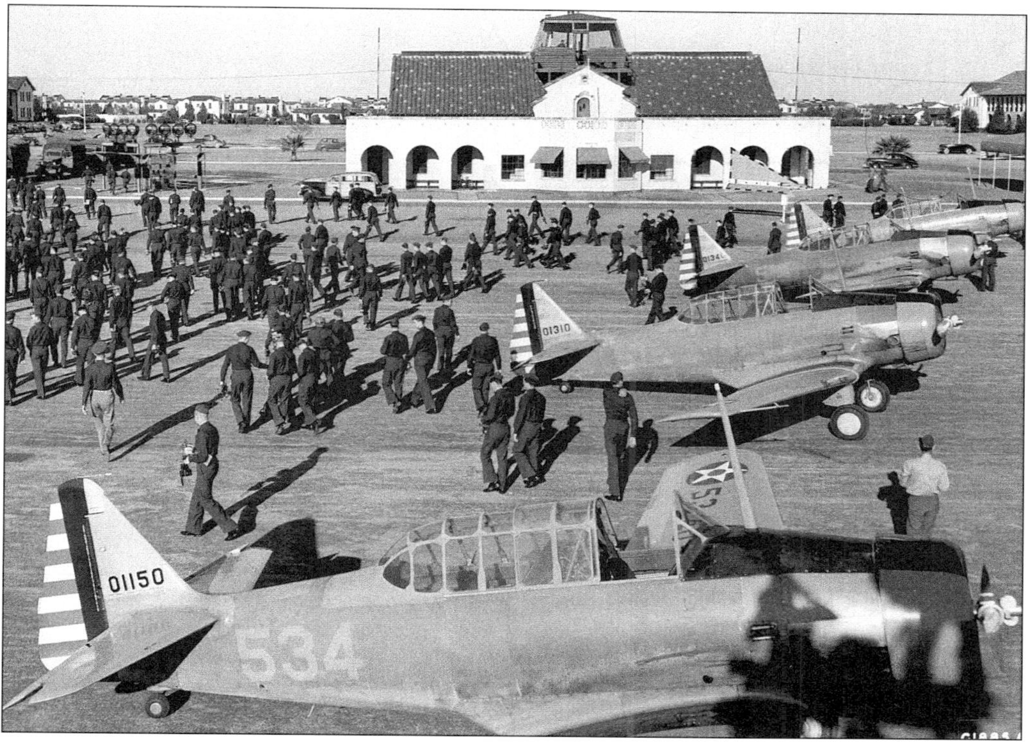

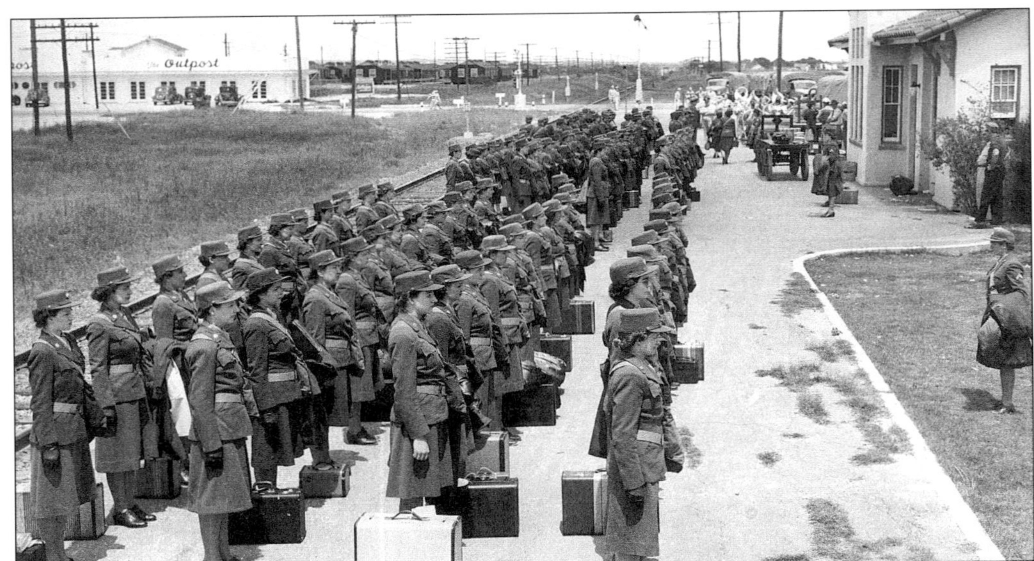

In April of 1943, the first members of the 727th Women's Army Auxiliary Corps (WAAC) Post Headquarters Company arrived at Randolph. The Army changed the WAAC designation to Women's Army Corp (WAC) in September 1943. In October of 1943, the WAC Post Headquarters Company became a WAC detachment. Shortly after the Air Force became an independent force, the WAC detachment became a Women in the Air Force (WAF) detachment in 1948. The Air Force finally integrated this detachment into the 12th Flying Training Wing, then stationed at Randolph in 1975. (Courtesy 12th Flying Training Wing, History Office, Randolph Air Force Base.)

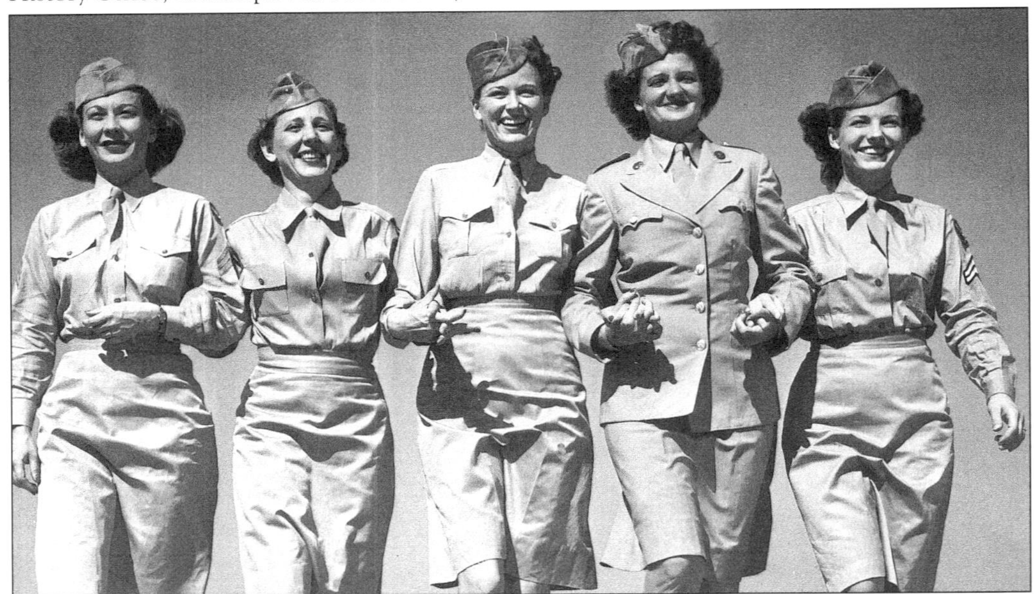

At the second anniversary of the Women's Air Corps in 1945 at Randolph, these two-year veterans link hands and arms. From left to right are the following: Sgt. Edna J. Daubert, Ssgt. Cora V. Kelly, Pfc. Helen Kempf, Pfc. Clara E. Ghist, and Cpl. Rose Yaremko. (Courtesy 12th Flying Training Wing, History Office, Randolph Air Force Base.)

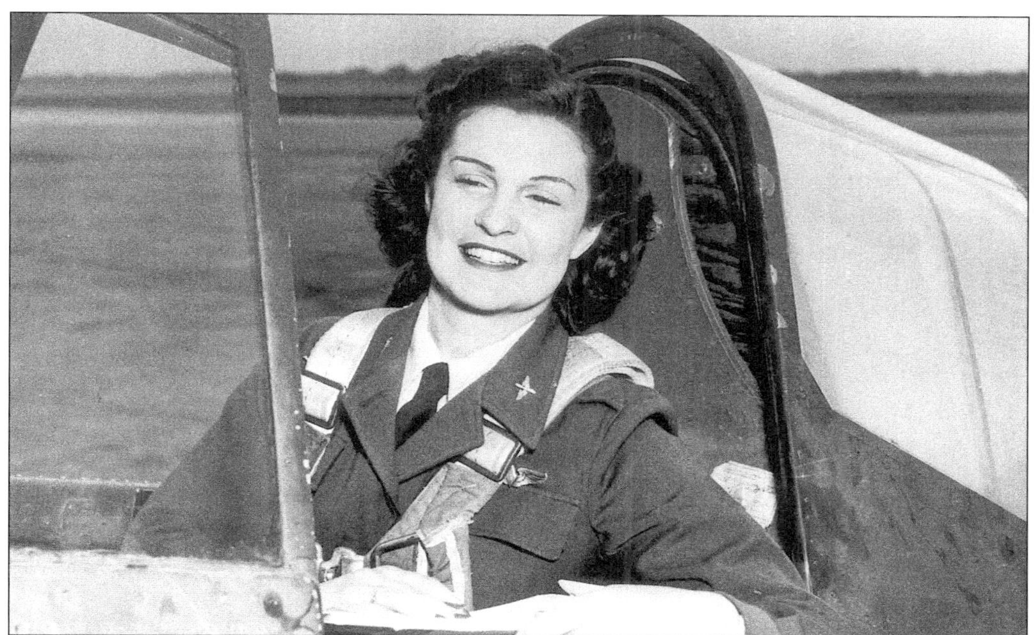

Betty J. Williams, a member of the Women Air Force Service Pilots (WASP) and an Engineering Test Pilot for the Army Air Forces (AAF) Central Instructors' School, sits in one of Randolph's planes. (Courtesy 12th Flying Training Wing, History Office, Randolph Air Force Base.)

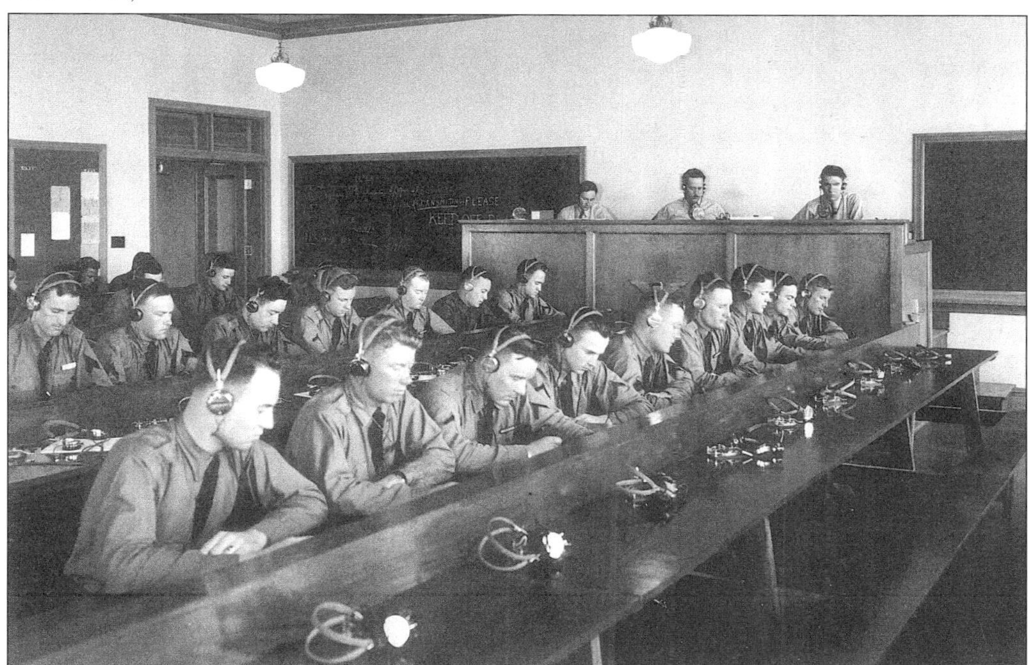

In order to fly at the best capacity, each pilot must learn radio code, and in this shot, a group of Randolph's cadets listen carefully in the radio buzzer. (Courtesy 12th Flying Training Wing, History Office, Randolph Air Force Base.)

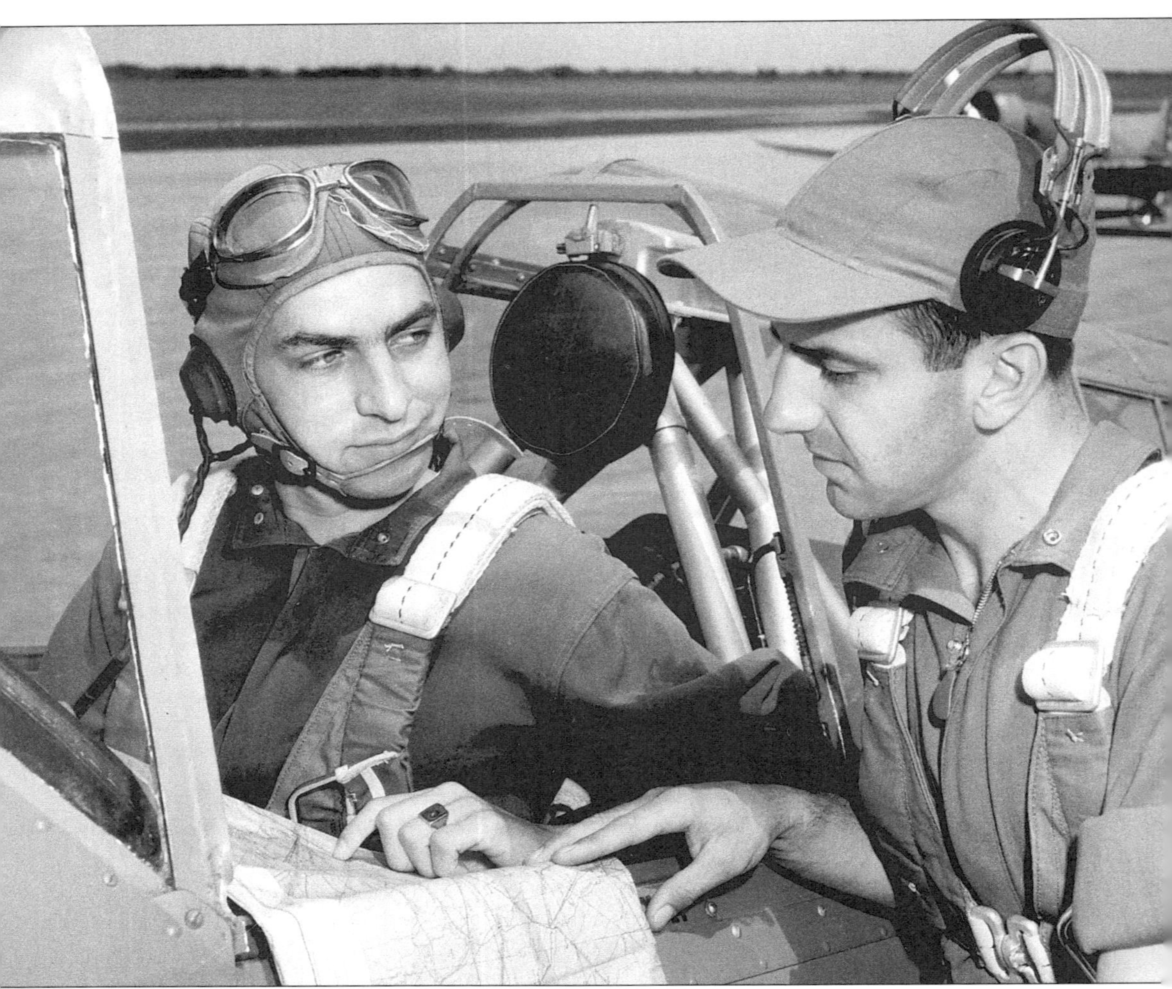

A student and an instructor examine a map together at Randolph. During flight training, students flew in the front cockpit and instructors in the rear, so if the student froze, the instructor could whack him on the head from behind. (Courtesy 12th Flying Training Wing, History Office, Randolph Air Force Base.)

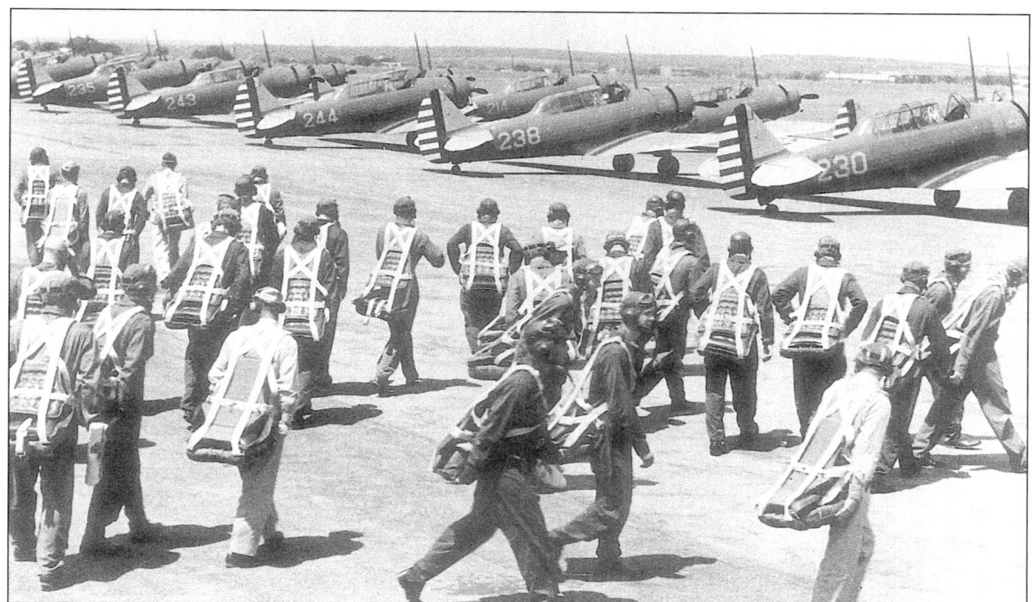

A group of Randolph's cadets and instructors advance with their gear towards these BT-9 planes. In the 1930s, cadets flew these planes for their basic training; the planes could fly as fast as 170 miles per hour. (Courtesy 12th Flying Training Wing, History Office, Randolph Air Force Base.)

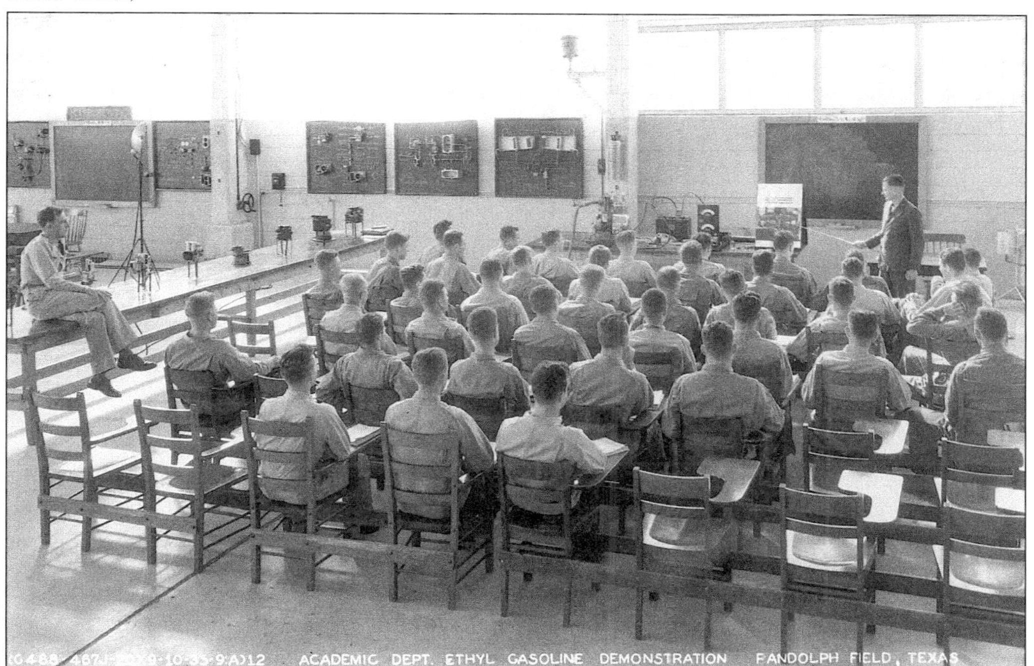

In a ground training session, Randolph's students learn about ethyl gasoline during a demonstration. When Randolph first opened, once pilots underwent intensive training, they could obtain a commission in the Army Air Corps in addition to their pilots' wings. (Courtesy 12th Flying Training Wing, History Office, Randolph Air Force Base.)

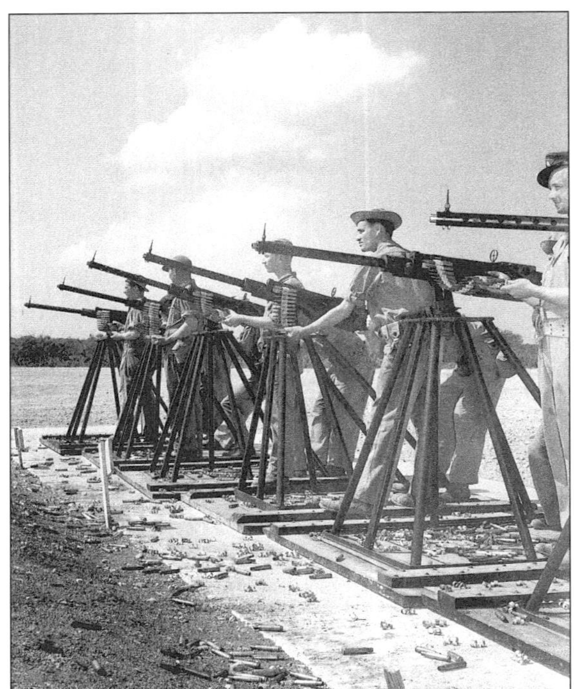

A group of unidentified future bombardier gunners shoot rounds during gunnery practice. Trainees often practiced on ground targets and targets towed behind training aircraft. (Courtesy 12th Flying Training Wing, History Office, Randolph Air Force Base.)

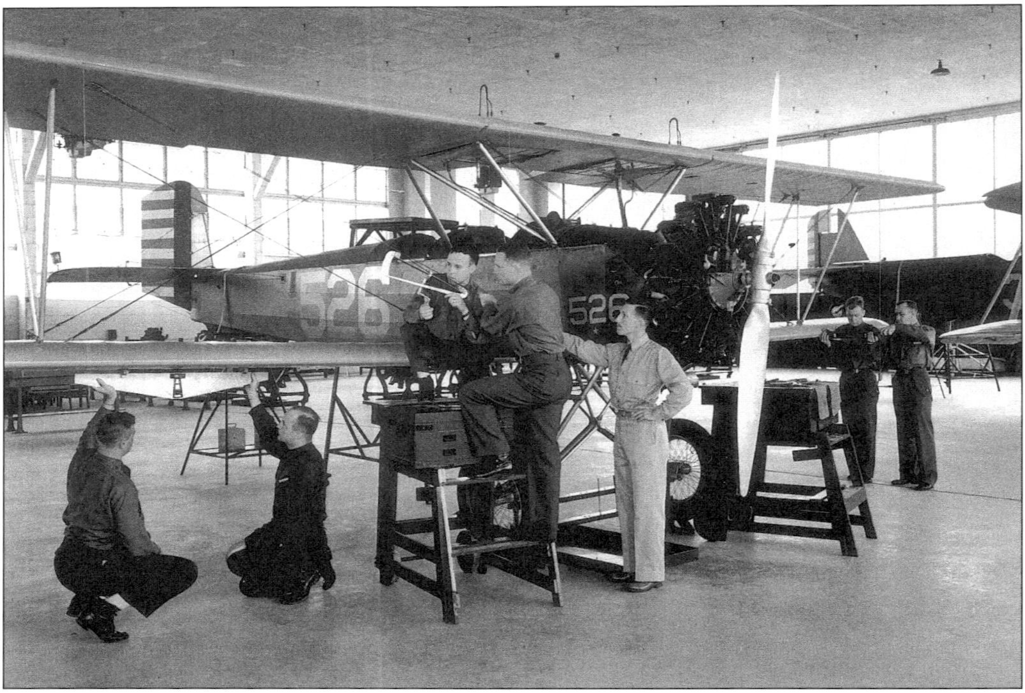

A group of Randolph's unidentified cadets learn about rigging during a ground training class in the 1930s. During the world wars, when pilots and other military citizens could not remain at San Antonio's military bases, civilians constructed and repaired planes. (Courtesy 12th Flying Training Wing, History Office, Randolph Air Force Base.)

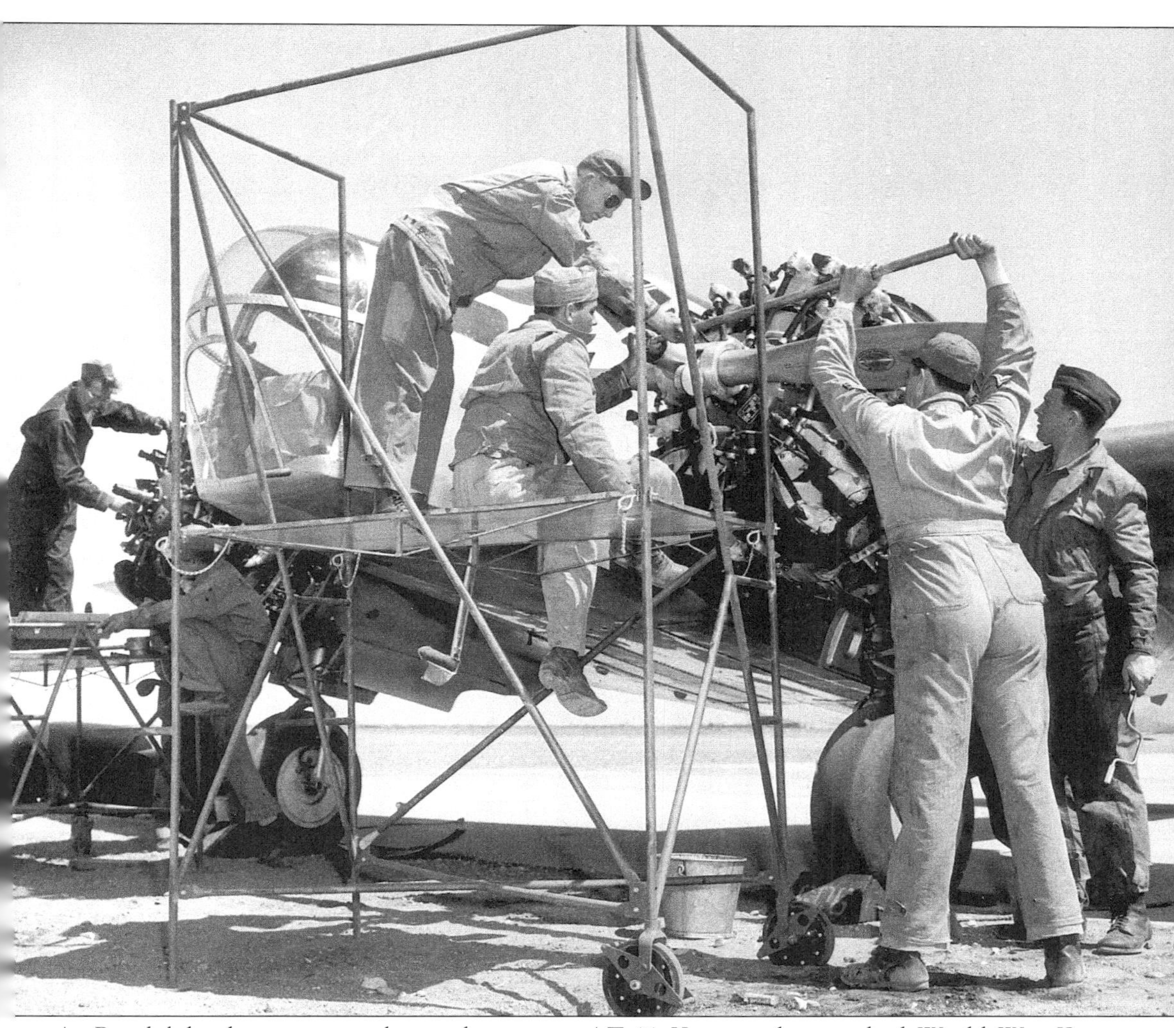

At Randolph, these men work together on an AT-11 Kansan, the standard World War II bombcrew trainer. Cadets who practiced flying these planes used sand-filled practice bombs. (Courtesy 12th Flying Training Wing, History Office, Randolph Air Force Base.)

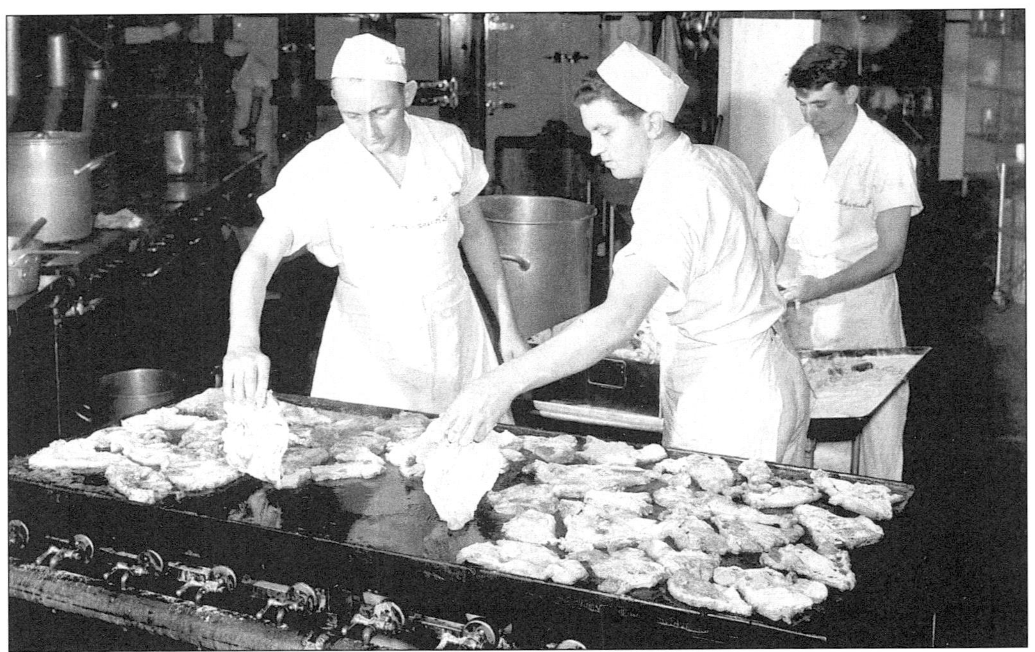

These cooks prepare food at Randolph. During mealtimes in the 1930s, cadets in upper training stages often issued orders to "dodos," or beginning cadets, who were ordered to provide entertainment during mealtimes. (Courtesy 12th Flying Training Wing, History Office, Randolph Air Force Base.)

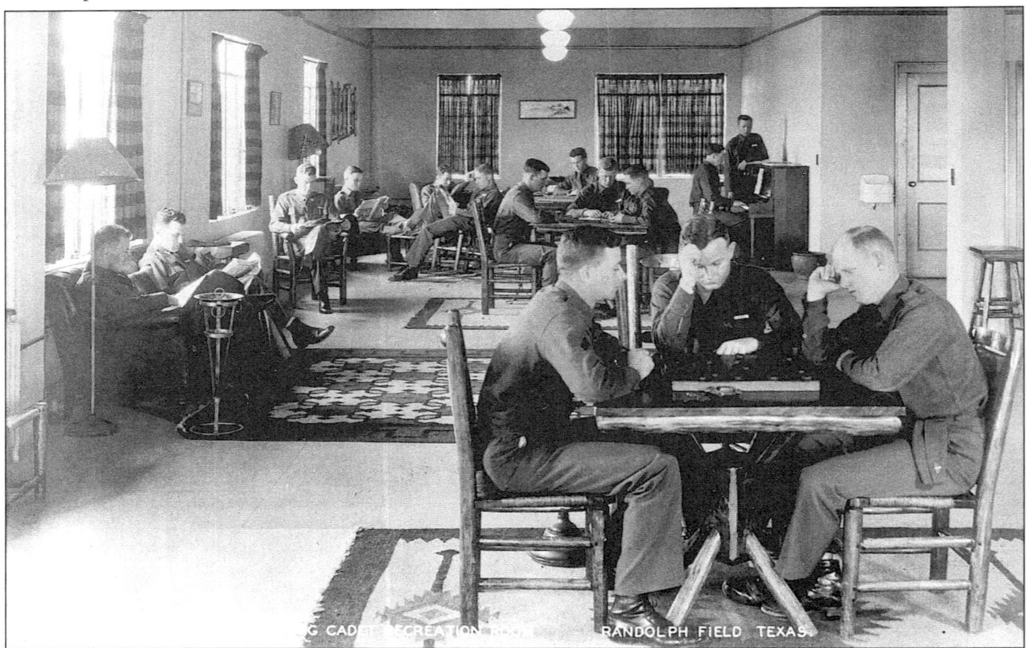

When upper-class cadets and "dodos" had a chance to relax, they could spend time in the Cadet Recreation Room, reading a magazine, listening to the piano, or playing checkers. (Courtesy 12th Flying Training Wing, History Office, Randolph Air Force Base.)

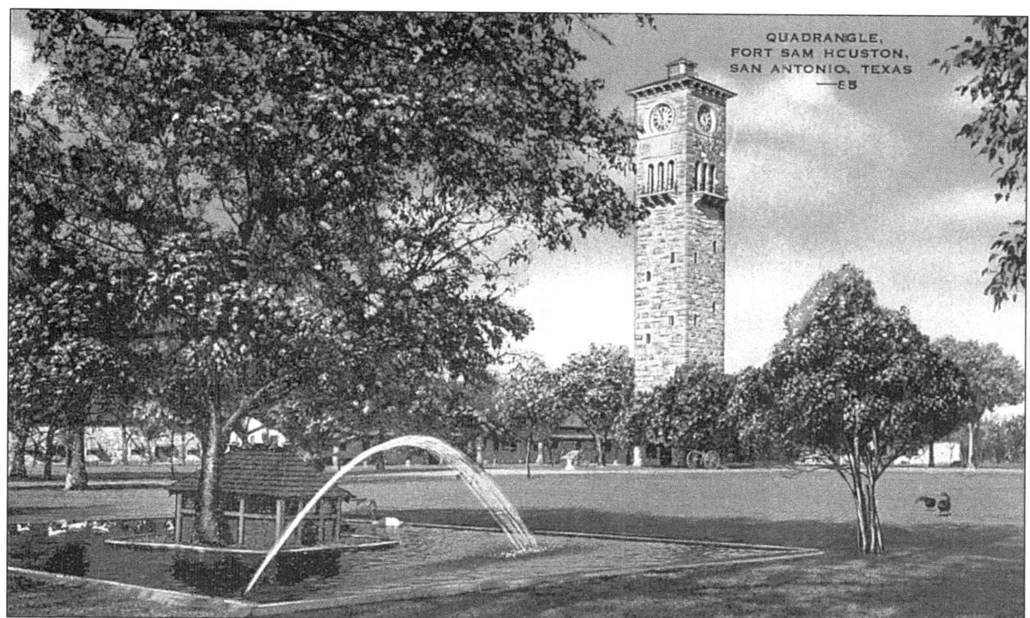

According to a tall tale, during a wild storm, a peacock skimped up to the top of this tower located in the Quadrangle at Fort Sam Houston Military Base and had to be escorted back down by firemen. Peacocks, as well as deer and chickens, amble around the original fort grounds near the tower that stands over 80 feet tall.

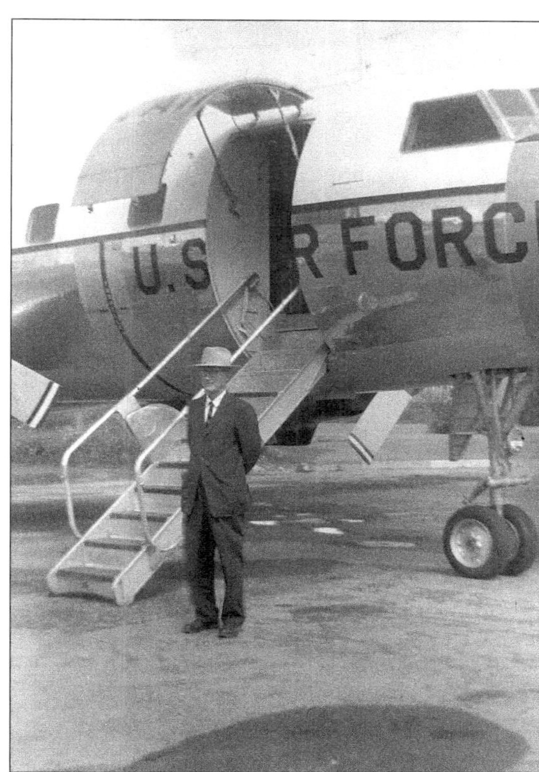

Although Joseph Idus never flew as a pilot during the world wars, he had the opportunity to fly in a U.S. Air Force plane in 1961. After the Second World War, Joseph Idus and his family settled in San Antonio and lived at Fort Sam Houston for a brief time. (Courtesy Thille Lambert Newton.)

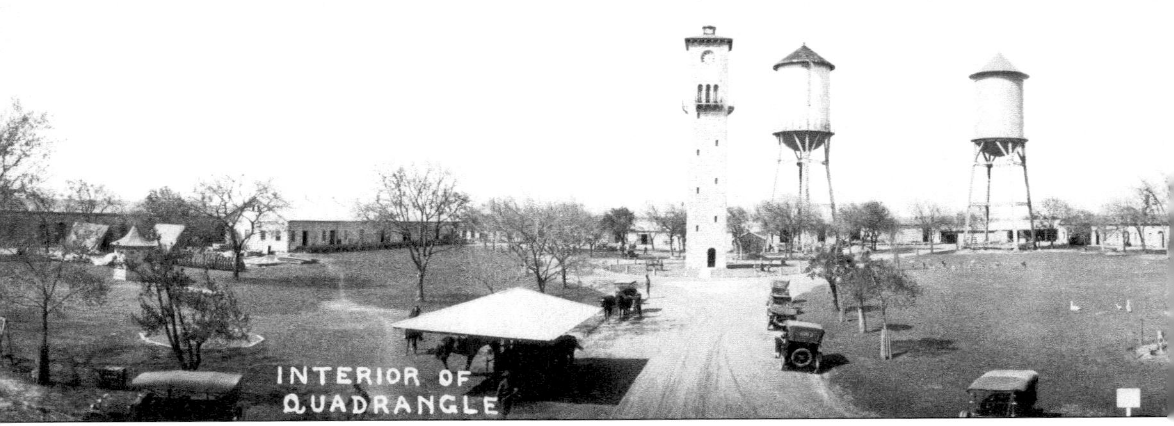

In this *c.* 1910 image of the Fort Sam Quadrangle, the Quartermaster Depot, or the limestone structure, surrounds the tower. The depot was built in the 1870s and enclosed a region of approximately 8 acres. Today, the Fort Sam Houston Bank faces the tower, and visitors must pass through a gate in order to step inside of the quadrangle. As a child, when my parents stopped at the bank, I often begged them to drive up to the gate, so I could greet the soldiers guarding the quadrangle. Although I wanted to stroke one of the deer, I usually ended by chasing them around the quadrangle until the stern looks of the guards frightened me. (Courtesy Fort Sam Houston Museum.)

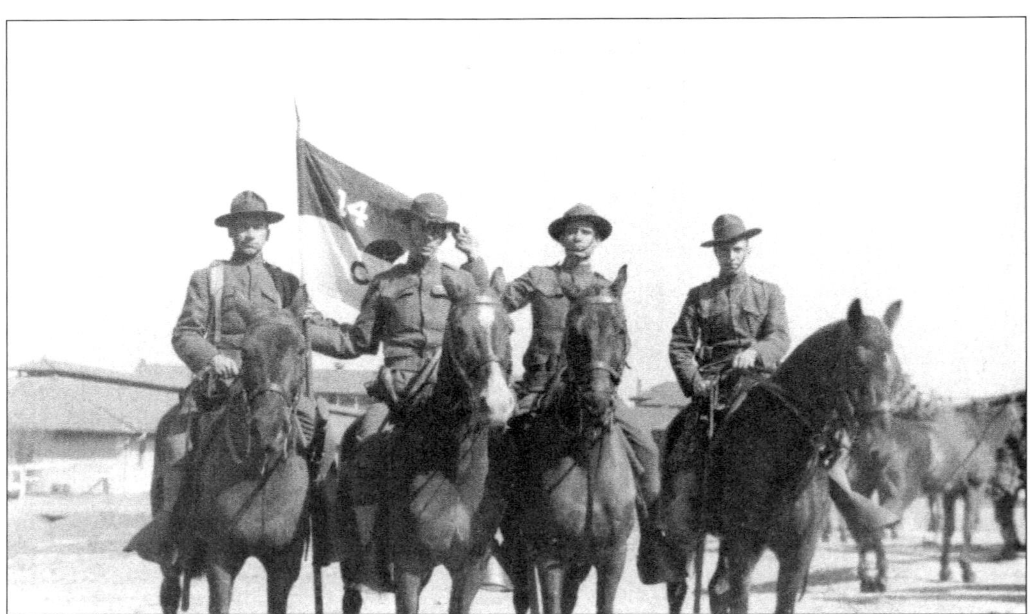

In 1918, the mounted cavalrymen of Troop C, 14th Cavalry, at Fort Sam Houston hold their regiment's flag. Joseph Idus hung his personal flag for his troop in his house, next to his polo mallet and sword. I never played polo, but I took riding lessons at Fort Sam's stables. Even though I spent many hours performing jumping exercises, I loved the trail rides, especially the "rolling hills" one. If I could get my horse into a steady canter, I felt as though the hills, not the horse, were moving. (Courtesy Fort Sam Houston Museum.)

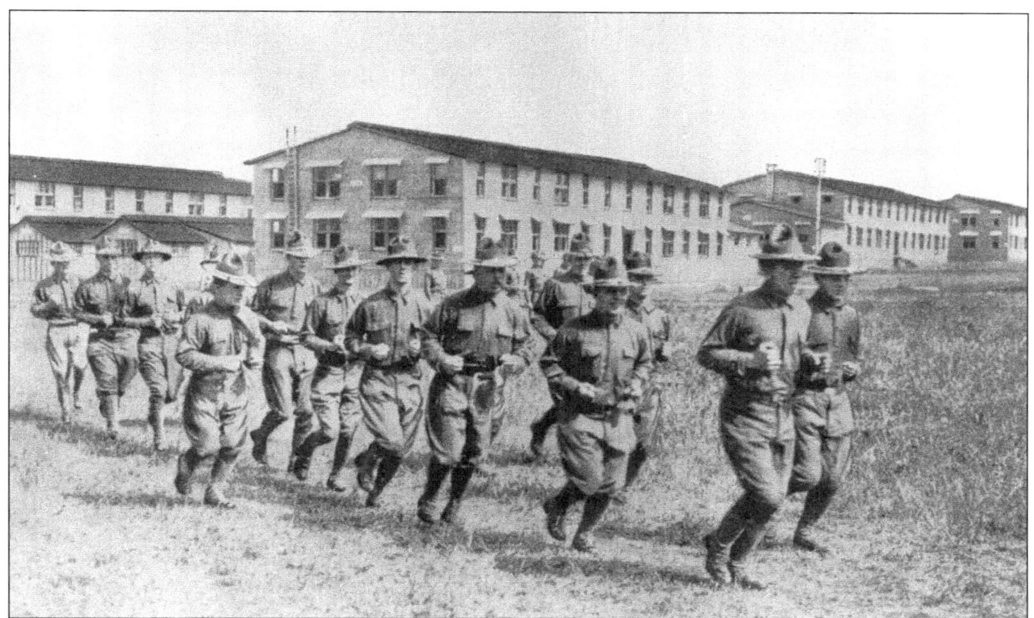

Camp Travis and its barracks, as seen in the background, became especially useful during World War I; at that time, the entire camp, adjacent to Fort Sam Houston, included approximately 1,500 structures. Here, soldiers perform their morning exercises c. 1910. Long after he retired from the army, my grandfather continued his morning exercises, and at the age of 80, he still could do 100 push-ups a day. (Courtesy Fort Sam Houston Museum.)

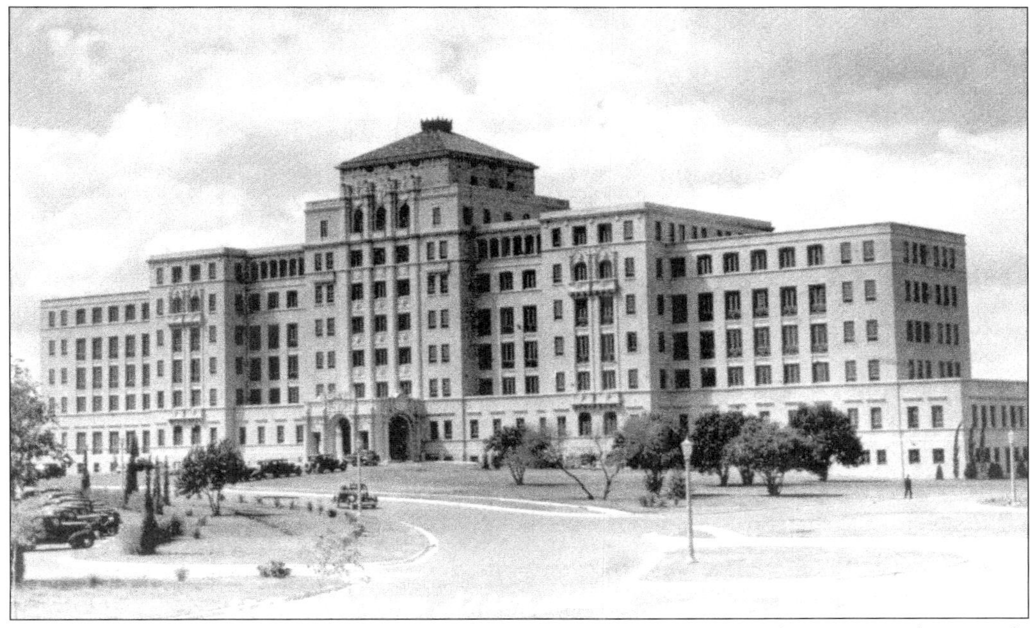

Station Hospital, also known as Brooke Army Hospital, was completed in 1937. When I rode horses on Fort Sam's trails, I often could spot the red rooftop of the hospital. (Courtesy Fort Sam Houston Museum.)

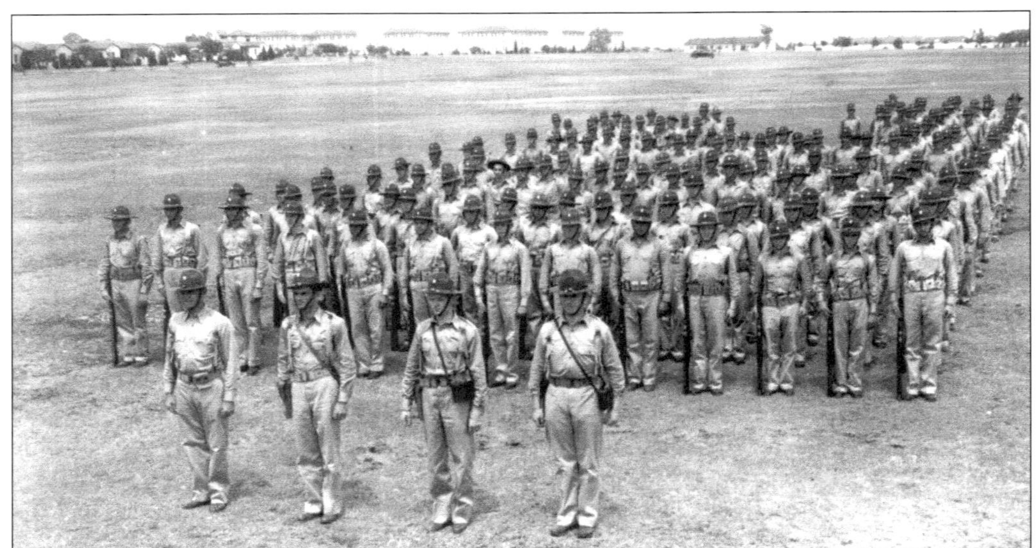

After completing the Provisional Infantry Division Tests on Fort Sam's Arthur MacArthur Field in 1939, the members of this infantry company, clad in summer uniforms, stand in formation. (Courtesy Fort Sam Houston Museum.)

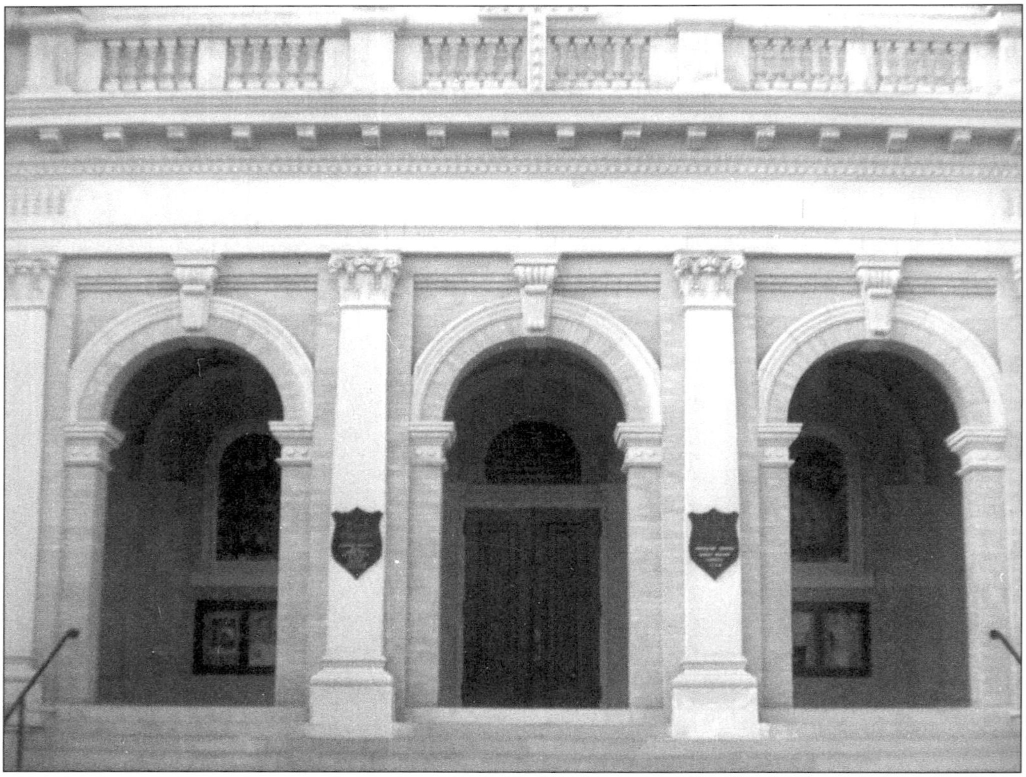

On June 30, 1961, my parents married in the Main Post Chapel, sometimes called the Gift Chapel, at Fort Sam Houston. William Howard Taft, former president of the United States, dedicated the chapel in 1909. (Courtesy Thille Lambert Newton.)

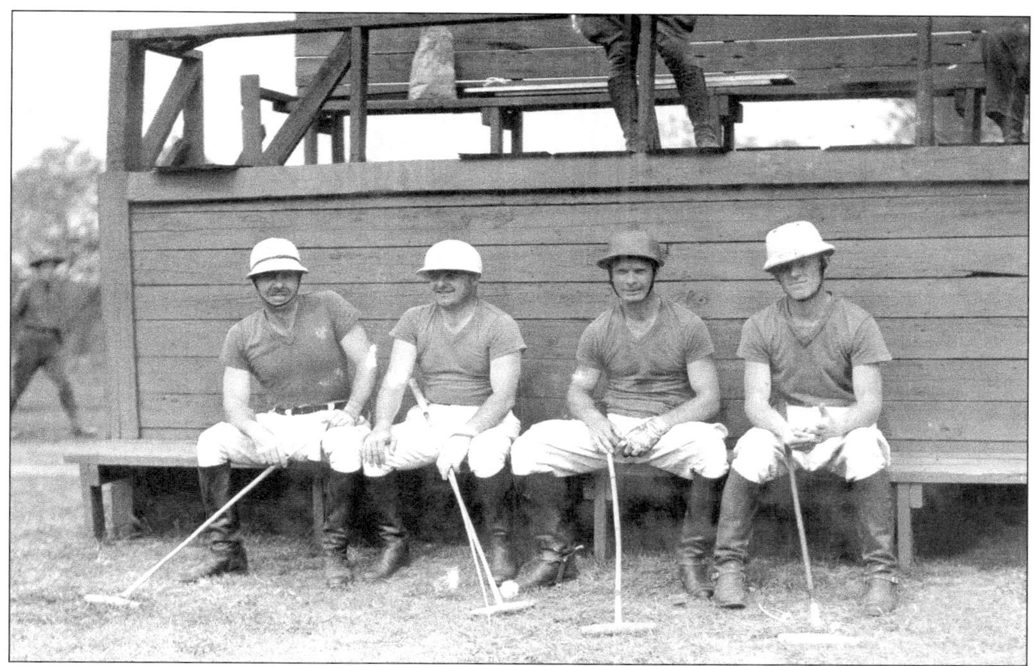

Above, the 15th Field Artillery Polo Team takes a break at Fort Sam Houston in this 1937 shot. Below, on horses, members of the same team wave their mallets in excitement; they won the Major Tate Trophy in 1937. My grandfather loved to watch polo matches, and on occasion, my family and I spent an afternoon at a match. After one game, I ran down into the field and found a lost polo ball. (Both courtesy Fort Sam Houston Museum.)

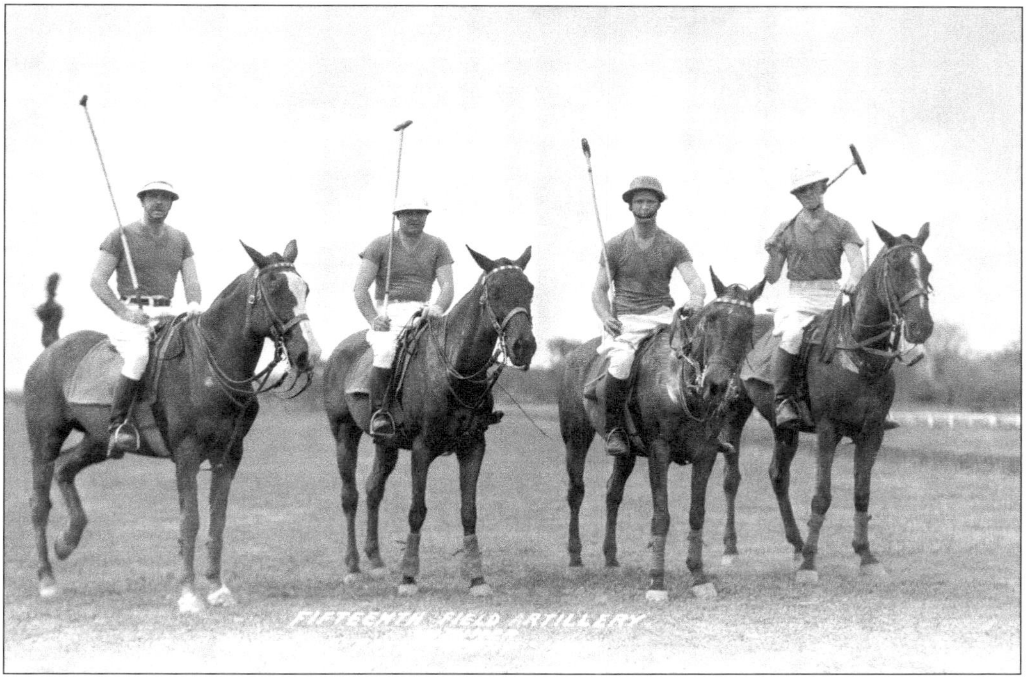

FIFTEENTH FIELD ARTILLERY

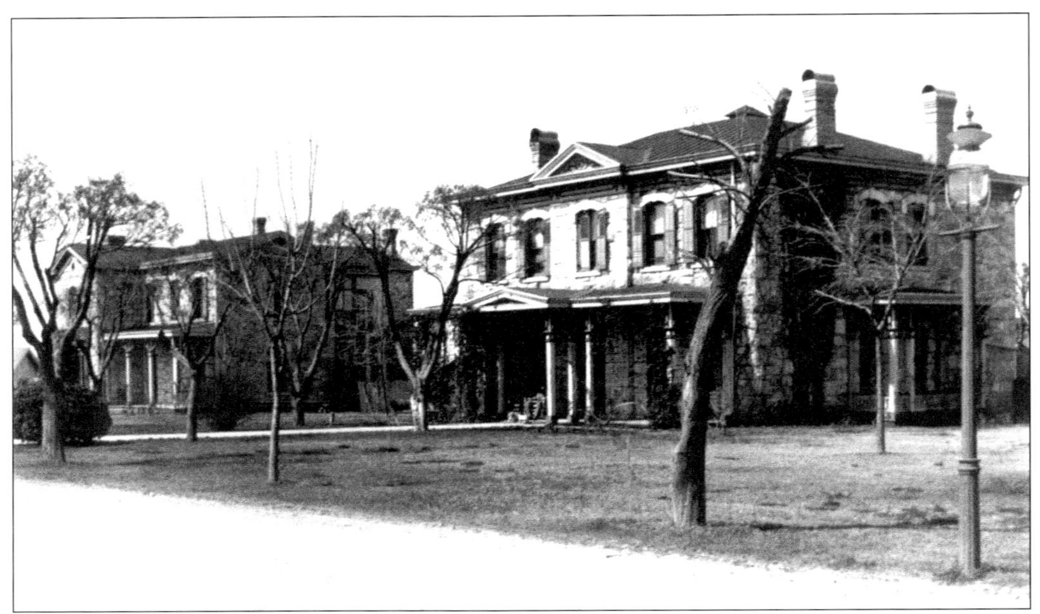

The Lower Post Officer Quarters at Fort Sam were designed by Alfred Giles. On the left are the company officers quarters and, on the right, the field officers quarters. Captain Benjamin Foulois dwelled in the field officers quarters in 1910 and 1911. (Courtesy Fort Sam Houston Museum.)

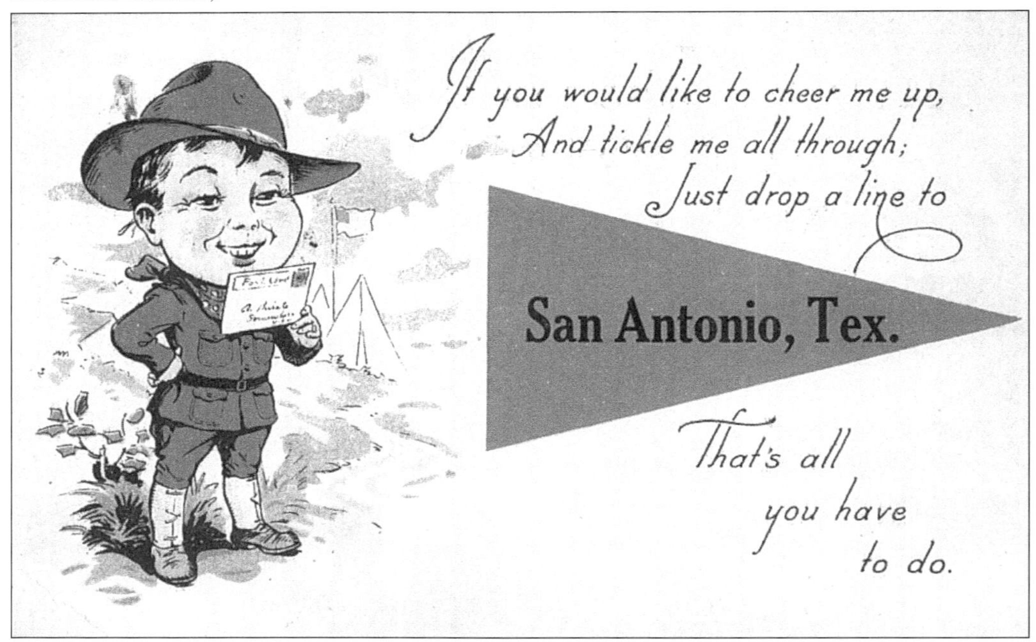

On this card postmarked January 28, 1918, from San Antonio, this soldier wrote to his girlfriend in Oklahoma City, "Why don't you write to me? I have written you two letters lately . . . I am going to leave for places unknown before many days . . ." Since this card also was stamped "Travis," this soldier probably was stationed at Camp Travis next to Fort Sam Houston and preparing to fight in World War I.

Eight

Deep Grooves:

The Hill Country

Although I have spent many worthwhile days in San Antonio's military bases, museums, schools, and missions, the Hill Country always beckons to me, calling me back to my ancestors' habitats. In my childhood, every spring, I stepped outside of my city house to test the air to see if I could go swimming or hiking. If it wasn't warm enough, I counted the days until school would end, but if it was, I hopped in my car, sometimes with friends, sometimes alone, and drove into the Hill Country. And today, whenever I return to my familiar spots in the area, such as the old train depot in Waring or Río Frio at the Lewis Ranch, I imagine my grandfather and his family treading the same spots, many of which they did.

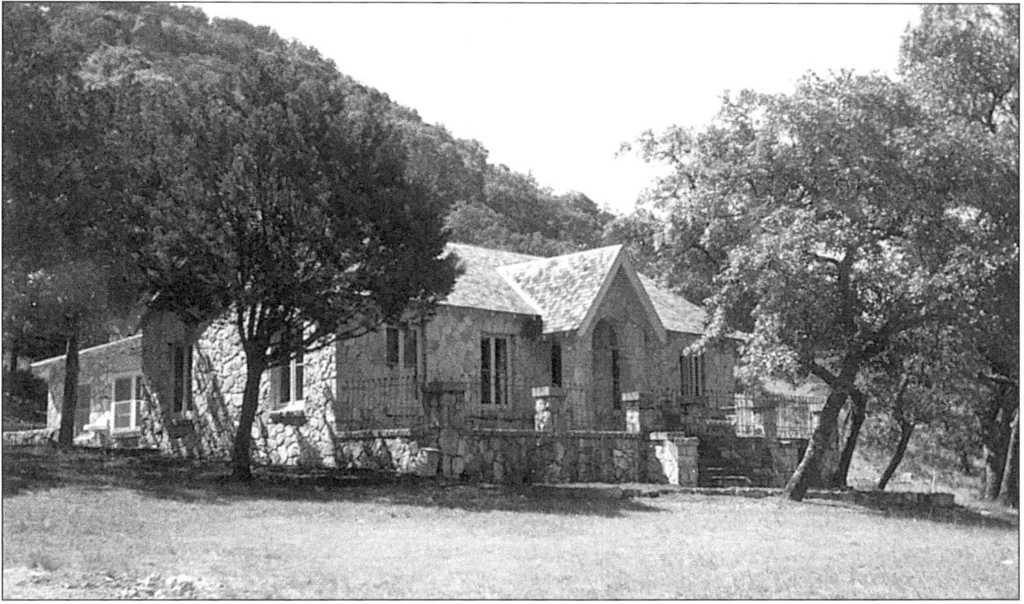

The sprawling porch and grounds of the H.W. Lewis Ranch, located in Leakey (pronounced Lay-key), provides ample room for adventurers to hunt rattlesnakes, to swim in the Río Frio, and to grill fresh lamb for dinner. As a child, exhausted after a long day of swinging on cattle gates and catching minnows in the river, I loved nothing more than eating that lamb as the Texas stars began to light up the Hill Country. Not long after this 1930s shot was taken of the Rock House, bedrooms and a Texas-sized patio were added to the right side. (Courtesy Eunice D. Lewis.)

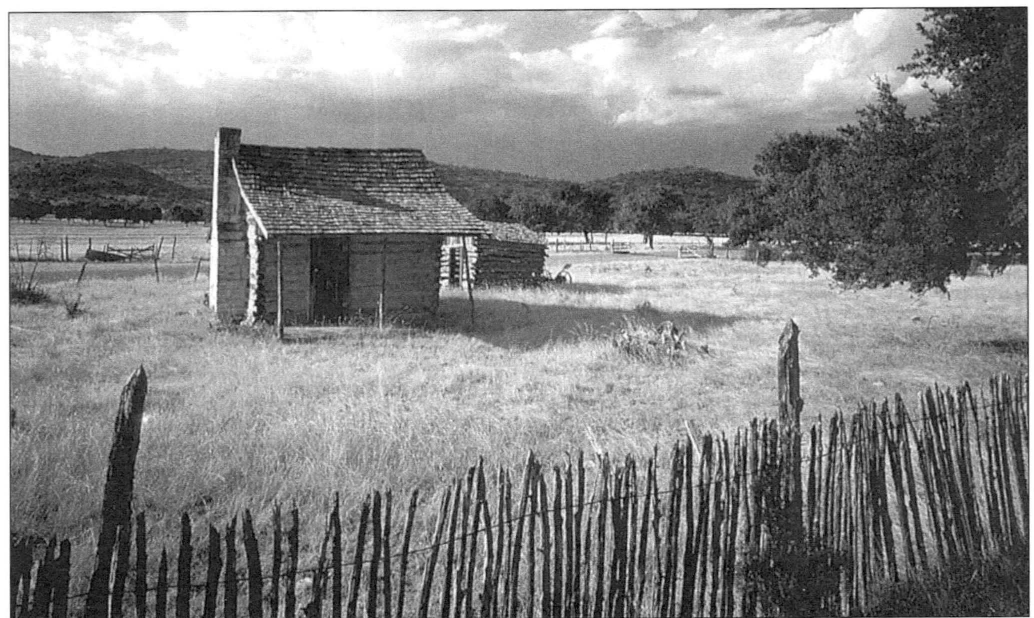

Eunice Lewis, the owner of the Lewis Ranch, once showed me this cabin of hand-hewn logs, only one of many marvelous sights on her ranch. After I peered at the log cabin from the dusty roads, I played with Eunice's nephews and niece who still live on the ranch. (Courtesy Texas Department of Transportation.)

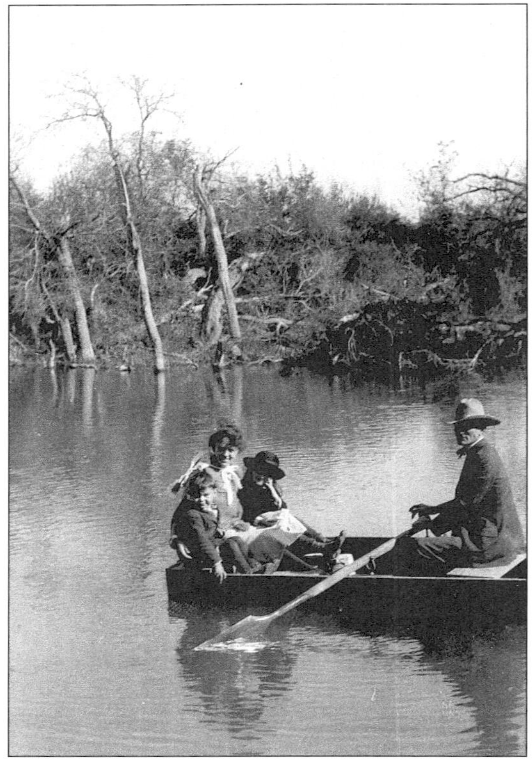

Eunice Lewis sometimes visited relatives at a nearby ranch, located near the Nueces River. Seated on the left end of a boat in the Nueces River are Mattie Tally with her nephew and niece, Wilson Lewis and Eunice Lewis, and on the right is Jake Tally. (Courtesy Eunice Lewis.)

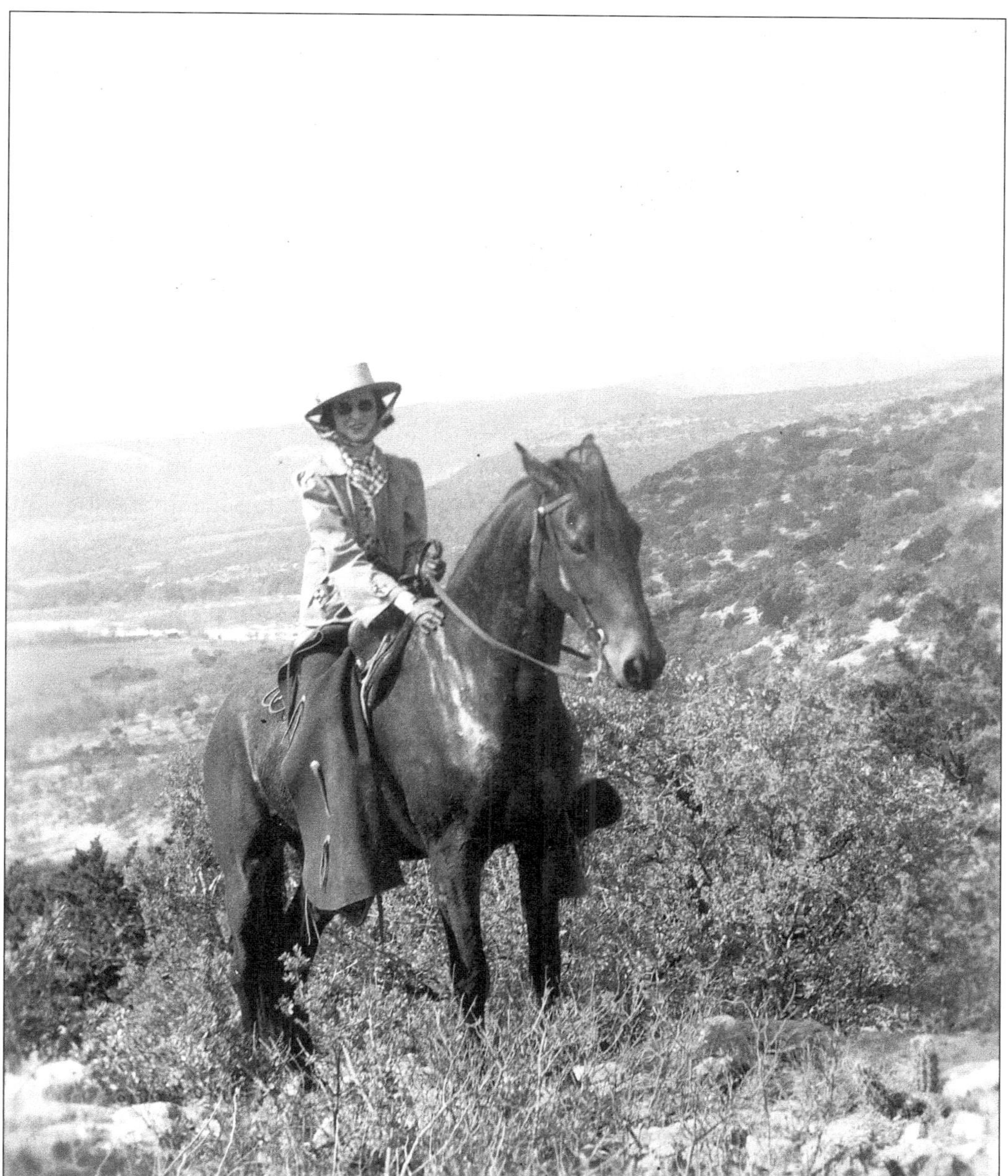

In the early 1940s, Eunice Lewis and her horse, Duke, enjoy the view of the Hill Country from a hill on the Lewis Ranch. Hiking at the ranch is almost as rewarding as riding, and Eunice's nephews, niece, and I often clambered up steep inclines and spied on deer. (Courtesy Eunice Lewis.)

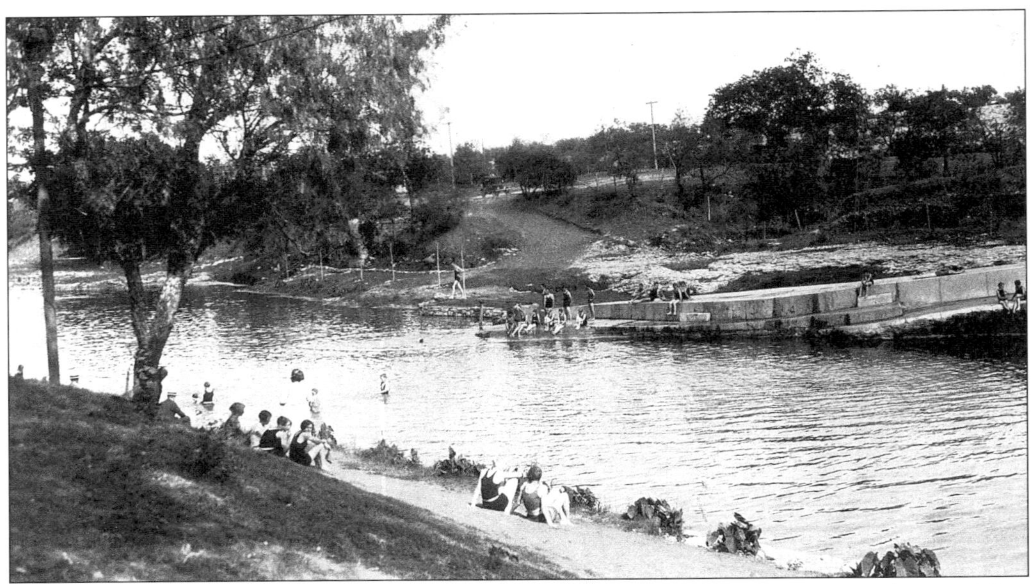

Landa Park, near the town of New Braunfels, which is about 30 minutes northeast of San Antonio, is one of the best swimming spots to which San Antonians flock. Although I like to jump into the swimming area at Landa Park, tubing down the Guadalupe River with friends is my favorite summer pastime. (Courtesy Carlita Hughes Kosty.)

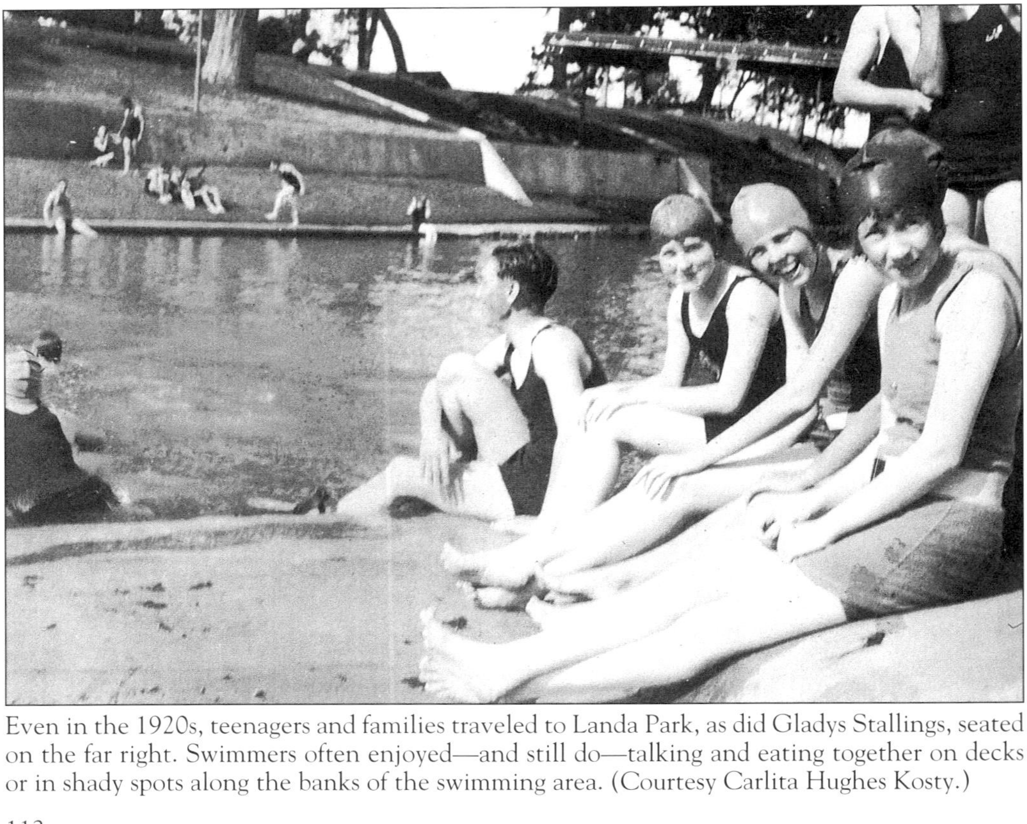

Even in the 1920s, teenagers and families traveled to Landa Park, as did Gladys Stallings, seated on the far right. Swimmers often enjoyed—and still do—talking and eating together on decks or in shady spots along the banks of the swimming area. (Courtesy Carlita Hughes Kosty.)

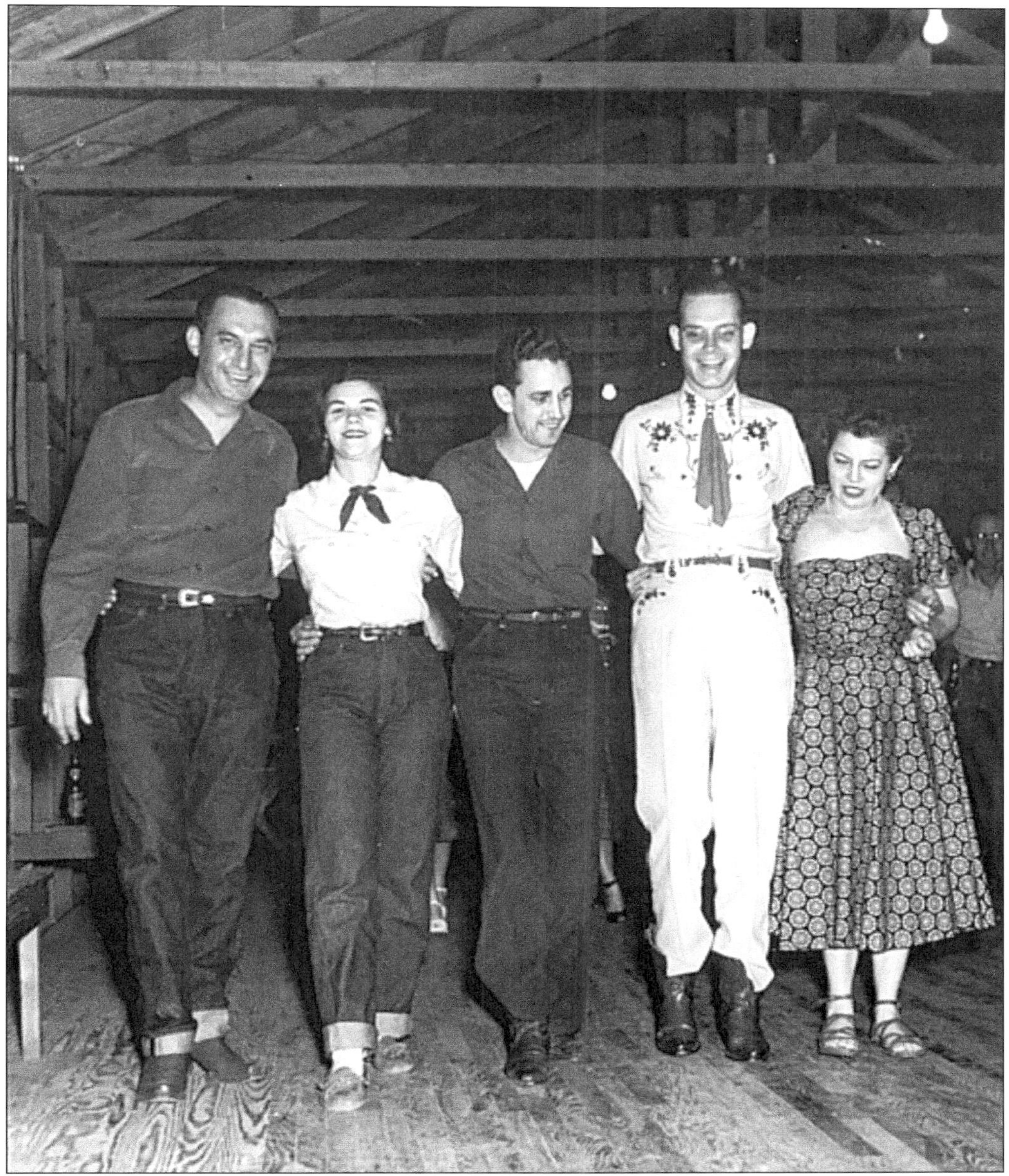

These unidentified couples gear up for some country-western dancing. When I was in high school, my friends and I often drove to a small town or to the Bluebonnet Palace for a night of boot scootin'. When we grew tired of two-stepping at Bluebonnet, we ventured to the indoor ring and watched daring riders try to hang onto steer for one minute. (Courtesy Daughters of the Republic of Texas Library, Elicson Collection, CN99.177.)

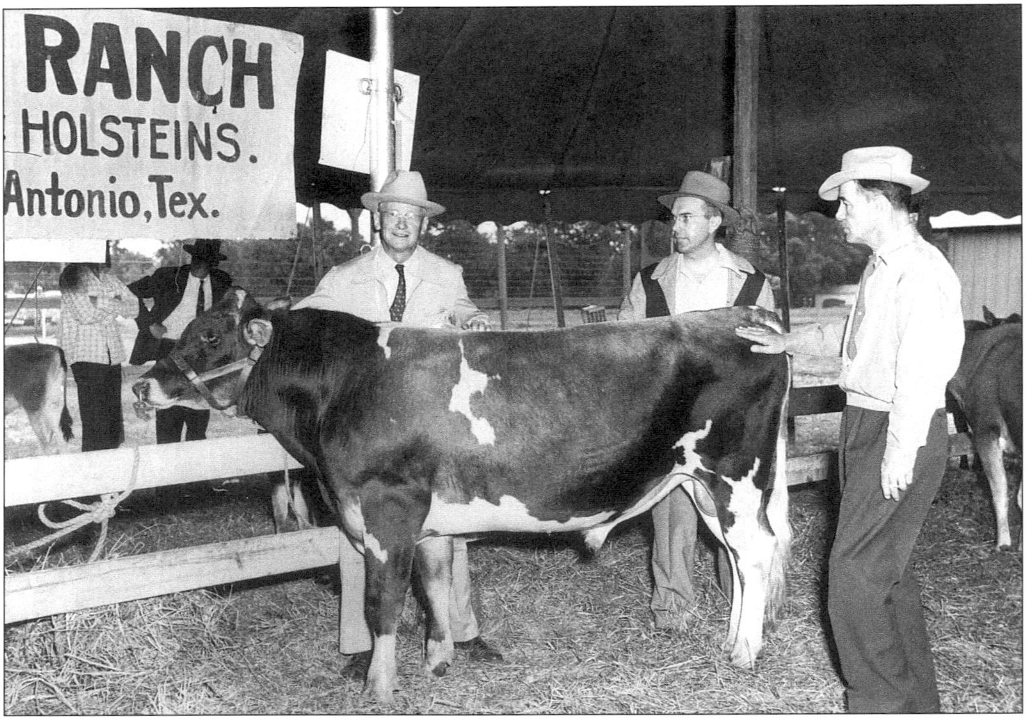

Rodeo Week takes place every February in San Antonio, and many farmers and ranchers travel to the city in hopes that their cattle might win a blue ribbon. These unidentified men stand next to a steer in a pen. Not only do judges pin ribbons, but the carnival also comes to town. Many San Antonians attend the night rodeo shows, which feature musicians such as Garth Brooks. (Courtesy Daughters of the Republic of Texas Library, Elicson Collection, CN99.176.)

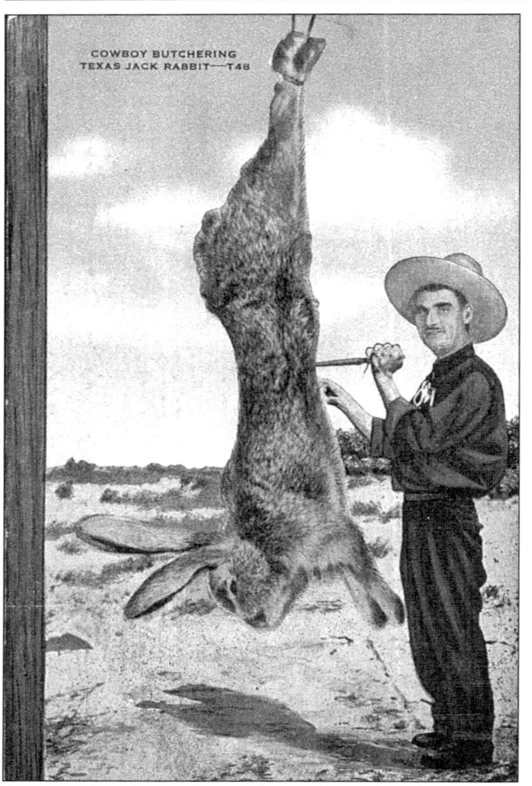

Texas jackrabbits usually are scrawny and dirt-colored and sometimes startle me. Although they may hide from cowboys and hunters, they also can be bold. Once, on a walk in the Hill Country, I froze when a movement in a bush frightened me. I expected to see a rattlesnake, but a jackrabbit popped out and scampered away.

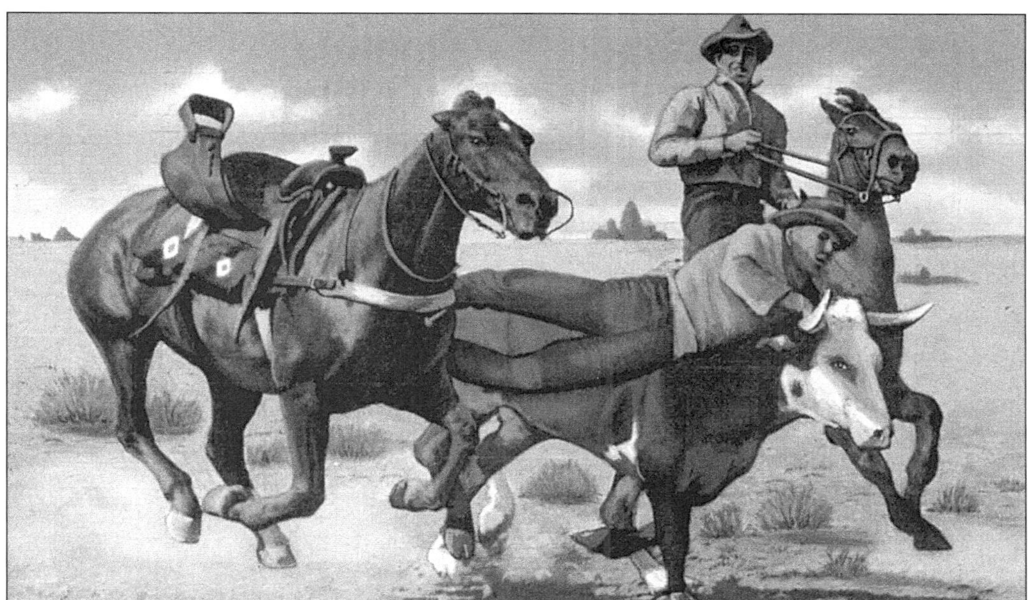

When "Bull Dogging a Hereford Steer in West Texas," if you "Miss Your Leap . . . Under the Hoofs You Go!" Even though professionals at the rodeos in San Antonio perform splendid leaping and roping feats, everyday ranchers might spend an afternoon "bull dogging." Cattle owners need to rope their cattle in order to brand them or to prevent them from straying. In the above postcard, a daring cowboy leaps onto a steer, and below, a cowboy ropes a calf.

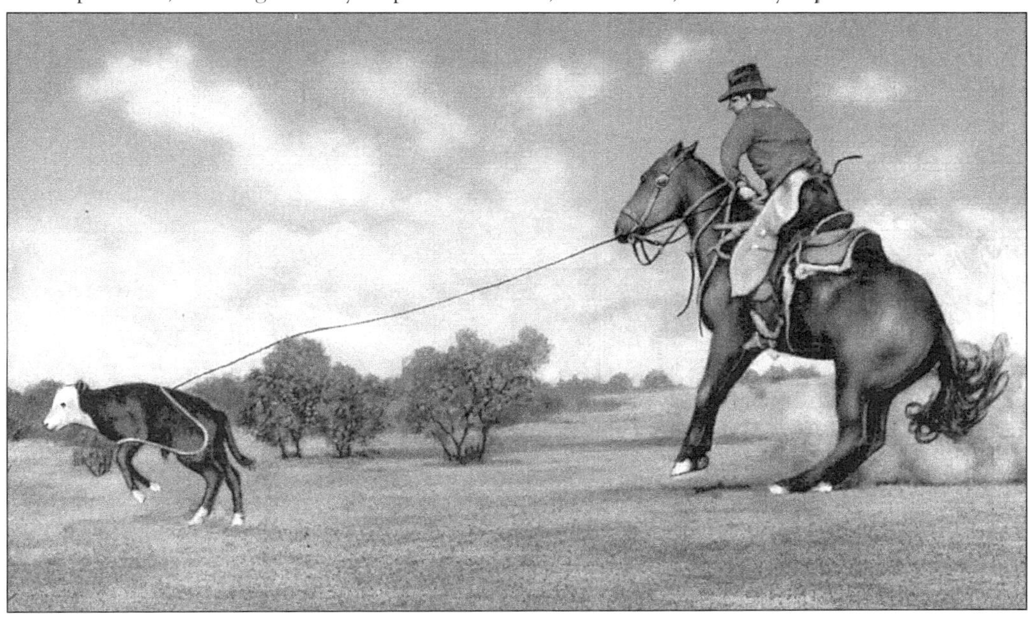

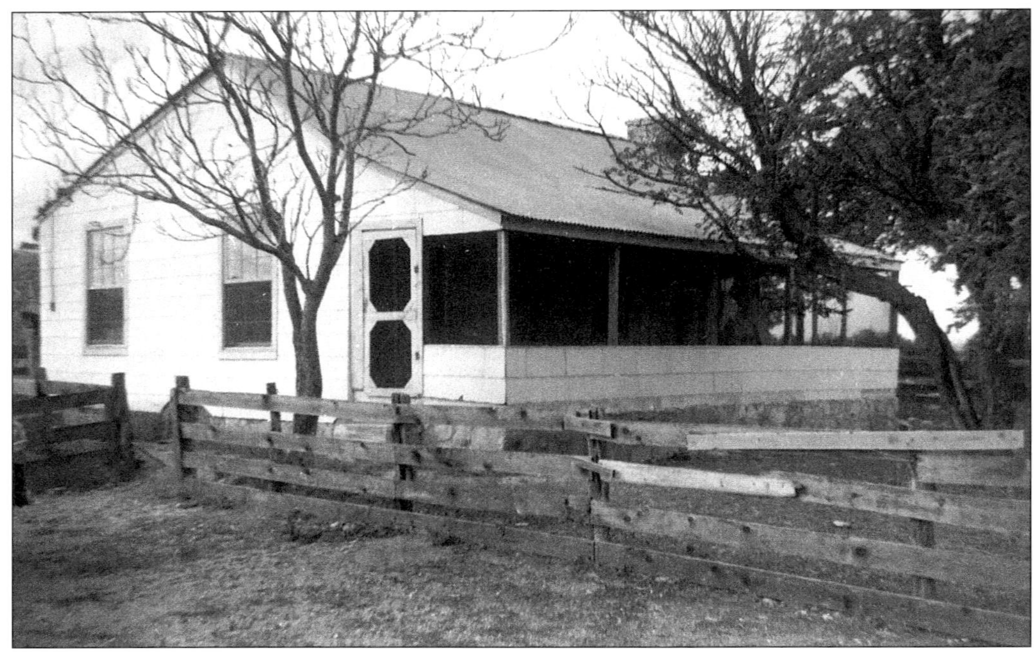

The Davenport family purchased their country property, now named the Davenport Ranch, in the 1950s. The ranch is located near the town of Dripping Springs, approximately an hour northeast of San Antonio. The ranchhouse in the above picture still stands on the property. Although the caretakers currently live in this house, another residence was built nearby in the 1970s. Below, the Davenport family enjoys a visit to the ranch in the 1950s; from left to right are Howard, Dick, Cynthia, and Maxine Davenport. On getaway weekends, the Davenports spent afternoons sitting on the shady porch of the house or walking through the countryside. (Both courtesy Cynthia Davenport Woodland.)

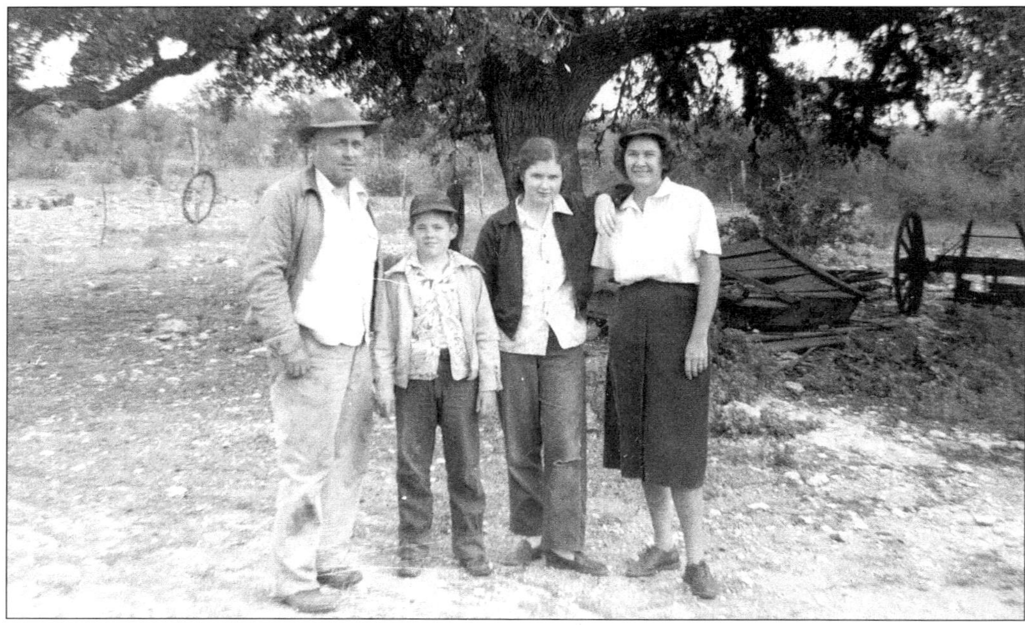

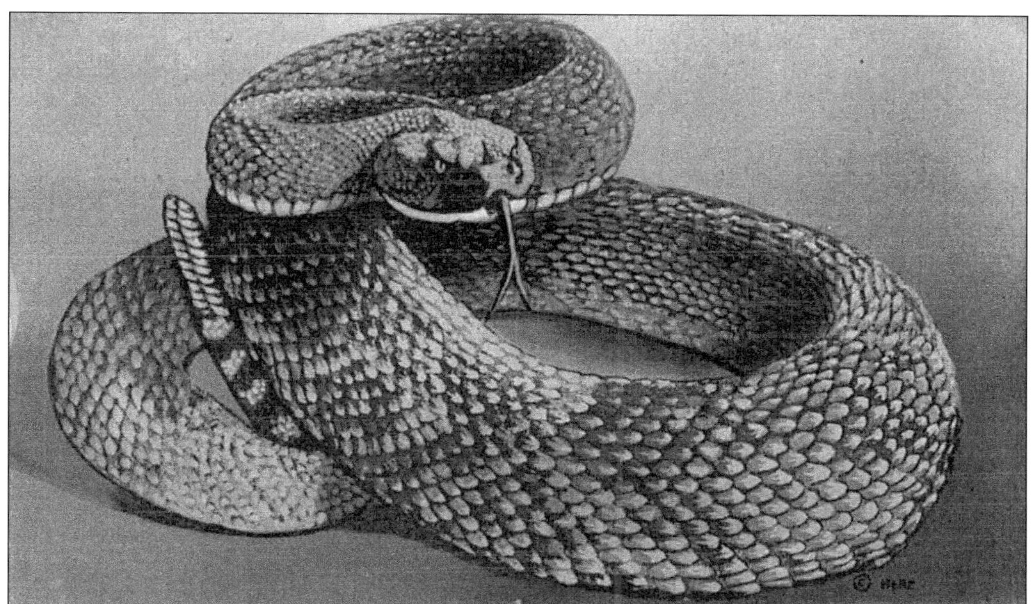

During a visit to the Davenport Ranch, my cousins and I spent the afternoon shooting cans until my uncle warned us to stay away from a spot where a coiled rattlesnake lay. Although the rattlesnake was asleep, its wide-open eyes and rattle kept us at a safe distance. Even near my house in the city, my parents often check the doghouse and yard for snakes before letting any children or dogs outside.

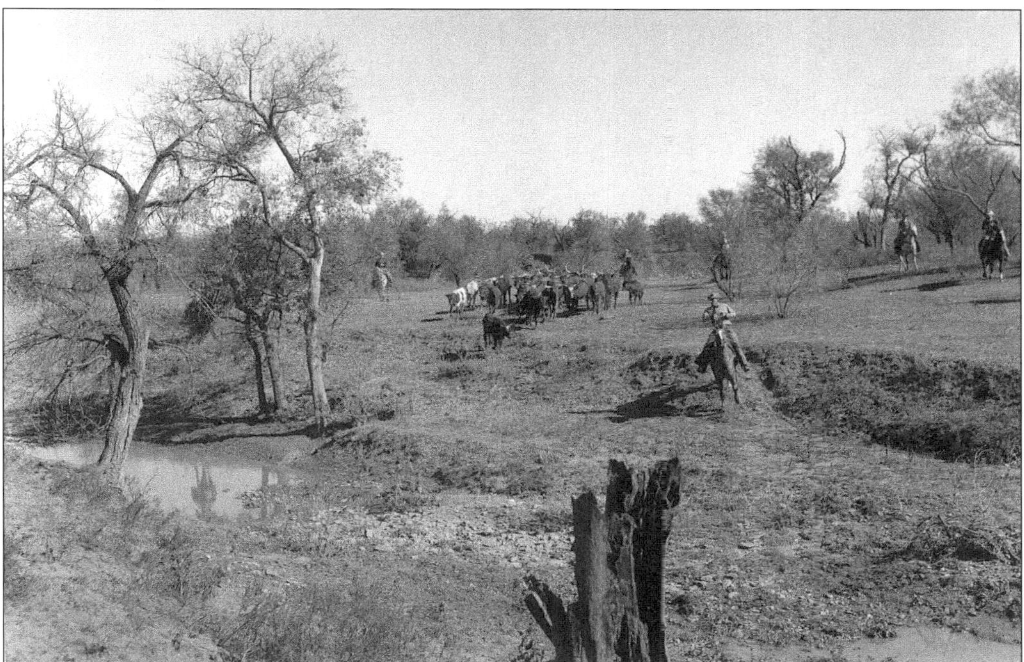

Although the Davenports are not full-time ranchers and use their ranch as a place to relax, nearby, serious ranchers like these unidentified cowboys spend their days rounding up, breeding, branding, and feeding cattle. (Courtesy Texas Department of Transportation.)

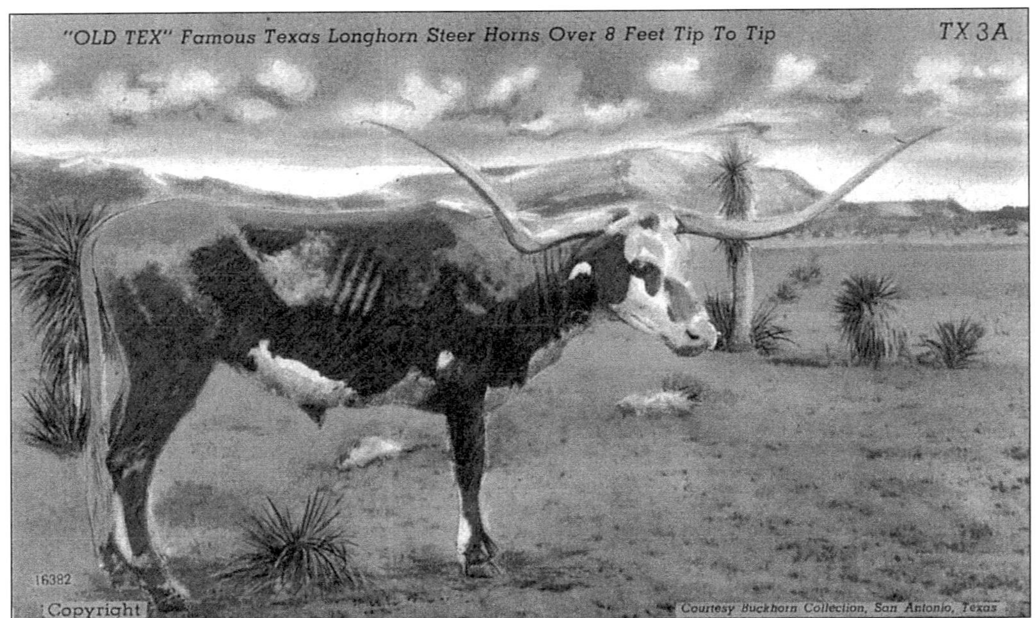

Although I've seen a real Texas longhorn, I made sure a solid fence stood between us. When the longhorn stood up, it put its horns on the ground as it pushed itself up. No matter how heavy the beast's horns are, they still can move fast. Once, my youngest cousin wanted to pet a longhorn, but fortunately, his friend saw the menacing look in its eyes and swooped my cousin out of harm's way.

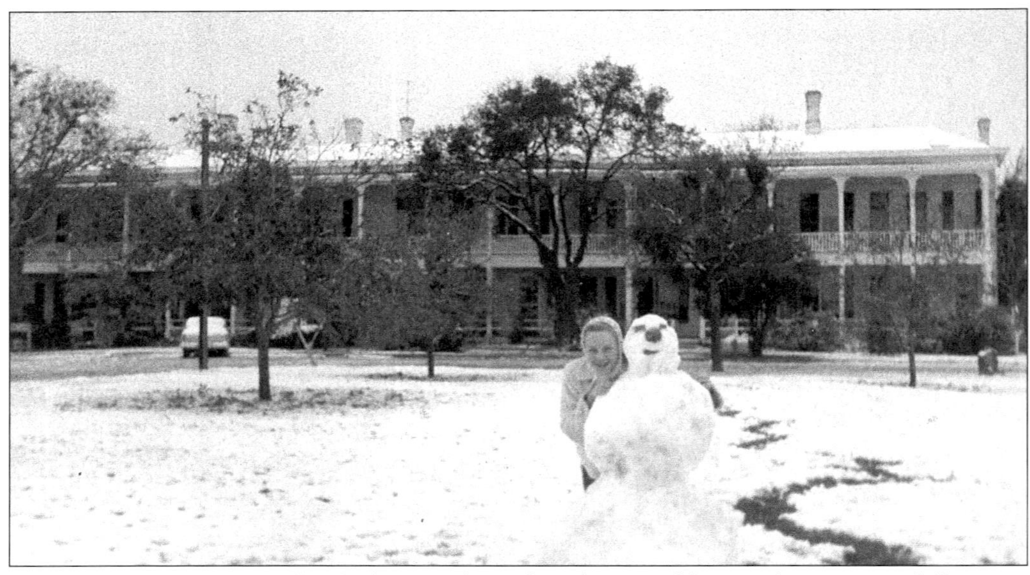

During a rare snow in 1958, Carlita Hughes's friends invited her to drive to Kendall Inn in Boerne, located roughly 30 miles northwest of San Antonio, for a day of fun. Standing behind a snowman, Carlita enjoyed the unusual sight of the Hill Country's snow-speckled land and houses. (Courtesy Carlita Hughes Kosty.)

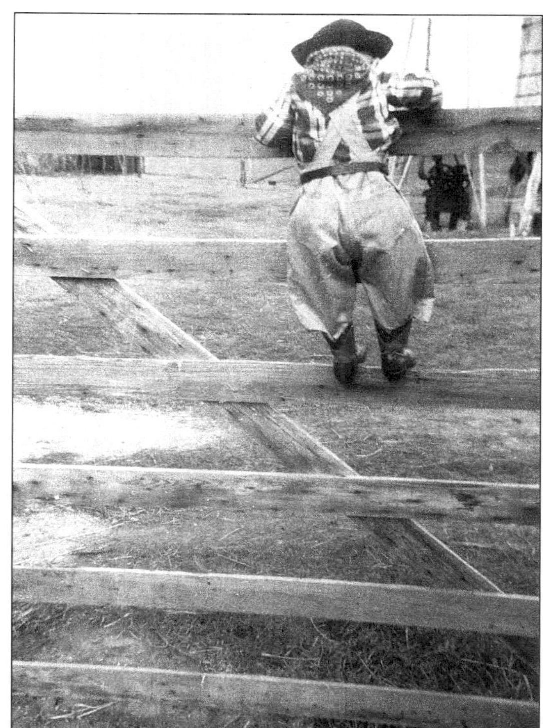

Do Texans really have oil fields in their backyards and wear cowboy hats and boots? Bill and Randy Woods, long-time natives of the Lone Star State, certainly do. In the above photo, Randy, aged four, leans into a corral near Luling. In the lower photo, his father, Bill, stands proudly on his land. (Both courtesy Brice Woods and family.)

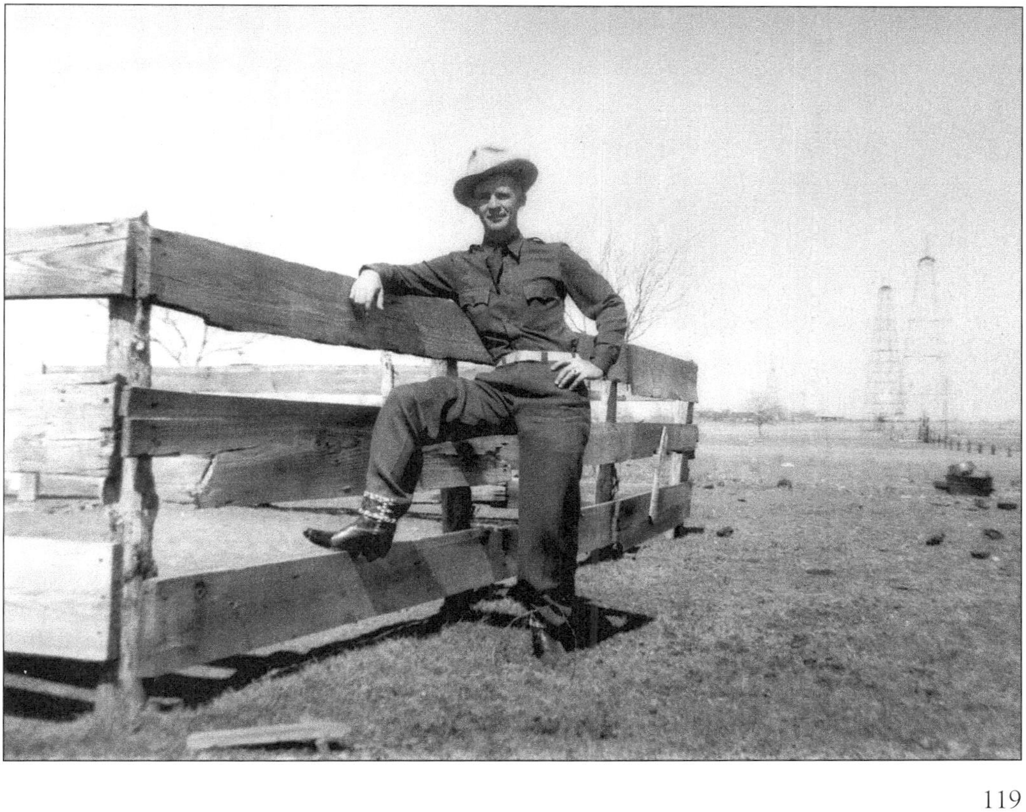

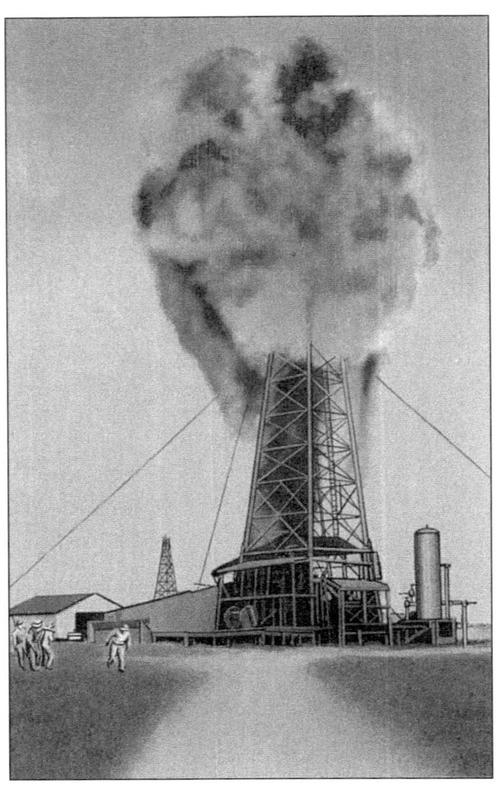

When I drive through the Hill Country, I sometimes spot pump jacks and oil wells, although I've never seen a well spurt oil or flames. In this image, "the well was being 'shot' to increase oil production. Rocks thrown out hit steel. Sparks, explosion, and fire resulted."

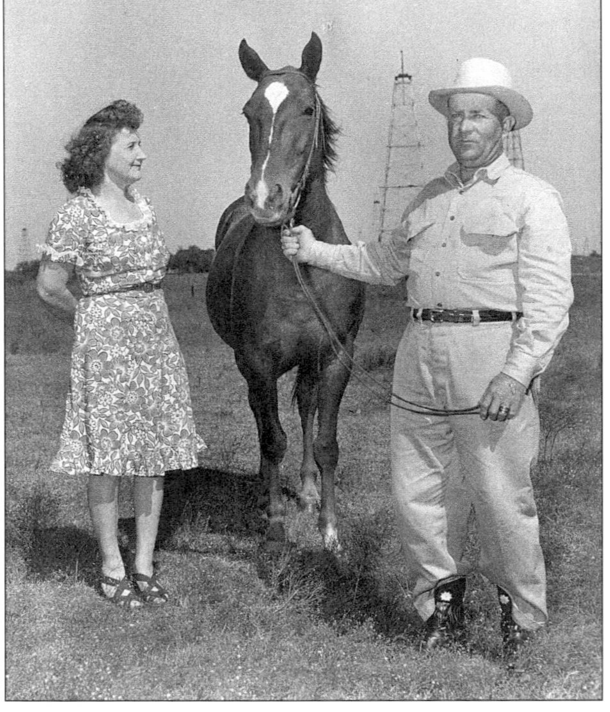

Jettie and Joe Keeton model one of their favorite horses, Fly, near their racehorse farm just outside of the town of Luling. Joe, who worked for the Magnolia Oil Company near Luling for 30 years, also raised quarter horses and let them run in the open range. (Courtesy Brice Woods and family.)

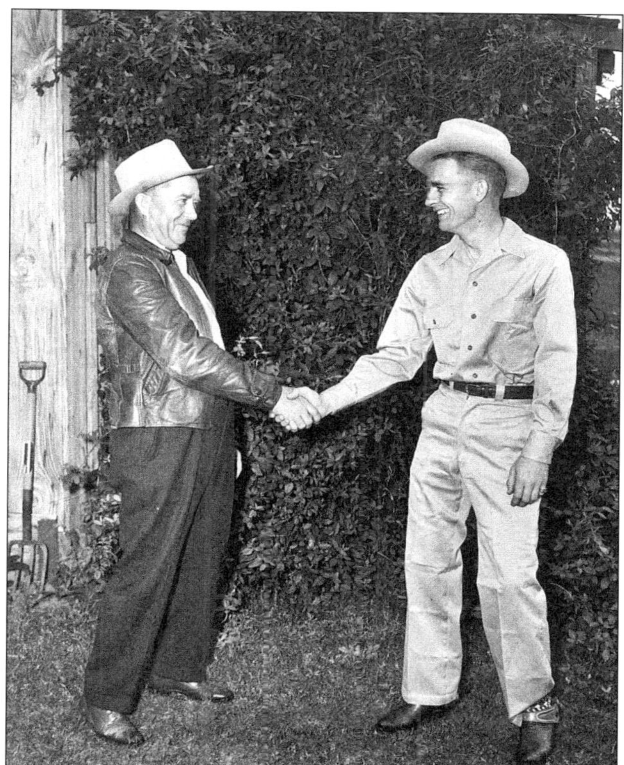

Getting ready for a gallop through the plains, Walter Wade "Bud" Keeton shakes hands with an old ranch hand—his father, Joe—outside of their country house. And as a seasoned veteran of the United States Air Force for 30 years, namely at Randolph Air Force base, Bill Woods (below) kneels in front of his prize game. The flat land and oil wells in the distance are common Texas landmarks. (Both courtesy Brice Woods and family.)

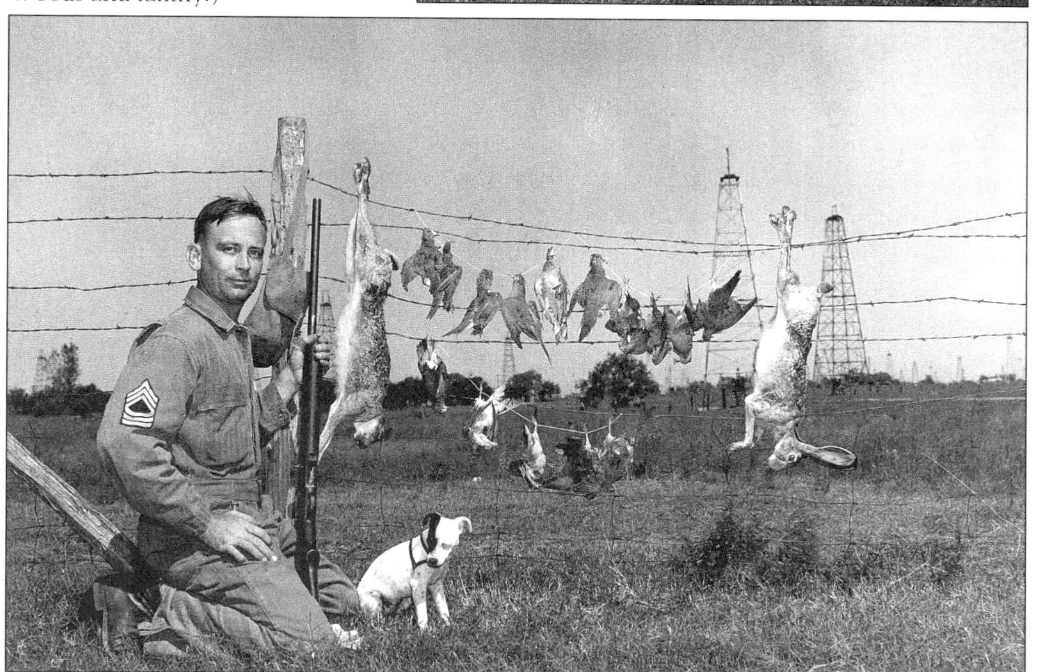

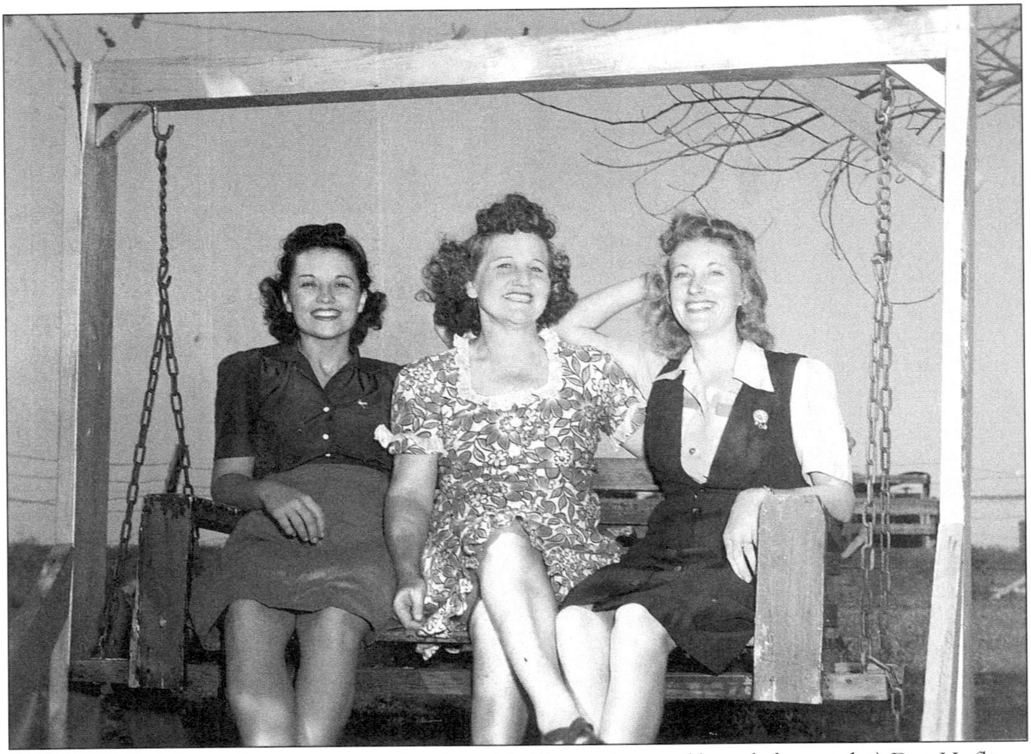

Seated in a swing in the country under the wide Texas sky are (from left to right) Dot Hofling, Jettie Keeton, and Margaret Woods. (Courtesy Brice Woods and family.)

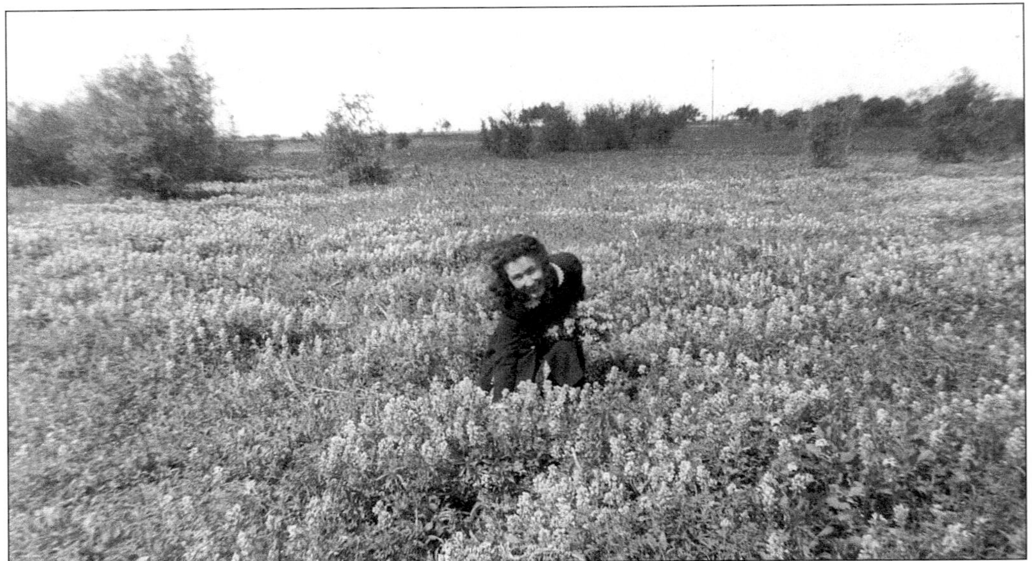

Mickey Stickley kneels in a field of bluebonnets outside of Randolph Air Force Base in 1942. Texans love to roll in their bluebonnets, the state flower. Since water is scarce, so are flowers of any kind; therefore, by law, picking bluebonnets is forbidden throughout the state. (Courtesy Brice Woods and family.)

By pulling his hat forward, this cowboy is missing a great sight—the Texas Hill Country. Whenever I visit home, I always head west on I-10 toward Waring and Welfare, two small towns just northwest of San Antonio. After stopping for lunch at Po-Po's outside of Welfare, I'll drive past the Waring General Store and stand by the bridge to look at the brush, the creek, and the Hill Country. (Courtesy Texas Department of Transportation.)

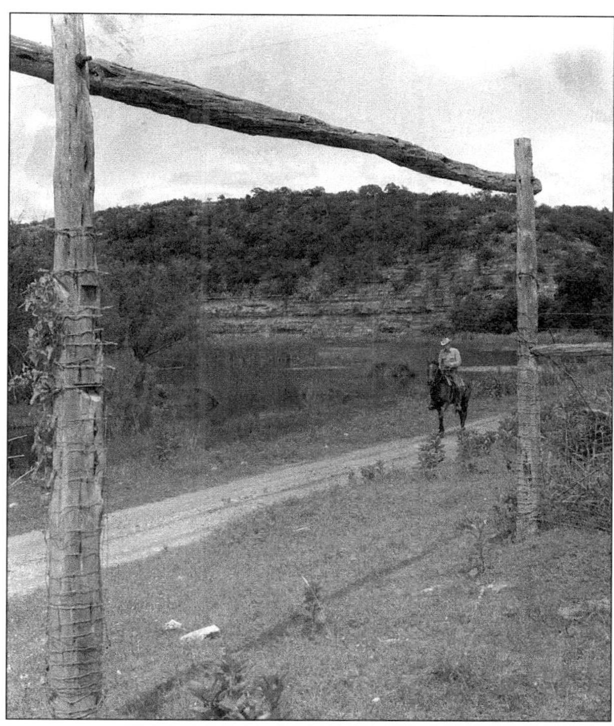

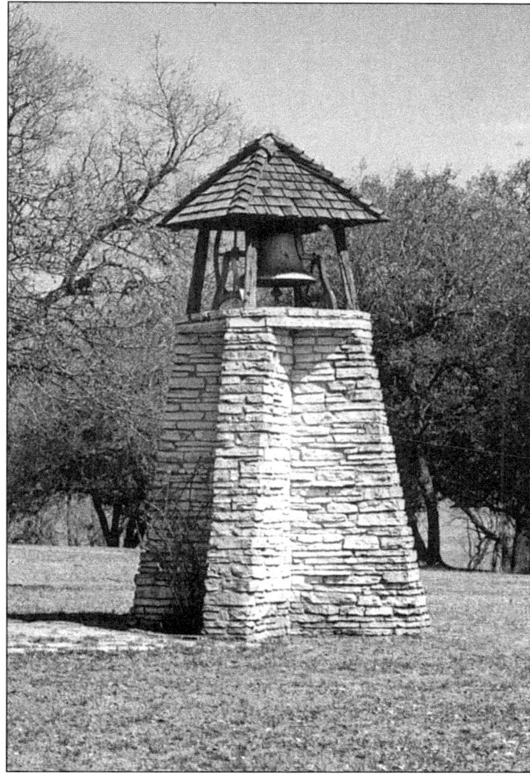

As a camper at Camp Capers in Waring, I knew I was in the Hill Country when the sound of this bell woke me in the morning. For nine summers, I attended this camp, and I always looked forward to my next visit, so I could watch for more armadillos or take a camp hike down to Waring or to the Guadalupe River. (Courtesy The Episcopal Diocese of West Texas.)

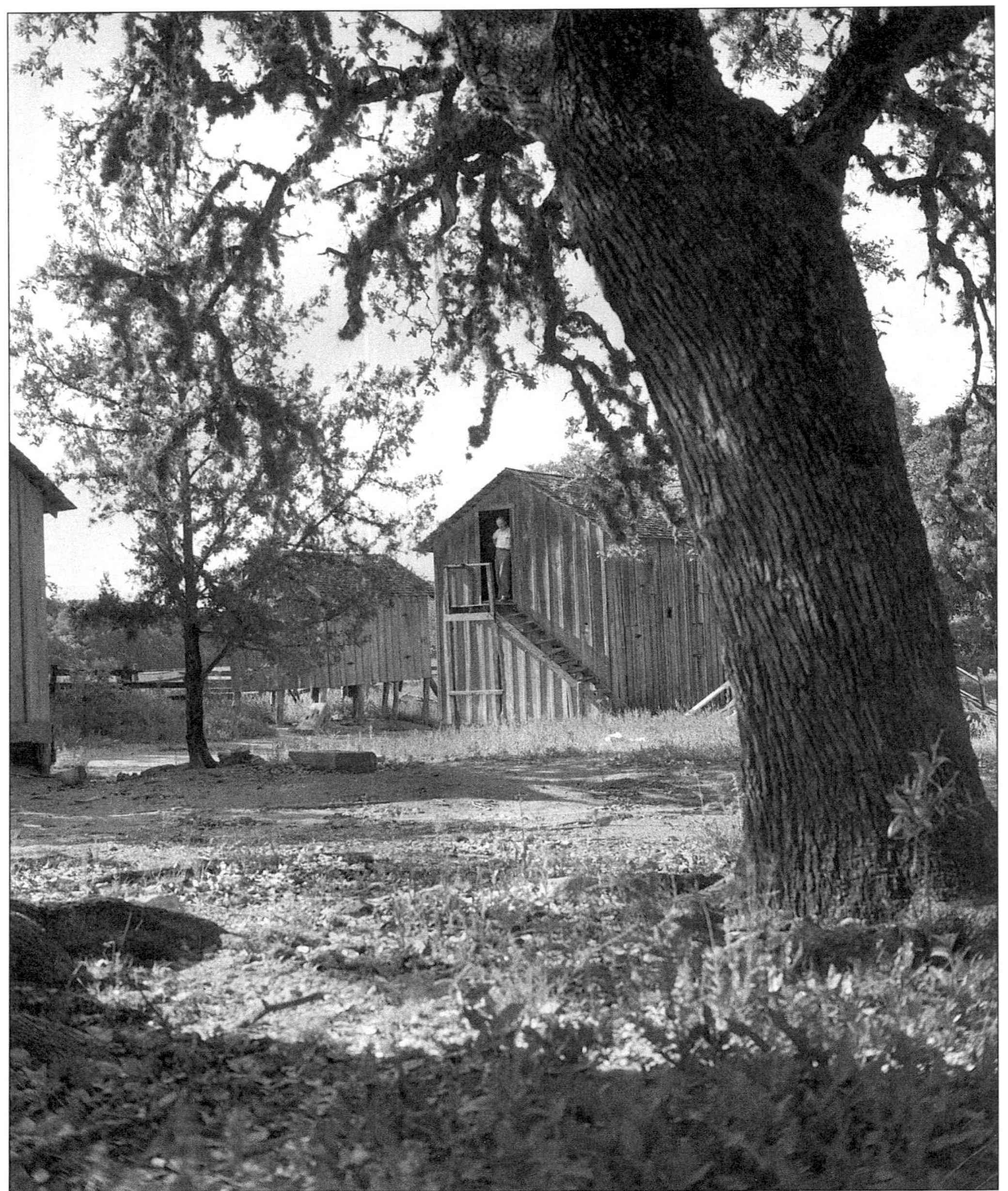

Although these unidentified structures on the property of Camp Capers are no longer used, this 1940s image shows the beauty of this part of the Hill Country. Even after hundreds of burrs adhered to my shoes and socks, as a camper, I continued to walk through unused areas of the camp, sometimes stopping to peer into old wooden structures like these that remain in remote areas. (Courtesy The Episcopal Diocese of West Texas.)

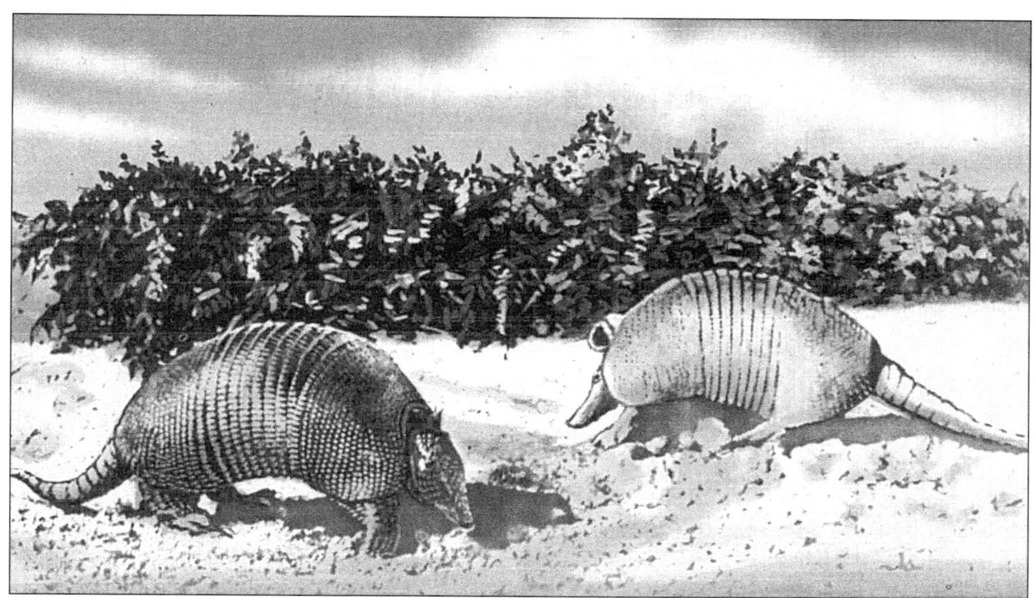

Sometimes during hikes at Camp Capers, the counselors signaled the campers to be quiet; I always tried to conceal my excitement when this happened, because I knew someone had spotted an armadillo. Although the campers often wanted to keep the armadillo, the counselors never trapped these quiet creatures; they let them run into the brush.

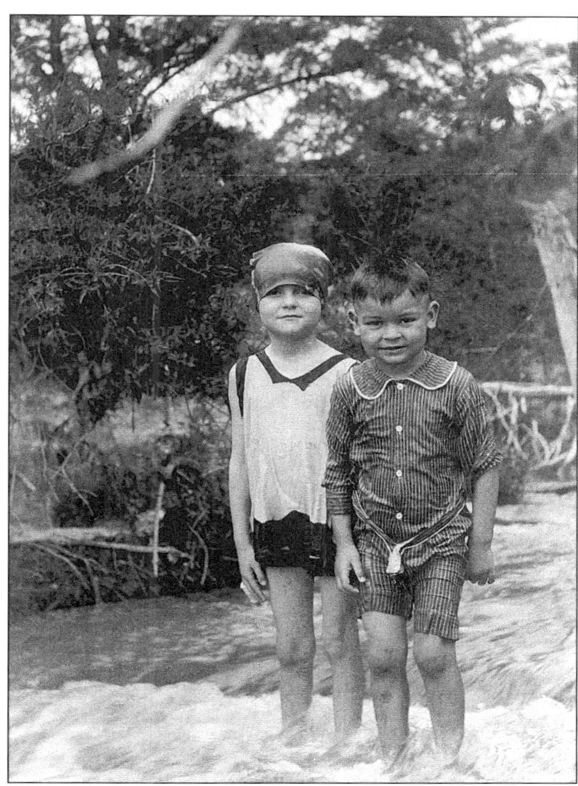

In their 1920s-style swimsuits, Eunice Lewis and her brother, Wilson Lewis, stand in the cool waters of the dazzling Guadalupe River, which winds through Center Point and Waring, as well as other small towns nestled in the hill country. (Courtesy Eunice Lewis.)

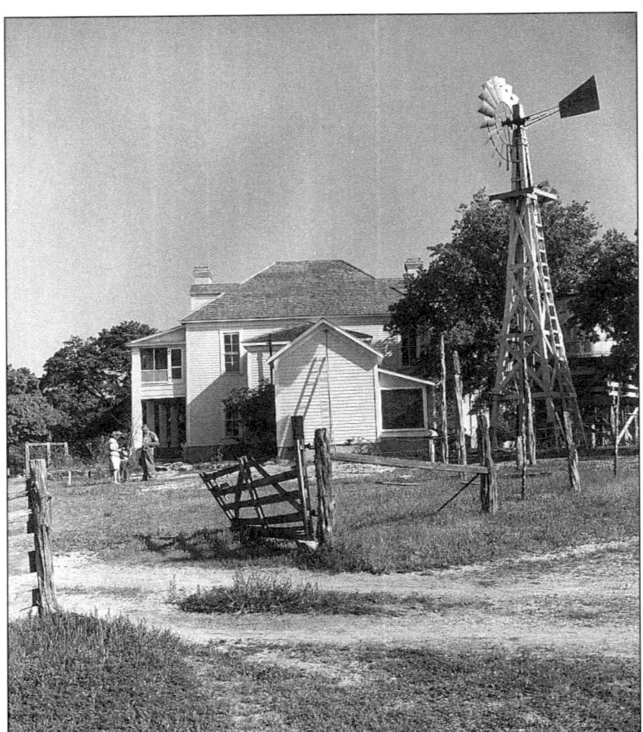

This house was named Steves Hall after the Steves family, who donated the property that became Camp Capers to the Episcopal Diocese of West Texas in the 1940s. Although the house was demolished in the 1970s, the diocese built a new Steves Hall, which currently is the summer staff quarters. (Courtesy The Episcopal Diocese of West Texas.)

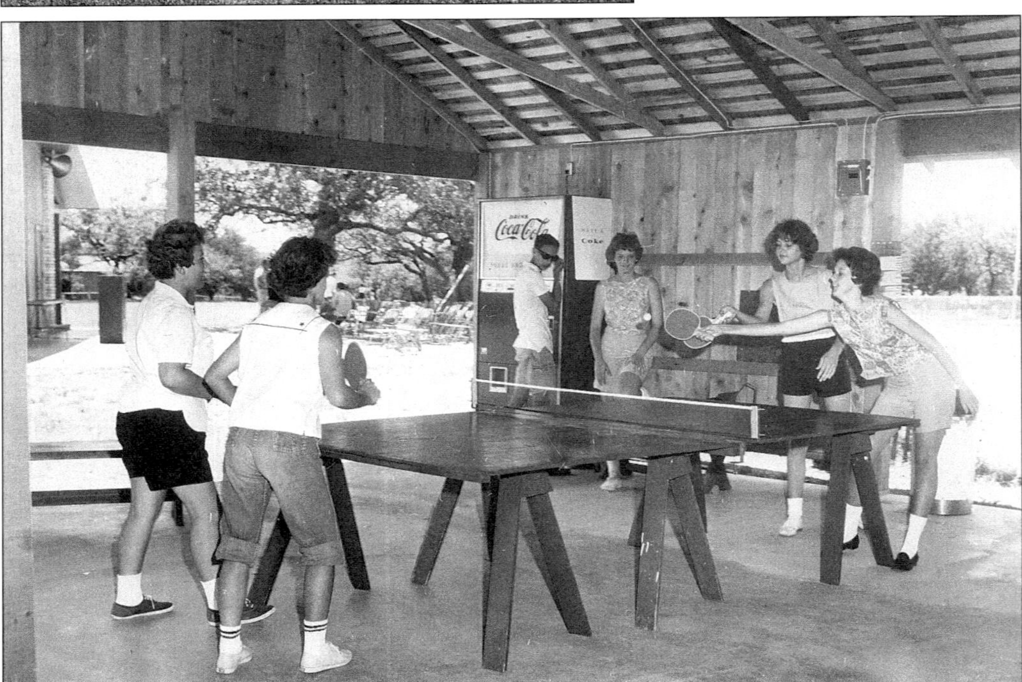

At Camp Capers in the 1950s, these campers enjoy a game of ping-pong. Although campers did not play ping-pong in my day, we hit tetherballs, held outdoor dances, and performed skits. (Courtesy The Episcopal Diocese of West Texas.)

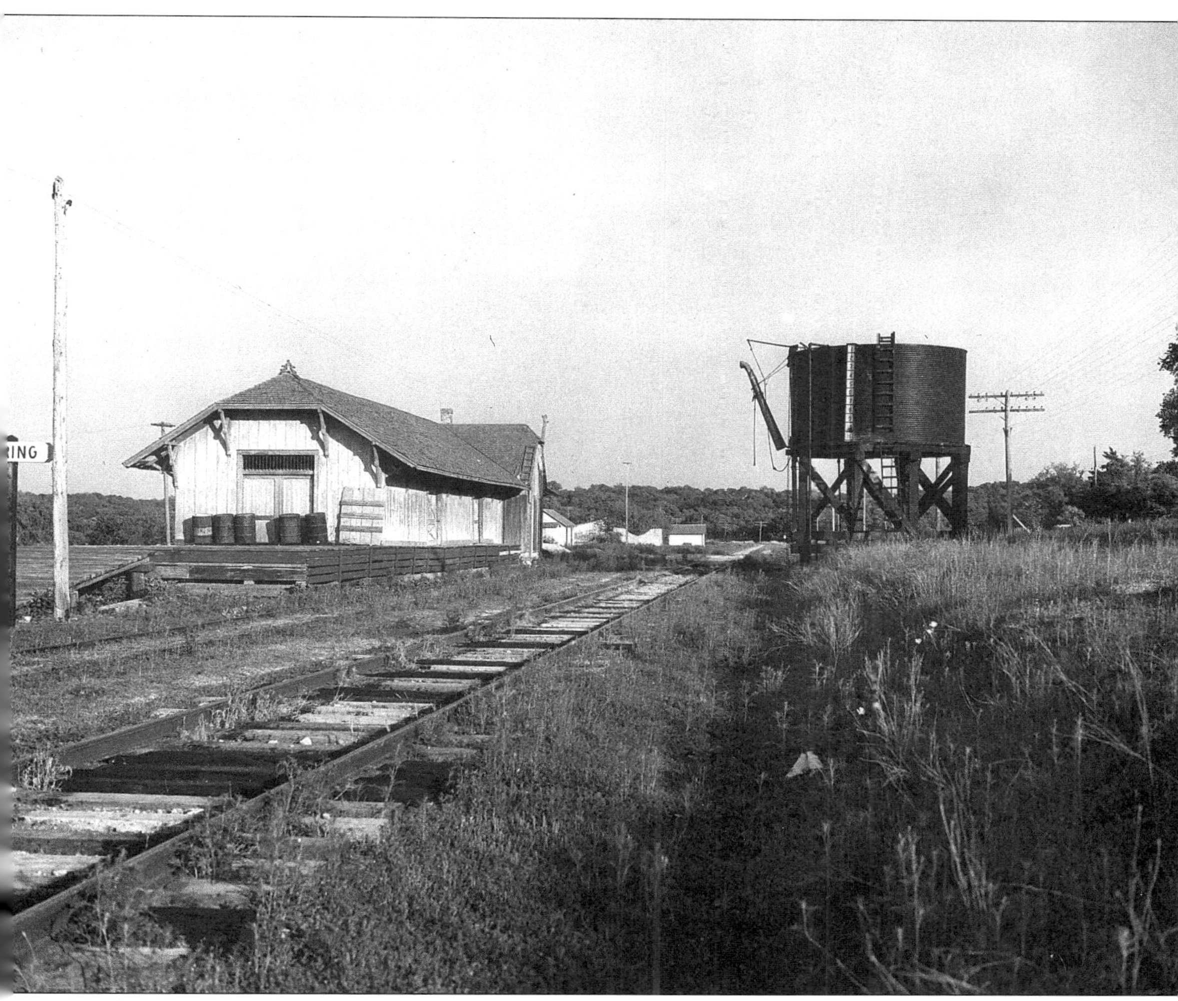

Near the Waring General Store is the old Waring depot. In this 1940s image, the railroad tracks and station appear in good condition, but today, most of the tracks are gone, and the building has collapsed. My grandfather's trains stopped at this depot when he traveled from Center Point to places such as San Antonio. (Courtesy The Episcopal Diocese of West Texas.)

Resources and Additional Readings

"A Brief History of Texas Military Institute." Texas Military Institute Alumni Directory 1995. White Plains, NY: Barnard C. Harris Publishing Company, Inc., 1995.

Carson, Chris and William McDonald, eds. *A Guide to San Antonio Architecture*. San Antonio: San Antonio Chapter of the American Institute of Architecture, 1986.

Daughters of the Republic of Texas. "The Alamo." July 21, 1998. <http://thealamo.org/>.

Eckhardt, Gregg A. "Brackenridge Park." March 28, 1999. <http://www.edwardsaquifer.net/bracken.html>.

Fort Sam Houston. "Fort Sam Houston: Home of Army Medicine." April 23, 1999. <http://www.samhou-usag.army.mil/>.

The History of Military Aviation in San Antonio. San Antonio: Air Education and Training Command History Office, 1996.

Jarboe, Jan. "Missions Accomplished." May 3, 1999. <http://www.texasmonthly.com/travel/virtual/mission/>.

Kellner, Marjorie. *Wagons, Ho! A History of Real County, Texas*. Dallas: Curtis Media, 1995.

Kownslar, Allan O. *The Texans, Their Land and History*. New York: Webster Division, McGraw-Hill, 1978.

Lambert, Joseph Idus. Reminiscences and Writings. Unpublished.

Maguire, Jack. *A Century of Fiesta in San Antonio*. Austin: Eakin Press, 1990.

Mayo, P. Randolph Jr. *Coca-Cola Heritage: A Photographic History of the Biedenharn Coca-Cola Bottling Business*. Austin: Best Printing Company, Inc., 1990.

National Park Service, U.S. Department of the Interior. "San Antonio Missions." July 19, 1999. <http://www.numedia.tddc.net/hot/hillcountry/sa/tours/missions/missions2.html>.

Orem, Harry. "Cambridge Album." July 5, 1998. <http://www.alamo-heights.k12.tx.us/campuses/cambridge/history.html>.

Paul, Lee. "The Alamo: 13 Days of Glory." July 19, 1999. <http://www.thehistorynet.com/WildWest/articles/02962_text.htm>.

Pfeiffer, Maria. "Brackenridge Park: An In-depth Historical Review." City of San Antonio Parks & Recreation Department. March 30, 1999. <http://www.ci.sat.tx.us/sapar/bracklg.htm>.

"A Brief History of Kelly Air Force Base." Kelly Air Force Base, Texas: Kelly Air Force Base, 1999.

St. Mary's University. "History." March 30, 1999. <http://www.stmarytx.edu/info/about/history.html>.

The San Antonio Express News. "Downtown San Antonio: Tower Life Building." July 18, 1999. <http://www.expressnews.com/cityguide/visitors/towlife.html>.

San Antonio Conservation Society. "Espada Aqueduct." March 30, 1998. <http://www.saconservation.org/prop12.html>.

Slattery, Sister Margaret Patrice. *Promises to Keep: A History of the Sisters of Charity of the Incarnate Word, San Antonio, Texas*. Vols. I-II. 1995.

Swartz, Mimi. "The Rose Window." Texas Monthly. April 8, 1999. <http://www.texasmonthly.com/archive/readme/window.html>.

Tarin, Randell G., "Alamo de Parras, The Untold Story of the Alamo's Early History." July 20, 1999. <http://www.flash.net/~alamo3/>.

Total Quality Management students. "Emily Morgan West, The Texas Yellow Rose." North Central Texas College. May 14, 1998. <http://www.nortexinfo.net/Texas_Quality/rose.html>.